# Praise for *Twist Your Fate*

"Theresa knows that stories have consequences. The stories we read and the stories we tell ourselves about ourselves. And so her book, *Twist Your Fate,* empowers the reader to tell themselves a different story about who they are, what their gifts and challenges might be, and how to collaborate with others in an effort to make the world a more connected place. I love the way Theresa framed all the transits, configurations, and cards in a way that is honest and strength-based. Because she highlights what is strong over what is wrong, the reader can manifest success by seeing where their success lies internally and externally. I'm so proud of Theresa for this valuable contribution!"

—Colin Bedell, author of *Queer Cosmos*
and weekly horoscope writer at *Cosmopolitan.com*

"As one of the greatest success stories in our own industry, Theresa Reed reveals the secret pathways toward prosperity through her ingenious approach to tarot and astrology. Who better than "The Tarot Lady" to expertly demonstrate how to utilize the stars and cards as your personal golden compass toward success? *Twist Your Fate* brilliantly empowers you to chart your own course toward the life you've always dreamed of living. There is no better guide through the golden doors of opportunity than the incomparable Theresa Reed."

—Elliot Adam, author *Fearless Tarot* and *Tarot in Love*

"If you're like me and like peanut butter in your chocolate and astrology in your tarot, Theresa Reed has written the perfect book for you. *Twist Your Fate* is chock full of insightful examples and brilliant exercises. She walks you through her method step-by-step, showing you how to adeptly blend astrology and tarot. With Theresa's method, you no longer have to just passively accept your circumstances as they are but can take the strengths that you have in your astrological chart, blend them with the guidance of the tarot, and totally transform your life. I love her take on both tarot and astrology, and the brand-new concepts she shares in this book make it the mash-up I've been dreaming of. A must for your magical bookshelf!"

—Madame Pamita, author of *Baba Yaga's Book of Witchcraft*,
*The Book of Candle Magic,* and *Madame Pamita's Magical Tarot*

"Regardless of what cards you're dealt in life, Theresa Reed has your back. In *Twist Your Fate,* Reed shrewdly shows how astrology and tarot can assist you in creating a successful life, making the best of whatever the stars might throw in your path. This brilliant book shows how the timeless insights of astrology and tarot can be used independently and in tandem to augment your strengths and mitigate your challenges to achieve your dreams. *Twist Your Fate* sheds light on the secrets that CEOs, celebrities, and politicians have secretly consulted to navigate success in an accessible manner to ensure they're victors and not a victims of fate."

—Mat Auryn, bestselling author of *Psychic Witch* and *Mastering Magick*

"This is one of the best books on utilizing astrology and tarot that I've ever read: accessible and useful, and absolutely packed with practical insights that anyone can feel confident using. Theresa Reed is one of the best tarot and astrology teachers out there, and *Twist Your Fate* is the perfect tool for anyone who wants to harness these practices for confidence and success. Blending practical insights and ready-to-use tools with exercises, journal prompts, and spreads, this book is a must-have for anyone who is looking to launch their own business, level up their career habits, and expand their understanding of how to best utilize specific planetary transits. Theresa shares an abundance of information in this book, but it's done in her signature warm, conversational style, making complicated, intricate astrological concepts incredibly accessible. *Twist Your Fate* is an absolute pleasure to read and includes everything that readers need to find professional success and satisfaction in a way that works for their unique natal chart. Highly recommended!"

—Meg Jones Wall, founder of 3am.tarot, and author of *Finding the Fool*

"Tarot card reader Theresa Reed delivers career guidance based in astrology and tarot in this accessible work. The author uses techniques from her practice to tell readers 'how to find potential paths best suited for your cosmic makeup and how to groove with the current movement of the cosmos.' She explains how to interpret one's sun, moon, and ascendant signs, and provides a modified birth chart in which the traditional 'houses' representing the different areas of life have been replaced by such professional considerations as 'public image/brand' and 'work environment.' Delving into tarot, Reed walks through how to use tarot spreads to gain clarity on questions; for example, she explains that in a spread of her own creation, the first card pulled from the deck 'shows the energy around the question,' the second indicates 'what you need to know,' and the third offers advice. Reed skillfully balances informativeness and entertainment, using playful prose ('I have a red-hot Scorpion Moon temper—and when I get angry, watch out!') that will keep beginners onboard as she explores more advanced material. The result is a fresh and fun fusion of two esoteric traditions that has something new for novice and experienced practitioners alike." *(Aug.)*

—*Publishers Weekly*


"In *Twist Your Fate*, Theresa Reed does what I love most. She shows her readers how they can work with the Sacred Arts of Astrology and Tarot to make their lives better right here and right now. And she does it in the way that I love most: with a caring, compassionate, and no-nonsense voice that breaks down complicated concepts in a way that makes them approachable and relatable. One of the biggest reasons people turn to astrology and tarot in the first place is to create more success and joy in their lives . . . with Theresa as your guide you are sure to do just that! This is a wonderful book and appropriate for those who are brand new or more seasoned practitioners. Get it, and start manifesting a brighter future, today!"

—Briana Saussy, author of *Making Magic* and *Star Child*


"Theresa Reed is one of the few people I know who can mash astrology and tarot to create a third entity—achievement of the life you desire. If you're new to any of this— no worries—as Theresa breaks everything down into manageable steps. That includes astrological transits, which I've always found difficult to understand, but no longer! If you want to take control of your future, this is the one book you need to own. Do the exercises, dig into your chart and tarot cards, and there really is no roadblock to what you can create."

—Nancy Hendrickson, author of *Ancestral Tarot* and *Ancestral Grimoire*

"There is truly no one out there who makes the mystic arts as exciting, digestible, and inspiring as Theresa Reed, and her latest offering is a testament to this. In *Twist Your Fate*, Theresa uses the ancient wisdom of astrology and tarot as empowering and supportive guides in creating a career that is nourishing, fulfilling, and deeply connected to the magick of the cosmos. Filled with wit, compassion, and plenty of exercises to learn how to read your birth chart, work with the tarot, and hone your intuition, this book is *the* guide for anyone who's looking to create a life that is abundantly and uniquely their own. Theresa makes business fun and exciting, and her decades of experience and deep care for her work shine through in every word. This book is a necessity for any spirituality-savvy business owner, entrepreneur, or occultist who wants to upgrade their professional life to be what they've always dreamed of."

—Gabriela Herstik, author of *Inner Witch, Sacred Sex*, and *Bewitching the Elements*

"Theresa Reed has done it again, and *Twist Your Fate* is a masterwork of astrology, tarot, and intuitive advice. Having such large subject matter to work with would make you think that all topics are jammed in there, without rhyme or reason. But no: Reed takes her time and weaves all three sections of the book into a final exercise in which you truly learn how to twist your fate and make your life extraordinary. We may not all be dealt hands that predestine us to glory and fame, but that doesn't mean we are fated to bemoan our circumstances either. You will not find trite axioms like 'follow your bliss' in this book, but practical advice that you can use immediately."

—Hilary Parry Haggerty, *www.tarotbyhilary.com*

"In *Twist Your Fate*, Theresa Reed takes you on a journey to discover yourself through your birth chart with a side of tarot. You discover what makes you tick and use this information to create the life you love. Theresa takes you by the hand and walks through reading your birth chart in an easy and fun way. Then, before you know it, you are using tarot, reading everyone's birth charts, and seeing Theresa in your mind's eye, saying, 'See, I told you; you got this.' This is an excellent resource for new and seasoned readers alike. She adds valuable tips and tricks to help you become a confident astrologer and tarot reader from her years of experience."

—Jen Sankey, professional witch and author of
*Enchanted Forest Felines Tarot* and *Stardust Wanderer Tarot*

"'What should I be doing with my life?' is in the top five for what clients ask about in sessions followed closely by, 'When should I do it?' *Twist Your Fate* is the perfect book to dive deeply to uncover those answers. Theresa Reed expertly takes the reader on a well-curated tour through their own chart from a work and karmic perspective in a way that is both technical and beginner-friendly. Not only does Theresa Reed give you the map for your calling, she also easily explains how to use charts and tarot in real time to plot your best trajectory through the year. I cannot recommend this book highly enough and will be personally using it until the cover falls off, and I have to buy another."

—Jenna Matlin, author of *Will You Give Me a Reading?*

"*Twist Your Fate* is a brilliant guide for enhancing your life through astrology. Theresa Reed shares her astrological tips for tuning your life to the cosmos to manifest big success and experience a deeper sense of life purpose. With her hard-won wisdom and trademark candor, Theresa gives us insider secrets to transform our unfortunate stars into guiding lights!"

—Shaheen Miro, author of *Lunar Alchemy*

"Inspiring and practical, *Twist Your Fate*, has it all! Theresa Reed has created a thorough and easy-to-digest resource to empower and inform you, wherever you're at in your journey."

—Jessica Lanyadoo, author of *Astrology For Real Relationships*
and host of *Ghost of a Podcast*

"If I'd had this book years ago, I wouldn't have wasted my energy, time, and talent in jobs that only led me to frustration. Theresa shines a light on how to use both astrology and tarot to help you find the path to your 'best destiny.' Not only does she break them down in a fun and accessible way—Theresa's trademark—she fully explains how you can combine both to help you live your life to its fullest potential. *Twist Your Fate* is your recipe for a well-balanced and delicious future."

—Rashunda Tramble, tarot reader and coauthor of *The Numinous Tarot Guide* and founder of *StayWokeTarot.com*

"There is no one out there better than Theresa Reed. *Twist Your Fate* is another invaluable resource for people who want to use Astrology and Tarot as tools to take control and create success in their lives. I know this book will be well-loved and well-used by everyone in my household!"

—Courtney Weber, author of *Hekate*

# TWIST YOUR FATE

# TWIST YOUR FATE

## Manifest Success
### with Astrology & Tarot

## THERESA REED

foreword by Monte Farber

**WEISER
BOOKS**

This edition first published in 2022 by Weiser Books, an imprint of
Red Wheel/Weiser, LLC
With offices at:
65 Parker Street, Suite 7
Newburyport, MA 01950
www.redwheelweiser.com

ISBN: 978-1-57863-768-3
Library of Congress Cataloging-in-Publication Data available upon request.

Cover and text design by Kathryn Sky-Peck
Interior tarot images from the Rider-Waite-Smith Tarot deck
Charts calculated by *astro.com*
Interior illustrations by Imaginary Party
Typeset in Roboto

Printed in the United States of America
IBI
10  9  8  7  6  5  4  3  2  1

*The stories in this book have been modified and names changed to protect privacy.*

*For Dad, the hardest working person I ever knew.*

# Contents

## Part Two: Tarot—Your New Business Cards

## Part Three: Make Intuition Do Its Job

## Part Four: Twist Your Fate

# Foreword

How I wish I had this book when I was learning astrology and tarot! The decades of work that Theresa has done has built the strong foundation for those of us who have dedicated ourselves to our understanding of astrology and tarot. She is unparalleled as a teacher—it is her special gift to make the seemingly difficult and esoteric easy to grasp. In *Twist Your Fate*, Theresa brings you inside the master's studio, and shares with you the same professional techniques she uses in her business and with her clients.

Theresa Reed is the rarest of friends. She's someone in whom I can confide and ask for her opinion when I need help with an important matter. I would do this even if she were not "The Tarot Lady" and the expert astrologer she is because, even though she can soar through the sky-realm of ideas, her lofty perspective is always merged with her down-to-Earth, life-lessons-learned practical way of framing the answers to the questions she receives—and she receives a lot of them.

We are living in a time where the dream of the mainstream acceptance of astrology, the tarot, and the importance of intuition is being realized. Like Theresa, my wife and artistic collaborator, Amy Zerner, and I have worked diligently on handcrafting the books we call "spiritual power-tools"—the cordless variety—and each day brings new confirmation that our efforts have borne fruit. Many of the most popular social media personalities have been kind enough to acknowledge to us how our books and kits have either started them on their journey or influenced them along the way. We welcome you, dear reader, into our extended family. Our goal, and this book you now hold in your hands, will empower you to improve your life on the spiritual, mental, and physical levels —that's right, all this fun and money, too! Because when it comes to using these tools to manifest success in business and life, there is no better guide than Theresa.

One of the many things I love about this book is that right from the beginning Theresa ties it into helping you to improve the way you make your living—it doesn't get more practical than that! Your time spent reading this book is one of the most beneficial things you can do. Doing the provided exercises, thinking about the many concepts that are a profoundly different way of looking at the world, and circling back to applying them to your life and the way you make your living will not only improve your life, but it will also improve the lives of those you care about, care for, and who care about you.

You will soon know what I mean when I say that astrology and tarot are not fortune-telling, but they can help you to make your fortune. Whenever I say that at a party, people always ask me if I have won the lottery. I always say yes and point to Amy.

"Twisting your fate" won't guarantee that you will win the lottery, but using the truly astounding amount of important information Theresa has shared with us in this book will make you feel that you *have* won the lottery—your own, personal, self-made fortune. Too often people think that their lives are written in the stars, that the birth chart is some sort of fated menu for the rest of their life. Nothing could be further from the truth. Your chart is about possibility and potential, and Theresa will teach you how to unlock that potential to reap the rewards of your best and brightest future.

Theresa always says, "Astrology creates the map. Tarot shows you the detours." When you look at that map from Theresa's astrological perspective, you will expand your consciousness and your understanding of your world on the most practical level. With that insight in hand, Theresa then shows you how to use the tarot as a guide to navigate the strengths and weaknesses, the potentials and pitfalls of your birthchart so that you can "twist your fate" (that is, be the author of your own life) to accomplish just about any goal you set out to accomplish. Not sure of your goals? With Theresa's astrological guidance, you'll learn how to recognize them; with her tarot guidance you'll learn how to manifest them.

Learning to interpret your chart and listening to what the tarot is trying to tell you will greatly increase your intuition—and that puts you in a much better mind/body/spirit state to know whether or not you have a (nanoparticle-sized) chance of winning the lottery. You'll learn to not waste your money on a ticket.

However, your chance of winning the game-of-life lottery *will* be improved by allowing Theresa to guide you on the journey to self-understanding she has mapped out for you in the pages of this book. There are no guarantees, of course—no one is guaranteed another breath, let alone winning the lottery. But since life does not come with an instruction manual, becoming aware and empowered using the information in this book, and incorporating it into your life through the suggested journaling and exercises, will help put you in the positive state of mind that we all need to function efficiently and enjoy life in this hectic and challenging world.

Looking at life through the lens of astrology, tarot, and developing your intuition is also a lot of fun. Theresa's sense of humor is as legendary as her ability to help people, and it is here for your enjoyment over all the pages of this book. Facing up to the self-knowledge that you are about to be offered does require a sense of humor. We all need to be able to laugh when we read her delineations of our astrology placements and realize, "Oh my gosh! That's me!" Expect that to happen quite a few times.

Astrology and tarot add spice to our lives, but no one can live just on spices. Theresa Reed's real-world approach to both practices, and her unique take on integrating them and understanding your intuition's power, are a complete and supremely nourishing meal, one that helps satisfy the hunger we all have for understanding the meaning of our lives. Let's eat!

—Monte Farber

author of *Mindful Astrology* and the bestselling *Enchanted Tarot*

# Introduction

**M**any years ago, I found myself on a beach in the Florida Keys. I can't swim, and the sun is not my friend, so this was certainly not my idea of a good time. In fact, I was miserable. It wasn't just the heat. My life had hit a brick wall after a series of stupid decisions, and I wasn't sure what my next move would be. I was rudderless.

As I laid on a blanket, contemplating my sad state of affairs, a hippie plopped down on the blanket next to me and said he wanted to read my palm. Suspicious of his motives (hippie dudes always seemed to have other agendas with me), I carefully jutted out my hand while keeping a lit cigarette burning in the other, just in case I had to make a fast move. He studied the lines and said a few things about being "sensitive" and other stuff I no longer remember. The only thing that stuck out: he told me I would be in business for myself and that I would be successful.

I scoffed at this idea. Business? What would *I* do?

I couldn't imagine running anything, especially since the only thing I seemed to be good at was running away from my problems. Plus, the odds were stacked against me. I grew up poor, didn't have a college degree, zero money in the bank (truth: I didn't even have an account), and no one to bail me out.

Business success seemed like something for lucky folks or rich guys, ala Gordon Gecko. Certainly not for some free-spirited ragamuffin like me!

Fast forward a few years later, and I'm a full-time self-employed tarot reader. I've had a business for thirty years as of this writing, and I'm now the author of many books. The hippie was right!

Was it luck? Talent? Hard work? I would say a little bit from all three. Turns out I've also got some damn good business instincts. Who'd a thought that (except that hippie!)?

But there has been another secret to my success: I stopped being a flake, got serious about something I loved, and started making better decisions. The latter got accelerated when I began using the same tools for myself that I used for my clients: tarot and astrology.

I will also say this: I wasn't an overnight sensation. It took time. Like I said: I had a lot of strikes against me. There was one more I didn't list, and that was my messy astrology chart.

I've got the kind of natal chart that elicits gasps from many astrologers. There are so many "bad" aspects, it's a wonder I've been able to achieve anything. I've had plenty of predictions that seemed to point to a frustrating future. For a time, that was true.

But one thing I've learned through the years is how to work with the gifts and challenges in my natal chart. I've also found ways to manage the transits of the stars in the skies to move with the energy rather than against the flow. I've tossed tarot cards when I needed guidance, and I've strengthened my intuition through trial and error.

Looking back on my life, I can say one thing for sure: if you've been dealt a difficult set of cards or a not-so-great astrological blueprint like mine, it doesn't mean you're stuck with it. You can take control and find your way, too.

In this book, I share the astrology and tarot techniques I've used for myself and my clients for many years. You'll learn how to find potential paths best suited for your cosmic makeup and how to groove with the current movement of the cosmos. I'm also revealing career and entrepreneur-centered tarot interpretations for better business decision making. Lastly, I've got a few techniques to help you develop your own instincts (yes, you have them too—we all have intuition!). My goal is to give you the tools to navigate the hard stuff and carve out a destiny you love (or at the very least, know how to manage the challenging aspects).

There is no such thing as a "bad" astrology chart, nor is your fate sealed in hardened wax. You have options, and you get to choose how you show up. As I always say: the cards tell a story, but you write the ending.

Let's find your happy (or happier) ending.

xo

Theresa

# How to Use This Book

## *"What do you want to be when you grow up?"*

We're asked that from the time we can form sentences. Some people seem to know what they want to do right from the jump. Most of us seem to find our way . . . eventually. There are also some folks who have circumstances beyond their control that hinder their ability to move ahead. In contrast, others have everything handed on a silver platter, yet they drift from one thing to another. A lot of us "wing it."

I went through various phases of wanting to do different things: sail the seven seas (ironic since I cannot swim), be a makeup artist to the stars, draw cartoons, be a psychiatrist, front a rock band, or be a muse to some heavy-metalhead. None of these plans worked out (well, except the last one). Instead, I bopped around a bit with a series of odd jobs (and strange relationships) before I found my way.

Thirty years later, I realize that every decision I made for my career got better when I used tarot and astrology to guide the way.

Look, there's a lot of pressure to "know" what you want—especially for kids fresh out of school. There's also a tremendous amount of stress placed on your shoulders to stay on a path, even when you discover you don't love it. (Fun story: I once had a factory job for a few months, hated it, quit, and then had to deal with the fallout from my family, who were convinced I would never have another "great job" like that one!)

Life isn't a neat, straight line. The journey is more like a million squiggles. Plans change. People do, too. We can want different things at different times in our lives. There is no "one way" or "right way." There's just *your* way.

Bottom line: you've got a life, and you want to succeed. Sick of navigating without a compass? No problem-o! With tarot and astrology, you'll always know which way to go . . . and when. (Type-A personalities and Virgos—get ready to rejoice!) Even if you get lost, you can find detours and new routes.

In this book, you're getting all of my favorite astrological and tarot techniques to help you make sense out of this puzzle called life. Our focus will center on vocation and purpose, not romance or relationships (that's for another book). You'll learn how to move with the cosmos in a way that allows for success with less stress, whether you're fresh out of college, a mid-life person in the middle of a downsize, a badass entrepreneur, or working for a company with your eyes on bigger prizes. Every single thing I'm sharing in this book is exactly what I've used for myself or in client sessions.

**I'd like you to do a few things before we begin:**

Get a journal. It can be any kind as long as you enjoy writing in it. Heck, it can be digital if you prefer. A journal is a vital tool for self-development. As you work your way through this book, there will be prompts and exercises to help you absorb the information. Your journal will be a record of your ever-evolving journey. I have kept many over the years. That's where I discovered some of my most profound epiphanies. (Psst . . . feel free to scribble all over this book and write in the margins, too! Use it up!)

Next, you'll need a copy of your birth chart (also known as a natal chart). You can use astrology software like Solar Fire or Time Passages. Or you can find free chart services online (my favorite is *astro.com*). If you order a chart online, what you'll receive looks very much like the illustration on page 5. To get an accurate birth chart, you'll need your date, time of birth, and birthplace. You can find this on your birth certificate. If your certificate doesn't have all the info, you may need to rely on a parent's memory. But suppose you've been adopted, or your mom's memory isn't reliable. In that case, you can explore getting a "rectified chart," a specialized service where the astrologer will look at critical events in your life and use those to determine your birth time. Also, rest assured: if worse comes to worst, we can use a solar chart, which will have a ton of helpful info for you! I promise not to leave you high and dry! (A solar chart is constructed by placing the Sun on the Ascendant with each house associated with an entire sign. For example, if you have a Gemini Sun, Gemini will be your Rising Sign and on your 1st house. Cancer will be on your 2nd while Leo will be on your 3rd and so on. This is what astrologers use when they write horoscopes for newspapers.)

I also recommend getting astrology software for your computer or smartphone. You'll need it to look at the transits. Again, at this time, the best is Solar Fire for PCs and Time Passages for Mac.

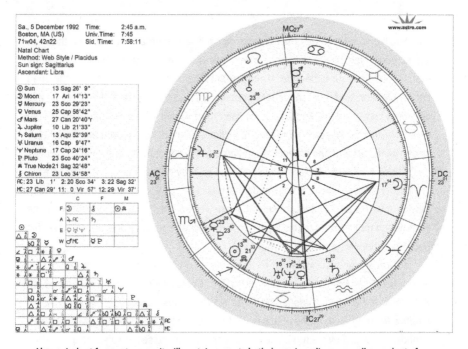

Sa., 5 December 1992  Time:      2:45 a.m.
Boston, MA (US)        Univ.Time: 7:45
71w04, 42n22          Sid. Time: 7:58:11
Natal Chart
Method: Web Style / Placidus
Sun sign: Sagittarius
Ascendant: Libra

| ⊙ Sun | 13 Sag 26' 9" |
| ☽ Moon | 17 Ari 14'13" |
| ☿ Mercury | 23 Sco 29'23" |
| ♀ Venus | 25 Cap 58'42" |
| ♂ Mars | 27 Can 20'40"r |
| ♃ Jupiter | 10 Lib 21'33" |
| ♄ Saturn | 13 Aqu 52'39" |
| ♅ Uranus | 16 Cap 9'47" |
| Ψ Neptune | 17 Cap 24'16" |
| ♇ Pluto | 23 Sco 40'24" |
| ☊ True Node | 21 Sag 32'48" |
| ⚷ Chiron | 23 Leo 34'58" |
| AC: 23 Lib 1' | 2: 20 Sco 34' | 3: 22 Sag 32' |
| MC: 27 Can 29' | 11: 0 Vir 57' | 12: 29 Vir 37' |

www.astro.com

Above: A chart from *astro.com*. It will contain aspects both drawn in as lines, as well as a chart of those aspects. Below: the same birth chart in its simplest form, showing signs, planets, and houses.

You'll also want to get a set of tarot cards. There are many available on the market, so you'll have plenty to choose from. Pick one that makes you happy. Simple as that. If you're not sure, the *Rider Waite Smith* is the perfect starter deck. It's the one I cut my teeth on, and most modern tarot cards are based on the imagery. (Psst . . . this deck was created in 1909 so it's not inclusive. If you want a new, beautiful, reimagined version of this deck, repainted to restore inclusivity, check out *The Weiser Tarot*. I also strongly recommend *The Modern Witch Tarot,* another beautiful update—and diverse.)

These will be the tools you'll use for the journey ahead (plus your sixth sense!). We'll cover some of the astrology and tarot basics to get your feet wet if you're a total newbie. If you're an old hand, consider it a review! Also, I'm staying laser-focused on the information that matters to this topic. I'm keeping it as simple as possible to make this book user-friendly (and not overwhelming).

However, suppose you want to dive deep into astrology or tarot. In that case, I recommend grabbing a copy of my other two books: *Astrology for Real Life—A No B.S. Guide for the AstroCurious* and *Tarot: No Questions Asked—Mastering the Art of Intuitive Reading*. Both of these books will give you a strong foundation and build your confidence (plus, they are fun!). The recommended reading section also includes some more advanced books, organized by subject area, if you want more information on a particular aspect of astrology or tarot.

This book is divided into four sections: **astrology**, **tarot**, **intuition, and a bonus section** that provides an indepth exercise to show you how to put it all together so you can see what it means to "twist your fate." Together, astrology, tarot, and intuition will help you make great decisions, solve problems, brainstorm ideas, and ultimately find your best path, no matter where you are right now.

Along the way, you'll find anecdotes, fun exercises, journaling prompts, and valuable tips. There will be **Astrocises**  and **Tarotcises** .

Please do the activities—they will help you absorb the information down to your bones. Also, keep an eye out for "common sixth sense"—nuggets of level-headed wisdom sprinkled throughout the book, because sometimes you don't need a mystical solution—you just need to use your darn head!

Alright—we've got work to do. Let's roll!

# BUT FIRST . . . A WORD ABOUT FATE AND FREE WILL

When people come to a tarot reader or astrologer, they want to know what lies ahead. "What's my future? Will I get married? Am I going to be rich?" These are some of the typical questions that someone in my profession hears all the time.

People assume that their lives are laid out like some sort of preordained story, with a beginning, a middle, and hopefully, a happy ending. But it's not quite like that. Although some events may appear fated, our destiny is mostly in our hands.

There are some things you cannot control. For example, your birth and early childhood are not things you get to say much about. Although karma and reincarnation theorists say we choose our incarnation, I don't think it's that simple. Plus, that puts the blame on you for your early circumstances—and that's not fair, nor does it make sense.

Some people are born into advantageous situations—wealth, privilege, loving homes—while others struggle to survive. Systemic racism, poverty, and lack of education are among the things that make it difficult for a good chunk of the population to succeed; and no matter how great the stars are aligned, those situations are complicated and baked into our society.

While astrology and tarot can help you find the way or dictate certain things, neither is a perfect science. You'll often hear me say it's all theory. What we do with the information and our circumstances is where the magic happens. (Psst . . . sometimes the way up is to ask for help.)

Let me give you an example. Let's say two people are born on the same day, same time, and in the same town—so they have the same chart—but they are born into radically different circumstances. One is born into wealth and lives a life of privilege, while the other lives in poverty without access to the basics. We can say that fate has carved out a completely different destiny for these individuals, even though they have the same charts. They may have the same astrological events happening simultaneously. Still, their circumstances are different, and prospects are unique for each.

Now let's say that they grow up, and the first one (the one born into wealth) struggles with addiction. In contrast, the second individual (the one less privileged) receives aid from a charity, goes to college on a scholarship, and starts to rise out of poverty. Different life experiences, different choices, two people with the same chart. The first one languishes in the land of "no success"; the second one creates a successful life.

Here's another example. A child is considered a gifted artist because they display talent at an early age. Perhaps they are a prodigy. But what if the child gets older and decides they don't really want to be an artist? What if they make a different choice and decide to run for governor or become a dog walker? Everyone thought this child would be the next Picasso . . . but that didn't happen. This child grew up and made a *choice*.

After many years of doing astrology and tarot, I fall somewhat in between the fate versus free will camp. I do believe some things are "meant to be" and cannot be explained. In some cases, we can get a glimpse of the future. Other times, the Universe surprises you.

We can also see where things are going based upon past and present decisions. Simple logic will tell you that if you eat bad food and never exercise, you'll probably end up with health problems. You don't need a crystal ball to see that outcome.

A good tarot reader or astrologer will look at all these possibilities, then study the cards or stars to see where you can make a change. From there, the future is up to you. That doesn't mean it's going to be easy. For some, making change is hard, especially if they're fearful of what that entails (not everyone likes change) or if their situation requires many sacrifices and help to get there.

I do believe you can twist your fate—you can bend it and shape it every which-way. I've done it, and I want you to have that same power to manifest your best destiny.

## Journaling prompt:

Have you ever experienced a situation that felt fated? How did you handle it? Did you ever feel a decision completely changed your path? Where do you think you'd be now if you had made a different choice? Journal your thoughts.

## Common Sixth Sense:

When someone is going through a rough patch, it's never helpful to say, "Everything happens for a reason." We often say that because other people's struggles make us uncomfortable. If a loved one is in pain or can't seem to find their way, a better response would be "I'm really sorry you're going through this. How can I help?"

PART ONE

# Cover
# Your
# Ass-trology

# The Fast 'n Furious Astrology Review

**B**efore we dive into making astrology work for you, you need to grasp the basics. If you're familiar with astrology, this is a quick review. For newbies, consider this your *CliffNotes* version. (And for those who are newbies, I recommend my book *Astrology for Real Life* for an in-depth course in learning astrology.)

## WHAT IS A NATAL CHART?

When an astrologer refers to a natal chart, they are talking about your birth chart, which is a map of where the planets were stationed in the sky at the time of your birth. The natal chart shows your potential, as well as possible struggles.

The natal chart gives clues to your life purpose, but remember: much can change depending on your choices, lived experience, and how you manage ongoing transits.

## WHAT'S A TRANSIT?

A transit means the current movement of the planets in the sky. Astrologers compare transits to your natal chart, which determines where you're going, what's possible, and potential problems you might want to avoid.

## BREAKING DOWN THE BONES OF A NATAL CHART

When you first glance at a natal chart, you may be confused. It looks like a big ole pizza with all kinds of mystical symbols (like pieces of pepperoni!). Don't worry—it's not that hard! Once you learn the basics, you're good to go—and over time, you can choose to go down many astrological rabbit holes (like this book!).

Think of astrology (and tarot, for that matter) as a language. When you first begin speaking a new language, you probably feel a bit timid. But with practice, it gets easier. One of the fastest ways to learn is immersing yourself with a fluent teacher (that's me!).

Deep breaths—let's hit it! Intermediate and advanced astrology friends—you can skim through this stuff, skip it totally, or devour—up to you!

**There are four essential components to astrology that you need to know:**

**The Planets**—The planets show what is operating. For example, the Moon is associated with emotions.

**The Signs**—The signs show how the energy of that planet is being expressed. For example, Aries tends to be passionate, original, and bold, while Taurus's energy is slower-paced, sensual, and stubborn.

**The Houses**—The houses show where everything is taking place or the areas of your life that are being impacted. This is where you might be highly focused or where you'll work out certain aspects of your fate. For example, the 7th house is the relationship sector of your chart. A cluster of planets here could mean that significant partnerships could play a big role in your life, or your major lessons may come through the people in your orbit.

**The Aspects**—the aspects show if the energy between the planets is favorable or tricky. A "good" aspect might give you a certain amount of luck or talent, whereas a "bad" aspect might indicate where you've got work to do.

**Bonus! These guys are good to know:**

**The Nodes**—these lunar points in the sky show your karmic destiny. By the way, these are not planets. The Nodes are determined by mathematical calculations. There are two nodes, North and South.

The South Node, also known as the dragon's tail, symbolizes gifts and talents from past incarnations. It's the place you naturally go, because it's easy or the path of least resistance (kinda like your astrological pillow fort!).

The North Node, also called the dragon's head, is the "way out," the karma we are here to work on, or the path of integration. The North Node is challenging, but if we lean into it, magic happens!

**Chiron**—Chiron is referred to as the "wounded healer." In your chart, this asteroid represents where you can find great strength once you've worked through your wounds. For example, I had a client with Chiron in the 4th house. She had a horrible childhood, which required a lot of work to overcome. Helping other families, particularly children, became her life's mission. She's been working as a family therapist for decades.

**The ruling planet**—this is the most important planet in your chart. It's your "guiding force." You can determine the ruling planet by looking at the sign on your Ascendant. If you're a Virgo rising, your ruling planet would be Mercury.

Okay, now that we've got a brief outline, let's get a little more detail. The keywords will give you enough astro-vocabulary for chart interpretation.

# The Signs

There are twelve signs in the zodiac. Each one is associated with a symbol, element, quality, and statement.

## Aries ♈

Symbol: Ram
Element: Fire
Quality: Cardinal
Ruling Planet: Mars

Aries is passionate, intense, fiery, and pro-active. They love to take the initiative and can always be found where the action is. Aries can be impulsive, and when they go that route, they tend to burn bridges even while blazing trails. A bit of restraint keeps them fired up and going strong.

## Taurus ♉

Symbol: Bull
Element: Earth
Quality: Fixed
Ruling Planet: Venus

Taurus is slow-moving, patient, reliable, and down-to-earth. They adore luxury, fine meals, and beautiful things. Security is essential to them—most of their efforts will be geared toward creating a safety net. Two traits to guard against: possessiveness and stubbornness.

## Gemini ♊

Symbol: The Twins
Element: Air
Quality: Mutable
Ruling Planet: Mercury

Gemini is quick-witted, sharp-tongued, curious, and intellectual. They love to learn and are perpetual students. Always on the go, it's hard to pin them down. At times, they can be superficial—or flighty.

## Cancer ♋

Symbol: The Crab
Element: Water
Quality: Cardinal
Ruling Planet: The Moon

Cancer is sensitive, tender-hearted, and motherly. Nurturing comes naturally to them, and they can be psychic, too. The negative side of Cancer is clinginess, possessiveness, and a tendency to smother the ones they love.

## Leo ♌

Symbol: The Lion
Element: Fire
Quality: Fixed
Ruling Planet: The Sun

Leo is bold, noble, glamorous, generous, and passionate. They have a regal bearing and want to be respected. When they don't get that, they can be pretty dramatic. No one roars as loudly as a Leo scorned. The center of attention is their favorite spot to be in—they must be careful this doesn't lead to a self-centered approach to life.

## Virgo ♍

Symbol: The Virgin
Element: Earth
Quality: Mutable
Ruling Planet: Mercury

Virgo lives to serve. They are meticulous, analytical, and adept at sorting out the details. Work is their favorite thing in the world, and if you work with them, you may have a hard time matching their attention to the small stuff. Virgos can be nasty critics and fussbudgets. Learning to relax can curb that.

## Libra ♎

Symbol: The Scales
Element: Air
Quality: Cardinal
Ruling Planet: Venus

Libra loves balance, harmony, and justice. If something isn't fair, they will do what they can to fix matters. Art and beauty are essential to them. If they are in ugly, chaotic environments, they wilt. Passive-aggressiveness and indecision can wreck their relationships, which are their lifeblood. If they can't just get along, they'll quickly move on to the next one.

## Scorpio ♏

Symbol: The Scorpion
Element: Water
Quality: Fixed
Ruling Planet: (Traditional) Mars and (Modern) Pluto

Scorpio gets a rep for being "extra." They are spicy, secretive, intense, and full of passion (sounds great to me!). Every one of them seems to have a built-in bullshit detector. Lesser qualities are vindictiveness, possessiveness, and a tendency to shut people out when they're pissed.

## Sagittarius

Symbol: The Archer
Element: Fire
Quality: Mutable
Ruling Planet: Jupiter

Sagittarius is a truth-teller. They seek freedom, justice, adventure, and possess a fine moral compass. Ever the wanderer, exploring parts unknown satisfies their need to see what's out there. They must watch out that they don't become flaky, unreliable, or self-righteous.

## Capricorn ♑

Symbol: The Goat
Element: Earth
Quality: Cardinal
Ruling Planet: Saturn

Capricorn is the CEO of the zodiac. They get shit done. In fact, they are born to lead. Get behind a Capricorn, and you'll reach the top of any mountain. They are also grounded, pragmatic, and dependable. But they can also be social climbers, willing to step on whatever heads they need to satisfy their ambitions. When they do that, they quickly discover it's lonely at the top.

## Aquarius ♒

Symbol: The Water Bearer
Element: Air
Quality: Fixed
Ruling Planet: (Traditional) Saturn and (Modern) Uranus

Aquarius is eccentric, innovative, and independent. They've got tons of friends from every walk of life—and are tolerant folks, even when others don't show them the same. Humanitarian pursuits make their souls happy, but they can come off as cold at times.

## Pisces ♓

Symbol: The Fish
Element: Water
Quality: Mutable
Ruling Planet: (Traditional) Jupiter and (Modern) Neptune

Pisces is emotional, poetic, compassionate, and intuitive. They are naturally drawn to creativity or the healing arts. They are gentle types and easily hurt. Sometimes they will seek an escape, which in worse case scenarios, can spiral into addiction.

# The Planets

Each planet represents a different part of you—or your life. Combined with the zodiac signs, you get a composite picture of your strengths, weaknesses, and potential.

## THE PERSONAL PLANETS:

### The Sun

The Sun is your basic personality. It shows how you shine and gives clues to what you're here to do.

### The Moon

The Moon represents your emotional life, how you react to situations, what you need to feel secure, and how you parent.

### Mercury

Mercury is the messenger, and it indicates how you communicate, think, and process information.

## Venus

Venus rules love, relationships, and how you like to be romanced. It's also associated with beauty, luxury, and cash attraction.

## Mars

Mars is your drive, ambition, and energy. It's how you lead, fight, and get it on. (This will be important for career matters.)

# THE SOCIAL PLANETS:

## Jupiter

Jupiter is where you are lucky. This is your talent and where you can expand.

## Saturn

Saturn rules limitations and lessons. Once you understand Saturn, you'll be ready to rock your world. Here's the gist: no one likes Saturn because it's a hard taskmaster. BUT the rewards come when you embrace the work.

# THE OUTER PLANETS:

These three bad boys are more concerned with a generation due to their slow movement. However, where they land in the natal chart and how they interact with other planets could be powerful stuff.

## Uranus

Uranus is the rebel planet. On its own, it indicates where shake-ups and wakeups happen. Unpredictable changes are Uranus's domain. Uranus also rules technology, innovation, and humanitarianism. It's the collective in a nutshell.

## Ψ Neptune

Neptune rules illusions, spirituality, creativity, and sacrifice. It's also associated with escapism and addiction.

## ♇ Pluto

Pluto was demoted to a dwarf planet, but astrologers beg to differ. This faraway orb is connected with transformation, regeneration, and power.

# The Houses

There are twelve houses in the astrological chart. Each one represents a different part of your life.

**Life themes represented by the houses.**

**1st**—This is your public image or how you present yourself to the world.

**2nd**—The 2nd house is associated with money and values.

**3rd**—This house is all about communication, mind, short trips, siblings, and early education.

**4th**—This is your home base or foundation. It can also have something to say about family.

**5th**—The 5th rules creativity, fame, children, speculation, and self-expression, as well as games and leisure.

**6th**—Health and work fall under the 6th house.

**7th**—Relationships of all kinds and out in the open enemies are 7th house subjects.

**8th**—Taxes, death, joint finances, inheritances, and sex are associated with the 8th house.

**9th**—Religion, philosophy, higher education, travel, and publishing—you can find them all in the 9th house.

**10th**—Career, reputation, politics, and fame.

**11th**—This is the house that symbolizes your social circle, network, community, and goals.

**12th**—The 12th house is the private you. This symbolizes secrets, subconscious, inner work, rest, and hidden enemies.

**For careerists and entrepreneurs,** I have presented on page 21 a modified version of house meanings to help you plot out bold business moves.

**1st**—The 1st house is your public image or brand.

**2nd**—The 2nd house is how you make money, handle it, and your business values.

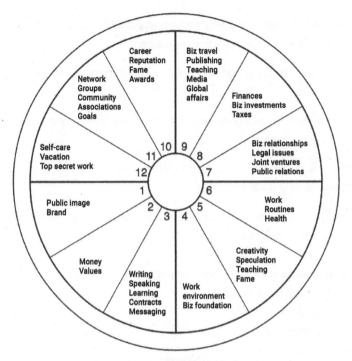

**Business themes represented by the houses.**

**3rd—**The 3rd house is associated with writing, speaking, learning, contracts, and brand messaging.

**4th—**The 4th house is your working environment as well as your business foundation.

**5th—**The 5th is associated with creativity, speculation, monetary gain from real estate, teaching, entertainment industry, and one of the fame houses.

**6th—**The 6th house is work, routines, and health.

**7th—**The 7th house is your partnership zone. It also rules legal issues, binding agreements, joint ventures, competitors, public relations, and advertising. If you have a business enemy, observe this house.

**8th—**The 8th house is associated with business investments, taxes, joint finances, debt collection, legacy work, budgets, insurance, and loans.

**9th—**The 9th house is connected to business travel, publishers, teaching, writers, global affairs, and media.

**10th—**The 10th house is associated with reputation, fame, awards, ambition, public life, and overall career direction.

**11th—**The 11th house rules community, network, online groups, goals, associations, humanitarian work, and wishes.

**12th—**The 12th house is your self-care zone. It's associated with rest, vacations, secrets, behind-the-scenes activities, and secret enemies.

**There are four points in the natal chart that you'll want to mark down:**
The Ascendant (or Rising Sign)
The Imum Coeli (or Nadir)
The Descendant
The Midheaven

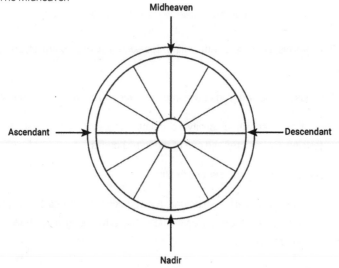

These are known as the "cardinal points," and much like the main points on a compass, they show where you've been and where to go. They also hold clues to how you interact with the world.

The Ascendant is located to the left of the astrology chart and is associated with the 1st house. This is your image. Planets on the Ascendant are important both in the natal chart and also in transits because they affect how you're presenting yourself.

The Imum Coeli (or Nadir) is at the bottom of the chart and the cusp of the 4th house. This rules your root—it's where you're coming from. When a planet lands here, it can impact your home life or your business foundation. Transits over the 4th house cusp can suggest a change of residence, family, or a chance to rebuild the foundation of your life . . . or business.

The Descendant is to the right of the chart on the cusp of your 7th house and tells a lot about the people in your life and how you interact with them. Planets in this house could point out areas where compromises are needed and where healing can happen. On the career front, transits in this house can give you clues about contracts, business partnerships, as well as PR campaigns.

The Midheaven is super important, and you should probably put a big ole circle over it. This shows where you're going, who you're becoming, and your most tremendous potential. It's at the top of your chart, on the cusp of your 10th house. When you lean into your Midheaven, you can see how to show up in the world as the very best version of you. This is your success point—and if you work with it, you could see significant gains. We'll be covering this just up ahead.

**A note about house systems:** there are many house systems to choose from. Two of the most popular are Placidus and Whole Signs. I prefer Placidus, but you might not. Test a few out and find one that makes sense for YOU. Your astrology software settings will allow you to choose your fave.

# The Aspects

There are plenty of aspects to consider, but I only work with the main guys. Aspects are geometric angles between the planets. They indicate if the planets are getting along . . . or not. When you're experiencing transits that impact the planets in your natal chart, they can show opportunities or potential problems.

 **Conjunction—0°** This is the most intense aspect and, therefore, the most important. A conjunction is two planets in the same sign, same degree (or close). This intensifies the energy for good or ill.

 **Sextile—60°** A sextile is a favorable aspect. It means the planets are playing nice.

**Square—90°** In my opinion, squares are the second most crucial aspect. Here, the planets are fighting with each other. They need to learn how to work together. When they do, great success is possible.

**Trine—120°** Trines are lovely. The planets are feeling groovy, getting along, and making things easy as can be. They can make you lazy, though.

**Opposition—180°** The planets are directly across from each other and refusing to cooperate. But opposites do attract! The way out: meet in the middle.

# Astrocise:

Grab your chart and take a gander at where everything sits. Now, fill in the blanks below:

My Sun is in sign_____ . It is in the _____ house.

My Moon is in sign _____ . It is in the _____ house.

My Mercury is in sign_____ . It is in the _____ house.

My Venus is in sign _____ . It is in the _____ house.

My Mars is in sign _____ . It is in the _____ house.

My Jupiter is in sign _____ . It is in the _____ house.

My Saturn is in sign_____ . It is in the _____ house.

My Uranus is in sign _____ . It is in the _____ house.

My Neptune is in sign_____ . It is in the _____ house.

My Pluto is in sign _____ . It is in the _____ house.

My Chiron is in sign_____ . It is in the_____ house.

My North Node is in sign_____ . It is in the _____ house.

My South Node is in sign _____ . It is in the_____ house.

The sign on the cusp of my Ascendant is _____ .

The sign on the cusp of my Imum Coeli is _____ .

The sign on the cusp of my Descendant is _____ .

The sign on the cusp of my Midheaven is _____ .

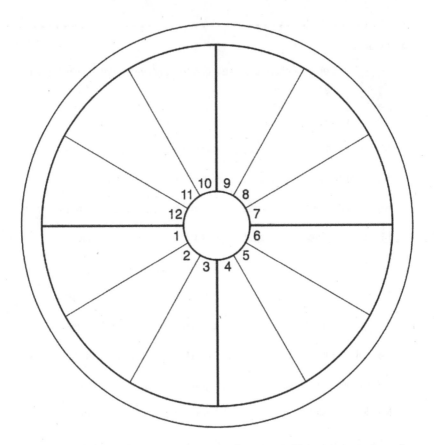

Take a minute to fill in your information from page 25 in the chart above (use the symbol cheat sheet below for symbols!). Note the keywords associated with each house where the signs and planets sit.

| Signs | | Planets | |
|---|---|---|---|
| ♈ Aries | ♎ Libra | ☉ Sun | ♃ Jupiter |
| ♉ Taurus | ♏ Scorpio | ☽ Moon | ♄ Saturn |
| ♊ Gemini | ♐ Sagittarius | ☿ Mercury | ♅ Uranus |
| ♋ Cancer | ♑ Capricorn | ♀ Venus | ♆ Neptune |
| ♌ Leo | ♒ Aquarius | ♂ Mars | ♇ Pluto |
| ♍ Virgo | ♓ Pisces | | |

# The Astrological "Secret Sauce"

O ur fast and furious review looked at the bare bones of your natal chart. But astrology is not just planets, signs, houses, and aspects. Each zodiac sign is classified by an element, a quality (also called a modality), and a rulership. Think of these components as ingredients in a recipe. When you understand these ingredients, you know why each sign has its own unique flavor.

## YOUR ELEMENTAL NATURE

The elements play a significant role in astrology (and tarot, too, for that matter). Think of them as forces of nature that shape your cosmic identity. Like the weather, they show patterns—and those patterns help us to better understand our tendencies, personality traits, and approach to life.

**There are four elements: Fire, Earth, Air, and Water.**

## Fire

Fire creates warmth. Think about sitting in front of a bonfire under a starlit night with a group of friends as you discuss your dreams for the future, and you'll know the magic of Fire. It helps to create comfort as it heats our homes and meals. But it must be handled with great care because it can quickly burn things down to a crisp.

Fire signs are passionate, intense, and warm. They can be impulsive and hard to control. When they get an idea, they are off and running—and not too concerned about the bridges burnt while blazing every trail. Every one of them has boatloads of courage, which is why you'll often find them in leadership positions. They're bold, enthusiastic, and exciting to be around.

*The Fire signs are: Aries, Leo, and Sagittarius.*

# Earth

Earth is grounded, practical, and abundant. It provides stability and opportunities to grow the things that nourish us. This is where we plant the seeds for the future, tend to what matters, and create. It's our security. But it can be unmovable, a hard, impenetrable rock. When that happens, everything dries up, and not much can flourish.

Earth signs are pragmatic and solid. You know where you stand with them. They love to take care of the people around them, and they can always be counted on. Material things give them comfort, and security is essential. But sometimes, they can become possessive and stubborn. When they go that route, it is impossible to reason with them. They will let their guard down only if they feel safe . . . or in control.

*The Earth signs are: Taurus, Virgo, and Capricorn.*

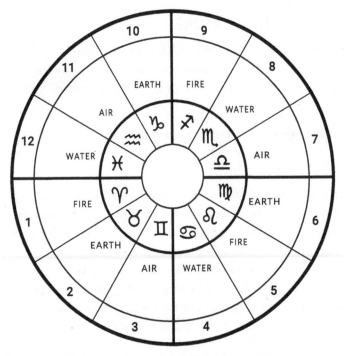

The four elements associated with their house and sign.

## Air

Air is adaptable, intelligent, and always on the move. You cannot contain it. It's all around you, but you cannot see it. Air can cool our bodies and provide relief on a sweltering day. But it is unpredictable. It can stir up dust, whip the ocean into a frenzy, and tear down entire villages. When Air is swirling out of control, we must hold on or risk being blown away.

Air signs are intellectuals. They live in the realm of ideas and love to communicate. Social activity is vital—each of them enjoys an active social life. You'll often find Air signs flitting about from one cool scene to another. Because they are changeable, they do not like to be tied down. If you push, they run like a deer, leaving everyone confused. Air signs must work on grounding, or they risk scattering their forces to the winds.

*The Air signs are: Gemini, Libra, and Aquarius.*

## Water

Water is deep, fluid, and mysterious. Without Water, the earth would die. It creates the conditions for life. Think of for a moment how the planet—and even humans—are mostly made of Water. Water flows but can be stagnant too. It can overpower, drown, and evaporate. When it's calm, it's beautiful, but when stirred up, Water can overwhelm.

Water signs are emotional, intuitive, and sensitive. It's easy for them to be in touch with their feelings and desires. They love to forge meaningful connections and will often take on a nurturing role. Depth is vital in their relationships. From time to time, they can get hung up on the past or emotionally charged situations. When that happens, they can wallow in silence—or they lose their objectivity, and their feelings get the best of them.

*The Water signs are: Cancer, Scorpio, or Pisces.*

- - - - - - - - - - - - - - - - - - - - - - - - - - - - - - - - - - - - - - - - - - - - - - - - - - - - - - -

## Astrocise

Count up the elements in your chart and fill in the boxes below with those numbers. Do you have an abundance of one element and perhaps a lack of another? How do you think the balance of elements shows up in your personality? Don't assume that a lack in one element is a negative. Perhaps you have no Fire—this does not mean you are fated with poor leadership skills. Remember: you have free will! These elemental traits show tendencies, period. It's up to you to recognize those tendencies and learn to spot where they provide strengths and weaknesses.

Fire

Earth

Air

Water

# QUALITY CONTROL

In addition to the elements, each sign is assigned a "quality," also known as "quadruplicities" or "modalities." The qualities will give you an idea of how each sign operates or acts.

**There are three qualities: Cardinal, Fixed, and Mutable.**

## Cardinal

Cardinal signs like to initiate things. They are the movers and shakers of the zodiac. The shadow side of this quality is selfishness with a "me first" mantra. The Cardinal signs are Aries, Cancer, Libra, and Capricorn. Each one also represents the start of the season.

## Fixed

Fixed signs like to maintain and sustain. Routines are essential to them. They are the "Reliable Rogers" in the zodiac. However, they don't like change and can be stubborn. The Fixed signs are Taurus, Leo, Scorpio, and Aquarius.

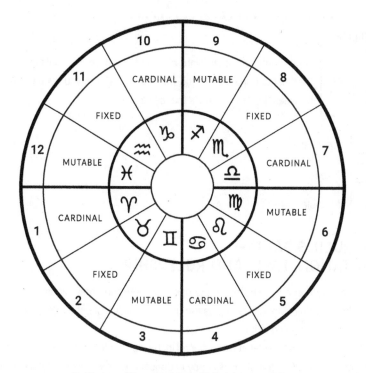

The three qualities associated with their house and sign.

## Mutable

Mutable signs are adaptable. They adore change and can go with the flow of life. But they can be restless and flaky. The Mutable signs are Gemini, Virgo, Sagittarius, and Pisces.

· · ·

If you have an abundance of one quality, the positive and negative aspects can shine through like a halogen light. Lacking one? Well, that can play out two ways. Either it's obvious as a hair on your chin—or you overcompensate in some way to fill the void.

## Astrocise

Go through your chart right now and count up the qualities. Are you Cardinal dominant? Lacking Mutable vibes? Are you evenly balanced between the three? What's that say about you?

☐ Cardinal

☐ Fixed

☐ Mutable

# THE RULING PARTY—
# EXALTATION, FALL, AND RULERSHIP

Someone long ago decided the planets operated better in some signs than others. While I beg to differ (Moon in Scorpios are great!), I didn't make the rules. There are a few categories you need to know:

Rulership refers to a planet being placed in the sign it rules. For example, the Moon rules Cancer. Therefore the Moon is happy in Cancer and able to express itself well.

## Detriment

Detriment happens when a planet is on the opposite side of the one it rules. The planet is uncomfortable and has trouble expressing the energy. For example, if the Moon was in Capricorn, it's opposite the ruler, Cancer. Therefore, it's not feeling groovy and may struggle to show emotions, which are associated with the Moon.

## Exaltation

Exaltation is the bomb-dot-com! Here, the planet is placed in a sign where it operates like a total boss with the absolute best expression. For example, if the Moon is in Taurus, it's exalted because someone decided that's the best placement. Moon in Taurus people are gentle, solid, and kindly. (Psst . . . they can be stubborn as a drunken mule so don't assume it's all peaches 'n cream!)

# Fall

When a planet is in the sign directly opposite the exalted version, it's considered to be in its fall. This means it's the worst expression of that planet. Pfft. Frankly, I think that's a bit extreme, but again—I didn't make these rules! For example, the opposite of the Moon in Taurus, which is exalted, would be the Moon in Scorpio (if you were here, you'd hear me hissing right now). Moon in Scorpio is considered the least favorable position because it's intense and volcanic. (If you have this placement, you're deep and psychic too—which is nifty!)

Below I've provided a handy dandy chart with everything mapped out for you. Memorize this stuff because you'll be graded on it (kidding!).

| Planet | Rulership | Detriment | Exaltation | Fall |
|--------|-----------|-----------|------------|------|
| Sun | Leo | Aquarius | Aries | Libra |
| Moon | Cancer | Capricorn | Taurus | Scorpio |
| Mercury | Gemini/Virgo | Sagittarius/Pisces | Virgo | Pisces |
| Venus | Taurus/Libra | Scorpio/Aries | Pisces | Virgo |
| Mars | Aries/Scorpio | Libra/Taurus | Capricorn | Cancer |
| Jupiter | Sagittarius/Pisces | Gemini/Virgo | Cancer | Capricorn |
| Saturn | Capricorn/Aquarius | Cancer/Leo | Libra | Aries |
| Uranus | Aquarius | Leo | Scorpio | Taurus |
| Neptune | Pisces | Virgo | Cancer | Capricorn |
| Pluto | Scorpio | Taurus | Leo | Aquarius |

• • •

Okay, that's our mini review. Now that we have the basics, we'll focus on using this stuff! By the way, if you feel you want a deeper dive into the foundational info, grab a copy of *Astrology For Real Life* or any astrology book you like. One of my faves: *The Astrologer's Handbook* by Frances Sakoian and Louis S. Acker. It's dense, dry, and complete.

Let's figure out what you need, how you roll, and how to twist your fate in the most beneficial way. Onward!

# The Big Three:
# Super-Natural You!

Before we start plotting and planning the best courses of action, you'll want to consider your cosmic makeup. Once you understand your needs and how you best operate in the world, you'll be less likely to waste your time on unsuitable vocations or paths.

Let's start with the Elemental basics.

## THE BIG THREE

There are three main points astrologers look at when trying to determine what you're all about:

**Your Sun**
**Your Moon**
**Your Ascendant**

My friend Amy Zerner coined the term "Celestial Trilogy" to describe these points. I call them the "Big Three." Most astrologers will tell you this trio gives enough information to get a clear picture of who you are and what makes you tick. Once you understand how these astrological bad boys impact your natal blueprint, you can start to make life path decisions that are right for you.

Let me explain.

No two people are the same. As you know from our mini-review, astrology is more than just the Sun Sign horoscopes you read in the newspaper. The planets line up differently for every person, which is why you rarely meet two identical Virgos. Astrology is complex, and so are humans. Factor in lived experience, and you'll see unique stories unfold.

Here's why these three points are so relevant:

## The Sun

Most of us know what our Sun is thanks to newspaper horoscopes. The Sun shows how you express YOU. This is your purpose or what you're here to do. Understand your Sun, and you get a pretty good idea of what paths might be right up your alley!

## The Ascendant

The Ascendant, or Rising Sign, is your self-image. This is the "you" people see, no matter what your Sun sign may be. This shows how you best do the work of your Sun Sign. For example, if you're a Cancer, you're here to nurture. If your Ascendant is Aries, that might happen through motivational speaking or perhaps some sort of leadership role in your community.

## The Moon

La Luna gives details about your emotional life—and what your soul needs. It's not enough to have a purpose—you must understand what supports you on a deeper level. If you're not satisfied emotionally, your work will become just a job, not a calling. Using our Cancer/Aries example, if the Moon was in Virgo, the individual would need mental stimulation, an orderly environment, and to be of service. That would tip the energy toward a leadership role in the community, perhaps in nonprofit or social work.

What about if the Moon was in Capricorn? Now the Cancer/Aries person needs to feel in control of their environment. Their happiness requires stability, security, and responsibility. All that Cardinal sign energy would also mean they need action and might be great at getting things moving. If this is you, the last thing you'd want to be doing is sitting behind a desk with monotonous duties! Instead, you'd be on the front line of a movement or directing the show in some way.

Here are a few more examples:

If you're a Leo Sun with a Taurus Moon and a Virgo Ascendant, this would mean you are creative with a huge heart. You love being on stage and don't mind having all eyes on you. In fact, you're content with stepping into the leadership role wherever you can. You can see the big picture and know how to take command without losing your nobility. The public face you present to the world is more cautious and detail oriented. Instead of that bold Leo, you're perceived as a shy kitten. The Taurus Moon grounds your personality and adds a practical, down-to-earth vibe to your emotional makeup. What you need is security. When you feel secure, you easily dance between the limelight and backstage, happily grabbing the mic while ensuring every element is perfectly arranged.

Notice we have two in the Earth element and one in Fire. The Sun and Moon are both Fixed. The Sun rules Leo while the Moon is exalted in Taurus. This shows a warm personality that always has its feet on the ground. Sure, there is drama from time to time, usually caused by resistance to change. But once you are willing to meet people halfway, you can get things done.

You're well suited for work that requires big-picture thinking combined with a love for minutia. You could be a fine actor, CEO, designer, writer, project manager, entrepreneur, public speaker, or teacher. What might make you unhappy: being around people who are sloppy or control-freaking out (you can do the second part just fine). Working in filthy conditions makes your heart sad—and you wilt if there isn't a sensible plan. Those folks who fly by the seat of their pants? Aggravating. You need to know what to expect and when you do, you shine.

Now, let's look at a different trilogy.

You're a Gemini Sun, Scorpio Moon, and Libra Rising. You're a curious sort (Gemini), you're deeper than the ocean (Scorpio), and a social butterfly (Libra). At times, you're restless, which may lead to a tendency to wander from thing to thing before finding your groove. Even when you do, part of you is looking at the horizon, wondering what's next. Unlike our other example, your attention isn't always fixed. Instead, you've got a million things happening in your circus-like brain. The image you present to the world: totally together, with a perfectly coordinated ensemble and courteous exterior. You're a diplomat in every situation. You might be feeling some type of way, but no one sees that. Instead, they're taken in by your charm and wit. But underneath all of that

Audrey Hepburn swagger lies a deep, intense personality. While you're flighty about some things, when it comes to partnerships, you want to merge. If your passion isn't matched or your loyalty breached, you're done. At times, you can be obsessive. When you go that route, the airy Gemini/Libra nature gets swallowed up. This can work to your advantage in a career that requires a great deal of concentration, but in relationships? Not so much.

Here we have two in the Air Element and one in Water. The Sun is Mutable, the Moon is Fixed, and the Ascendant is Cardinal. The Moon is in its Fall, which means it's the least favorable expression of La Luna. This shows a personality that is both glib and intense. They may be hard to pin down or understand. One day they're all about the latest Megan Thee Stallion CD, the next day, they've moved on to some obscure band from Japan. They're bewildering to those who come into contact with them but also the subject of fascination.

If this is you, you're happiest when you're working in one of your many passions—for example, a good cause. You'd also be most excellent working in fashion, journalism, or as a detective (your ability to win folks over makes you a triple threat at ferreting out information). What wouldn't work: something tedious with zero interaction. Picture being in a room by yourself sorting out nuts and bolts, and you'll know a special kind of hell. You're also not feeling your groove thing around boring talk or situations where you have to make a long-term commitment. You need to be where the intellectual action is—and there must always be an escape door.

While these are simplified descriptions, you can see how radically different these two people are. You might think: these two could never work together. How can they get along?

But guess what: they are incredibly close—and they work well together. This is my daughter and me. Ta-da! Once you understand your (or other people's) astrological makeup, you've got keys to doing your best work—and encouraging others to do the same. More importantly, you're not trying to fit into a mold that doesn't suit you. You can be who you are and respect other people's uniqueness as well.

Psst . . . knowing the Big Three is super helpful when hiring folks. You can bring out their best—and avoid putting them into positions they hate! The most critical point: the Moon. Never put someone in a job that doesn't align with their emotional makeup.

## ABOUT THE WEATHER

Another way to look at Elements in the Big Three is to view them as the "weather patterns" in your makeup.

For example, let's say you're an Aquarius Sun, Gemini Moon, and Libra Rising. This is all Air, which means you can be changeable at a moment's notice and like plenty of breathing room. However, from time to time, you're like an unpredictable storm, scattering your energy far and wide.

Now, let's consider a Virgo Sun, Aries Moon, and Sagittarius Rising. Earth, Fire, Fire. The weather becomes like a hot summer day, which can fry the surface. This means you're stable and down to earth but intense. You need to find ways to cool down if you want to avoid overheating.

Here are a few more:

Capricorn Sun, Aquarius Moon, Gemini Rising—a beautiful snowstorm. It can be cold, but underneath the surface, bulbs are growing in time for the spring.

Scorpio Sun, Taurus Moon, Leo Rising—a gorgeous, lazy spring day with lots of sun, a little shade, and flowers in full bloom. There is harmony, passion, but also an unwillingness to move.

Sagittarius Sun, Leo Moon, Gemini Rising—a roaring fire on a cool night. But if the wind goes in the wrong direction, we've got a wildfire burning out of control.

See how that works? You can get an idea of temperament by studying the "cosmic weather" in the Elements.

. . . . . . . . . . . . . . . . . . . . . . . . . . . . . . . . . . . . . . . .

## Astrocise

Fill in the blanks:

My Sun is: _____

My Moon is: _____

My Ascendant is: _____

I express my Sun best by: _____

My Ascendant allows me to express myself by: _____

My Moon says this is what I need to be fulfilled: _____

My Sun is a(n) _____ sign.

My Moon is a(n) _____ sign.

My Ascendant is a(n) _____ sign.

My Elemental Weather Pattern might be described as: _____ .

Psst . . . if you forgot what each sign or element is all about, use clues from the Astrology Basics and Elements sections.

· · · · · · · · · · · · · · · · · · · · · · · · · · · · · · · · · · · · · · · · · · · · · · · · · · · · · · · ·

## Bonus Astrocise

 Use this little worksheet for your employees, coworkers, business partners, or family! Then ask yourself (or them) this question: "Does your work make you happy?" Once you have the answer, look at the Big Three and see how it plays out. What advice might you give them if they aren't grooving on their job?

### Common Sixth Sense

Don't use astrology to make "astro-excuses." While your chart can give a blueprint for your personality, you don't get to say, "Sorry not sorry I'm a jerk—I can't help it because I'm a Pisces with a Leo Moon!" That doesn't wash, ever.

# The Midheaven—Looking Up

So, you've got an understanding of your Big Three. This knowledge allows you to be the "real you." But where to go with all that? There's one place to look for the answer: the Midheaven. The Midheaven is the highest point in your natal chart, situated on the cusp of the 10th house. If it were a compass, it would be North.

It illuminates your potential and shows how you can achieve success. This is how you need to share yourself (and your gifts) with the world. If you want to find your calling or a way to stand out in your industry, look up to the top of your chart. The Midheaven is your "north star."

Not only will the Midheaven point you toward your best path for success, but it can also help you find one that makes you happy. Applying the wisdom of your Midheaven will allow you to align with your purpose—and impact the world in the most positive, productive way.

For some, the Midheaven may feel at odds with the Big Three. Here's the deal: the Big Three shows how you operate and what you need to be happy—but if you embrace the Midheaven, you're stepping into your star power.

Using myself as an example, I'm friendly, but actually quite introverted. My Scorpio Moon loves nothing more than being at home alone, surrounded by a stack of books and a good cat. Too much time around people, and I'm drained. In my career, I preferred to stay under the radar as much as possible. I leaned into my Moon hard. While my soul felt happy staying firmly in my comfort zone, my Leo Midheaven wanted attention (typical Leo!).

Leo on the top of my chart is the mark of the performer. It's ideal for rock stars, main stage speakers, politicians, and celebrities. It's NOT shy—and loves being in the spotlight: If I embraced that . . . what would happen?

Let's begin by looking back to the past. As I said, I'm an introvert. I'm quiet by nature and like my own company. But back in high school, I took a drama class on a whim, convinced it would help me get out of my shell a bit. Every time I hit the stage, it was like a completely different person emerged. Suddenly, I was animated, fiery, and funny. My teacher thought I had comedic talent, and every role I auditioned for was mine. While I had never been popular, this allowed me to open up and make new friends. Being on stage boosted my confidence—and it was NATURAL, even though I still preferred being a lone wolf.

In short: I was "successful" onstage but never made that connection until much later.

After years of hiding out in my safe introvert space, I finally put up a website (something I was terrified to do because of the fear of being "seen"). This allowed me to build a brand—and my business soared. But what really opened doors for me: getting on stage. Speaking at industry events led to opportunities, and hosting live streams upped my game. Suddenly, I had lots of new people in my orbit—and watched my following grow by leaps and bounds (it was always slow as honey on a frigid day before). Putting a mic in my hand was great for my biz and me.

If I had kept running my biz via my Scorpio Moon's need for privacy, I would have been fine but, most likely, missed out on many possibilities. I wasn't using my full potential nor my talents for wit 'n sparkle.

See how that works?

Your "Big Three" gives clues about your personality. When you combine those planetary super-friends with the Midheaven, you can find a true path that allows for success on your terms.

Look, I still love being alone, and I do make plenty of time for my private life. But every day, I let my Leo Midheaven lead the way in my business, which helps me connect with and entertain people all over the world. While my social media platforms aren't major television (that might be TOO much for me), they are still a stage and one that gives me a place to share my thoughts, knowledge, and humor.

When I'm working with a client, we always begin by exploring the Big Three—and then we look to the Midheaven to see where they need to go and how they must show up to achieve their mission happily.

In this section, I've listed keywords for each sign, along with fears and possible careers. The 4th house is also significant. Because it opposes the 10th, it can shed light on what you need at the root to happily reach your Midheaven. (Psst . . . in children's charts, I like to look at the sign on the 4th house cusp to determine what kind of environment helps them reach their full potential.) Okay, let's rise 'n shine!

# Aries

If you've got an Aries Midheaven, you are a bold original. You're a trendsetter and natural leader. You can inspire others with your enthusiasm and courage. It's important never to play it too safe. Take risks, blaze trails, go where no one else has dared to go before. Stand up, speak out, and you'll lead the pack. Watch out for a tendency to be restless and impulsive. If you act before thinking, you might turn people off.

Sometimes, you may feel anxious about taking those first steps. You want to be a team player and never want to be seen as pushy, which may cause you to hold your fire at times. You must trust that you can take the lead and still maintain healthy relationships. Being first doesn't mean anyone else needs to get left behind.

**Fourth house needs:** With Libra on this cusp, you need permission to be an individual. If you're pushed into "people-pleasing mode" early on, you may feel timid about expressing your unique point of view. Parents of children with Aries Midheavens need to encourage their independence.

**Careers:** entrepreneur, motivational speaker, rescue, fire person, daredevil, inventor, or any profession requiring fast-thinking and leadership.

# Taurus

Taurus Midheaven folks are calm, practical, and artistic. If this is your Midheaven, you operate best in the world when you can immerse yourself in creativity. Security is essential, which means you might choose careers with an eye on making the most money. While there is nothing wrong with wanting financial security, if that is the only driving force, you may find yourself stuck in jobs that pay the bills but make you miserable. Instead, you must express your creative nature in some way. Even if you do not choose a career in the arts, there are many other ways to bring an imaginative flair into your work. Because Taurus is ruled by Venus, beauty and harmony are important. You want the world you inhabit to be beautiful and solid. Look for ways to help others feel good, safe, and secure—and you'll be richly rewarded.

A loss of control scares you. This could lead you to act possessive or domineering. If you feel yourself going in that direction, ask yourself what you can do to feel safe.

*Fourth house:* Scorpio on the 4th house cusp indicates family skeletons. There may be more than a few embarrassing secrets growing up, which could have created trust issues. You need to feel secure with the people around you. Parents of children with this Midheaven need to create a safe space for self-expression and be mindful of respecting the child's need for privacy.

*Careers:* beauty, art, design, financial management, chief financial officer, farming, gardening, childcare, real estate, builder, singer, massage therapist, luxury brand ambassador, or fashion.

## Gemini

You are here to communicate. Gemini Midheavens have keen minds, sharp wits, and the ability to talk about anything to anyone. If this is your Midheaven, you love to learn and share information. You also have a lot of strong opinions and are not afraid to say what's on your mind (that "no filter" thing applies well to you!). Academia is your natural home, but you may also enjoy flitting about from one passion project to another. You may have two careers—perhaps at the same time. You must be careful that your need for variety doesn't make you a "jack of all trades, master of none."

You dread being bored or trapped. You also don't like being made to feel stupid. These fears may cause you to flee when you're feeling stifled or judged. Learning how to stay put and finish the job will allow your brilliance to mature.

*Fourth house:* Sagittarius on the 4th house cusp means you need truth and freedom. You must be able to express yourself with sincerity. If your loved ones give you space, you thrive. Parents of children with Gemini Midheavens need to keep their minds and hands busy. Encourage them to learn a second language and make sure they have access to all the books.

*Careers:* academia, writer, speaker, playwright, journalist, interviewer, teacher, salesperson, translator, data entry, publishing, social media, server, bartender, or librarian.

## Cancer

Cancer Midheavens are the nurturers of the world. Whatever path they choose must allow their softness to shine through. Your greatest strength is your empathy. You are sensitive to other people's needs. This may lead you to take on the role of caregiver. People feel safe with you because they know you care deeply. That being said, you must be mindful that you don't try to dominate other people—or carry their problems with you. You can care without taking it all on. Many fine teachers and parents have this placement. They love children and are keenly interested in developing their potential.

You fear getting hurt, which may cause you to put on a hard shell. Sure, you look tough, but if no one gets to see your vulnerable side, you miss out on more profound connections. It's okay to cry—and to allow others to see those tears.

*Fourth house:* With Capricorn on the 4th house cusp, traditional values and steady support allow you to feel safe in the world. When you get that, you're expressing your emotions fully and giving others space to be themselves. Parents with Cancer Midheaven children need to give them responsibilities but also plenty of play time. Never force a Cancer Midheaven into an adult role when they're young.

*Careers:* caretaker, nurse, doctor, chef, interior design, home builder, architect, parent, childcare, teacher, physical therapist, counselor, therapist, real estate, social worker, or hospitality.

## Leo

Shy violet? Not you. Even if you prefer solitude, the Leo Midheaven says you belong to the people. This is the mark of the performer. Whatever you do, you do it with flair. When you embrace your natural showmanship, you capture the public's hearts—and the center stage. Express your feelings with boldness. Let your big heart lead the way. Grab the mic, shout it out loud, and never forget to leave 'em laughing. Above all, toot your horn once in a while. We're all here for that! Watch out for a tendency to worry too much about what other people think. If you let the critics get inside your head, you'll lose your place in the Sun.

Sometimes, the limelight scares you a little. You may not want to admit that because you don't want to be seen as a cowardly lion. At the same time, you worry about not getting recognized or appreciated. And then there's the concern you might be too "extra." It's okay to care about these things—as long as you don't let them convince you to play small. You're too big for that. Interestingly, I've met lots of Leo Midheavens who struggle with "imposter syndrome," a mindset where you doubt your achievements and secretly feel like a fraud.

*Fourth house:* You need to be around people who allow you to shine—and don't feel threatened by your big personality. That doesn't mean constant applause. Constructive criticism is essential, provided it doesn't wound. When you are allowed to express yourself fully, your inner child comes out to play without shame. Parents of children with Leo Midheavens need to praise their accomplishments and encourage them to be proud of who they are. Aquarius on the fourth house cusp may create a cool early environment—but little Leo Midheavens need all the warmth.

*Careers:* entertainment, actor, comedian, rock star, CEO, coach, teacher, public speaker, thought leader, author, director, artist, hostess, theater manager, special education teacher, animal trainer, dog groomer, PR executive, events planner, DJ, graphic designer, or cardiologist.

## Virgo

Face it: you're a perfectionist. You like sorting out the nuts and bolts—and putting them in order. You're intellectual and precise, with a sharp eye for details. Research, analyzing, and fixing come naturally to you. To-do lists make your heart happy—and routines keep your feet firmly on the earth. Too many shake-ups in your world aggravate your tender nerves. Virgo is associated with service, which means everything you do is centered around making the world a better place. You can always be counted on to lend a helping hand. Although you're good at spotting problems, you'll need to keep an eye on your critical side. When you learn to be tactful, your words land better.

You are your own worst critic. You may secretly worry that you don't measure up. Being needy or feeling helpless—terrifying to Virgo Midheavens. But guess what? Admitting you're not perfect and could use a helping hand eases up the pressure you put on yourself.

*Fourth house:* Pisces on the Imum Coeli means you need peaceful surroundings. An orderly home life will keep your stress levels low. Better yet: hang out with people who know how to go with the flow. This will help you learn to relax. Parents of Virgo Midheavens need to keep perfectionism in check. While there's nothing wrong with wanting things to be neat, too much pressure creates anxiety. By that same token, not enough structure has the same effect. Find the balance between order and flow.

*Careers:* nurse, teacher, doctor, dietician, researcher, scientist, dentist, therapist, spiritual advisor, organizer, gardener, veterinarian, civil servant, accountant, personal assistant, professional housekeeper, computer engineer, seamstress, IT expert, librarian, or curator.

## Libra

Libra Midheavens are diplomats. If this is your Midheaven, you probably enjoy working in partnerships. You're fair-minded and can always find a way to bring out the best in others. Everyone wants you on their side because they know you're a great team player. When dealing with the public, you emit grace and beauty. This makes you a natural in front of the camera. If you go into politics or the performing arts, the public will be interested in your every move. You must guard against indecisiveness and people-pleasing. Be yourself and trust your judgment (which is actually impeccable provided you remain cool and detached).

You never want to let anyone down. That's because you fear being alone. This can lead to codependency or a tendency to shove your own needs aside for others. You must learn that it's okay to put yourself first from time to time. Once you practice that, you'll achieve the balance you crave.

*Fourth house*: Your loved ones need to inspire you to stand on your own two feet as an individual. Aries on the 4th house cusp means independence must be encouraged. A beautiful home is essential—even if your means are modest, harmonious surroundings will make your spirit happy. An argumentative family will create stress—and chase you out of the nest. If your child has a Libra Midheaven, give them permission to do their own thing. Encourage them to express their needs and discourage the tendency to "people please."

*Careers:* artist, fashion designer, lawyer, judge, relationship expert, marriage counselor, art dealer, diplomat, politician, interior design, makeup artist, beautician, event planner, human resources, personal stylist, florist, publicist, mediation, art historian, makeup artist, or career counselor.

# Scorpio

Scorpio on the Midheaven means the public sees you as mysterious. Everyone knows you've got secrets. It's okay to keep them guessing but watch that this doesn't lead to hiding. Instead, you must find a way to step up and share your wisdom. You know things. Scorpio Midheavens are here to unravel the mysteries, share secrets, and transform people . . . or the world. You're no lightweight—you're made of the serious stuff. But you do have a wicked sense of humor and don't mind poking around in taboos. Be careful you don't push people away or cling too tightly to your opinions. The curmudgeon schtick quickly wears thin. Psst . . . you're also incredibly psychic—you see things no one else does. You never miss a thing.

You may have trust issues. The fear of betrayal means you don't like to be vulnerable. While others share their feelings, you remain mum. This doesn't allow people to get too close. When you learn to be open, you get the deep intimacy your soul craves.

**Fourth house:** Safety and honesty are your love languages. A comfortable space with loyal family members allows you to develop trust in people . . . and the universe. Routines add structure to your life and give you a sense of control. Parents of Scorpio Midheavens need to give them privacy and room to vent feelings without shame or blame. Taurus on the 4th house cusp means plenty of affection will help them learn to keep their hearts open.

**Careers:** detective, psychic, healer, researcher, politician, psychologist, forensic psychologist, occupational therapist, transformational speaker, medicine, sex worker, financial advisor, auditor, mortician, funeral director, medical examiner, sex therapist, massage therapist, tax expert, or market analyst.

# Sagittarius

Sagittarius Midheaven folks want to see the world. If this is your Midheaven, you need the freedom to explore. You don't need to be hemmed in. If you're tied down, you quickly rebel. You've got a fine moral compass and an optimistic outlook on life. People feel inspired by your faith. Education is a must—and you may choose to enter academia (once you're done traveling the globe). Life is an adventure—and even if you cannot be a jet setter, you'll find plenty of ways to keep things mentally stimulating. You must be honest in all of your dealings and never try to force your beliefs or ethics on other people. They're more than happy to follow your lead if you remain focused on lifting spirits and being a good example.

You despise being trapped, which may cause you to keep one foot out the door at all times. This can also lead to too many interests, not enough commitment. The continuous search for truth may be an excuse to avoid taking responsibility in the here and now.

**Fourth house:** With Gemini on the 4th house cusp, you need a mentally stimulating environment, but also plenty of "downtime." It's good for you to be bored from time to time. This allows your beautiful imagination to flourish. A spacious room of your own and plenty of time to explore the world around you keeps you content. Parents of Sagittarius Midheaven children need to be honest at all times. If the child perceives hypocrisy or manipulation, they will rebel swiftly. Talking it out is always the solution if problems arise.

**Careers:** travel agent, tour guide, religious scholar, philosopher, academia, import/export business, publisher, entrepreneur, professor, writer, athlete, coach, personal trainer, animal trainer, veterinarian, environmental engineer, landscaper, botanist, conservationist, forest ranger, magazine editor, travel blogger, broadcaster, or journalist.

## Capricorn

You can achieve stunning success if Capricorn is at your Midheaven. This is the ruler of the house, and if you have this placement, lucky you! You are a natural leader, born to take command of every stage, and able to rise to the top of every goal. Success is yours for the taking, provided you are willing to step into the role of authority figure. You're never afraid to work hard. You'll do what it takes to make the grade—and you'll inspire others to go for the gold, too. You're steady, organized, and ambitious. You're made of the CEO stuff. Keep your eyes on the prize, and you can win big. Just remember to make time for play and family. It gets lonely at the top.

The fear of failure? Capricorn Midheaven knows that oh-too-well. You never want to be seen as incapable. This can cause you to morph into a joyless workaholic—or a dictator. It's not the end of the world to fail. A few scrapes on the knees keep you humble.

**Fourth house:** You love your family and enjoy the day-to-day routines of structured home life. When you feel loved, you loosen up. You tend to be the one who protects the realm—it's nice when others have your back. You mustn't get thrust into an "adult role" at a young age. If you do, it will cause resentment later on. Parents of a Capricorn Midheaven need to be affectionate with these serious kiddos. Lots of hugs, kisses, and nurturing allow them to feel safe. Tap into that Cancer on the 4th house cusp and love 'em up!

**Careers:** CEO, boss, management, entrepreneur, organizer, business analyst, financial planner, creative director, film director, producer, health care administration, executive, builder, programmer, antique dealer, appraiser, teacher, purchasing manager, engineer, or customer service.

## Aquarius

If you have Aquarius on your Midheaven, you will always march to a different drumbeat. You are an innovator, disrupter, humanitarian, and cool rebel. You're never afraid to challenge the status quo—and always have an eye on future trends. Community is essential to you—and you may build, lead, or participate in groups that bring people together. You are known for being tolerant and idealistic. You don't like drama but can always get the most logical solution if you're caught in the middle. Always remember: whatever path you choose must be aligned with your ideals. Never conform just to please the general public. You're here to shake it all up and make people think. You may prefer to remain detached at times, but that coolness can leave people feeling like you don't care.

You want to be popular with all the people. This can lead to the anxiety of being disliked. If you let that lead, you may bend over backward to curry favor. That never feels good. In fact, it leaves you wondering if you're really liked . . . or not. Aquarius Midheavens can also feel anxious about intimacy. When someone gets too close, you pull back. Emotionally unavailable will keep everyone at arm's length . . . and once again, you're left doubting how the other side feels.

**Fourth house:** With Leo on the 4th house cusp, you need to be the center of attention in your home. If you were allowed to strut your stuff as a child, you probably have oodles of confidence. If you weren't, you might have neurotic feelings about not being "good enough." Parents of Aquarius Midheavens need to encourage their individuality.

It's also important for them to realize they can put themselves first once in a while. They don't always have to be taking it for the team.

*Careers:* artist, humanitarian, social worker, therapist, non-profit, scientist, computer programmer, IT tech, astronomer, astrologer, activist, environmentalist, environmental engineer, or performing artist.

## Pisces

You are here to heal and inspire. You're sensitive, psychic, and highly creative. Empathy plays a significant role in the way you interact with the public. You can sense how others are feeling—and it's easy for you to put yourself in their position. Because of this, you may be drawn to spiritual work or helping professions. No matter what path you choose, your gift of compassion will always shine forth. You must be careful that you don't deplete all of your energy trying to fix other people's problems. Learn to step back and let go.

On some level, you may worry about becoming dependent on others. This may cause you to put on a tough act. When you're scared, you lash out, and your words become sharp. If you start acting out, know you probably need to ask for help. The other side of this fear coin is escapism. When the going gets too rough, you may try to drown your sorrows or run like a deer.

*Fourth house:* Virgo on the 4th house cusp means a tidy home creates the calm you crave. You need unconditional love. When you are given permission to make a mistake, you learn the greatest gift of all: the ability to forgive yourself as well as you do others. Parents of children with Pisces Midheaven need to create sound structures to support these sensitive souls. They must also be mindful on how they deliver criticism because their words will be taken to heart.

*Careers:* artist, nurse, doctor, musician, writer, muse, psychic, poet, marine biologist, photographer, filmmaker, psychologist, physical therapist, caregiver, social worker, marketing, healer, massage therapist, human resources, or nonprofit.

## Astrocise

Check out your Big Three and Midheaven. Ask yourself these questions: What are the elements? Is there an even amount of Fire, Earth, Air, and Water—or does one element stand out? What does that tell you about your nature?

Are the qualities evenly distributed? Or do you see an abundance in Cardinal, Fixed, or Mutable? Are there any planets making good or challenging aspects to your Big Three and Midheaven? What does this say about you?

## Bonus Astrocise

One of my favorite things to do is pick a "theme song" for the Midheaven. Think of the soundtrack you'd like to have played in the background when you step onto a stage. Find one that matches up with the energy of your Midheaven. My song: "Prima Donna Like Me" by The Struts! *SOOOO* Leo!

### Common Sixth Sense

While the 4th house has suggestions for parents about what each Midheaven needs to thrive, all children need the same thing: unconditional love.

# Who's Living in Your 10th House?

**O**kay, we've established the importance of the Midheaven. But what if planets are occupying the 10th house? Guess what: this impacts your path, too.

The 10th house is associated with career, reputation, where you're going in life—planets in the 10th house impact how the world sees you—and possible career options. Let's explore what happens when one of the heavenly bodies is living here.

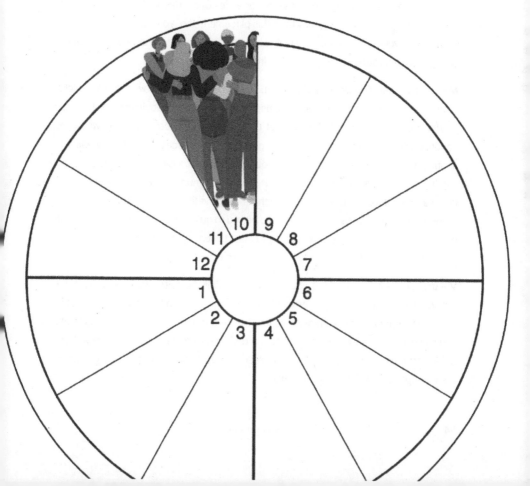

**Sun:** You need to shine brightly in your career. If you're working with the public in any way, you can excel. You take great pride in your work—and will probably attain a position of responsibility or power. Goals keep you happy—and the bigger they are, the better for you. Do not stifle your ambitions or play small. You're meant to be on the main stage, inspiring others through your positivity and bold leadership. This position of the Sun could bring honors and recognition. Keep it classy at all times. If you ever step away from your ethics, the fall from grace could be swift and your legacy damaged.

**Moon:** If you've got the Moon in your 10th house, you derive much emotional satisfaction from being in the public eye. You can connect with people through their emotions, which helps people feel safe in your presence. You have a nurturing quality about you, which means you'd be perfect in any career where you encourage other people's talents. For example, you might be a teacher or a life coach. People who use their emotions for work, such as actors, may have this placement. too. You are at your best when you express your feelings openly. The Moon in the 10th can also indicate many career changes. When you're no longer happy with your work, out you go.

**Mercury:** Mental stimulation is vital to you. If your career doesn't have that, you quickly grow bored and move on. Education is also essential for your happiness. You'll pursue knowledge to gain the skills for the best positions. Your success happens when you continuously upgrade your skillset through continuing education. You're a genius at sharing words and ideas, which makes you well-suited for a career in writing or speaking. If you're in a leadership position, your gift for communication makes you a skilled negotiator. Orators, speechwriters, preachers, and media types may have this placement. Your ability to organize and plan allows you to quickly move up the company ladder. However, you'll need to watch that you don't scheme your way to the top. If you're using trickery to achieve your goals, the victory may be shallow.

**Venus:** You want to be loved . . . you really do. Like Sally Field, it's vital for you to feel the public adores you. You may consciously choose a profession that allows you to build a fan base. For example, you might go into the performing arts. If you possess talent, you could achieve fame. Venus in the 10th often brings popularity and prestige with the public. After all, people do like you—they really do. Just remember to thank people on the way up. No one likes a social climber.

**Mars:** You've got fire in your belly. Mars in the 10th is here to blaze trails and make waves. You're bold—and not afraid to take risks. Careers that require courage are your specialty. You can motivate even the laziest sloth. What's important is that your path has action. You must be able to move about freely, or you get antsy. You'll need to be careful about being too aggressive with your ambitions, though. While Mars in the 10th produces great take-charge leaders, it can also indicate a bully. Power moves are fine—but using force will hurt your rep.

**Jupiter:** Jupiter in the 10th brings luck and opportunity. You may "fall into" certain careers or be blessed with an exceptional talent that effortlessly opens doors for you. It's easy for you to achieve lofty goals, and you may acquire a position of authority—or prominence in your industry. You've got an excellent moral compass, which guides your actions in business dealings or in the public arena. People feel inspired by your example. You're also keenly interested in broadening your horizons, which may mean plenty of travel and education. The more you learn, the more you'll earn. The public will trust you, but you must make sure you practice what you preach. A negatively aspected Jupiter in the 10th can produce a hypocrite. If you lean in that direction, you'll squander your good fortune.

**Saturn:** This is the best place for Saturn to hang out because Saturn is associated with Capricorn, which it rules. In other words, it's at home! If you have this planetary placement, you've got CEO skills and are disciplined as can be. Your goals are steep, but you have the single-minded persistence needed to reach the top, even if it takes forever. Integrity is essential, but you may be willing to bend the rules at times to suit your aims. Careers in business, entrepreneurship, and politics are natural for you. You're better at the boss role than the underling because you'll always want to take charge (and you're able to find the best way to do that). Always stick to your principles and keep your ambition tempered with service. If you're ambitious only for yourself, you'll be celebrating alone.

**Uranus:** You can think outside the box, which means you'll never be happy if you're stuck in a staid, conservative environment. You're innovative, unique, and inventive. A career based in science, technology, or anything that requires innovation is your jam. You're great at working in groups—and an excellent team player. You're known for your tolerance and humanitarianism. If you're in a space where ignorance exists, you'll change the game. Some may call you eccentric, but no one will ever accuse you of being boring. This placement can bring sudden changes of fortune. One day you're scrubbing floors; the next day, you're a rock star with a million-dollar contract. But do know: it's easy to end up right back where you started. Never take your success for granted.

**Neptune:** This placement of Neptune makes you perfect for any career that requires a bit of illusion: magician, actor, makeup artist, or photographer. You're mysterious, idealistic, and visionary. Psychics, healers, mystics, and spiritual leaders have this placement. Great sacrifices will be necessary along the way. You may have to give up certain things to achieve your lofty goals. That being said, you're not always reliable. You might promise more than you can deliver—or your ideas may be unrealistic, which might cause people to dismiss you as a flake. If your Neptune is afflicted, it can also indicate deception. Suppose you have a habit of lying your way into opportunities. In that case, you can quickly experience a fall from grace when your duplicity is uncovered.

**Pluto:** You are an agent of change, here to transform the world and the people in it. You're also highly psychic and can spot future trends. Your willpower is unmatched—and you possess a potent desire to make it to the top. You want to lead, which makes you unwilling to be on the bottom of the ladder for too long. Instead, you will do what you can to acquire as much power as possible. When afflicted, Pluto in the 10th house brings out the dictator—and powerful enemies. You'll want to manage your energy with care and grace if you want to avoid that scenario.

**North Node:** You're here to establish an emotional rapport with the public. If you do that, you'll go far—you could even become famous. Family is everything to you—and you may prefer to hunker down with your loved ones—but you're called to be in the public eye, so you must learn to step into the spotlight.

**South Node:** It's easy for you to take the lead because you've been a leader in past lives. However, you've been in the limelight before—in this lifetime, you need to give the spotlight to others. You must focus on family and home. If you put your career first (because it's easy), your home life will suffer greatly.

If you do not have any planets in the 10th house, that doesn't mean you won't have a career. Instead, you'll want to focus on the Midheaven for guidance.

## Astrocise

 If you have planets in your 10th house, how might they work with—or against—your Midheaven? For example, let's say your Midheaven is Pisces. If you have Neptune here, it might amplify your mystical tendencies. But if you have Mars, Uranus, and Pluto, this could create situations where your faith—or the public's faith in you—is tested. Ponder your planets in the 10th and journal possible ways those heavenly bodies impact your Midheaven.

**Note:** while I tend to focus on the 10th house, you might also want to check out what's going on in the other career houses, which are the 2nd and 6th. They can also hold a wealth of information about your vocation.

# The Nodes Know

he Nodes can reveal a great deal about destiny and karma. Astrologers look to them when trying to determine what you need to work on to reach your full potential.

What are the nodes? They are not planets! Instead, the lunar nodes are two mathematical points in space, where the Moon's orbit intersects with the ecliptic. They are always in pairs and directly opposite each other.

When you study astrology, you might see two variations of the nodes: the true node and the mean node. The true node correlates to the node's exact transit, while the mean node's transit is the average location of the Moon's node. Which one to use? I prefer the true node, but you might choose the mean.

The North Node, also called the Dragon's Head, is your karmic destiny. This is where you need to go to experience actualization. New opportunities are present, but they might feel uncomfortable. It's hard work, but if you lean into it, you will grow.

The South Node, also called the Dragon's Tail, is your gift and blessings. This is the good stuff you've brought in from past lives. However, it can become a comfort zone. You may rely on it too much as a way to avoid North Node issues. While there is nothing wrong with enjoying your South Node goodies, you'll miss out on the new opportunities the North Node brings. Master the North Node, and you'll realize your soul's purpose— why would you want to miss out on that?

Alright, here are some short interpretations for the Nodes:

## The Nodes through the Signs

**North Node Aries/ South Node Libra**—You must learn to assert yourself. Past lives spent focused on other people's needs allowed you to become a great team player. In this lifetime, you must step into the role of leader.

**North Node Taurus/ South Node Scorpio**—You are here to be resourceful and practical with your money. In your past life, you were pretty comfortable, dependent on others, and perhaps preoccupied with accumulating wealth. Now you can learn to rise above that, let go of materialism, and stand on your own two feet.

**North Node Gemini/ South Node Sagittarius**—You have great mental gifts and must communicate your ideas with the world. Remaining positive instead of critical will ensure you're rising to your full potential. In past lives, you may have been a truth seeker. Watch out that you do not become self-righteous. The need to be right in this life comes from finding truth in past lives.

**North Node Cancer/ South Node Capricorn**—Your task is to learn how to take care of your home—and family. You can create a family however you choose. Having a home base will anchor you. In the past life, you were centered on ambitions and status. It's easy for you to claim your place as a leader, but can you put your home life first?

**North Node Leo/ South Node Aquarius**—This lifetime needs to lead from the heart. You must remain true to yourself and not allow flattery to affect your decisions. Instead of worrying about what the group thinks, find your sovereignty—and your self-respect. In your past life, you were involved in communities where cooperation was essential. You learned to fit in for the good of the group. Now you must be your own person—but keep your ego in check.

**North Node Virgo/ South Node Pisces**—You are here to learn how to serve without the thought of rewards. You must watch tendencies to be intolerant. How can you give selflessly? In what way can you put others first? Master this, and you master yourself. Past lives may have found you flitting through life, chasing your muse, and avoiding responsibility. While this may have allowed for inspired art, this next lifetime demands you show up and do the work.

**North Node Libra/ South Node Aries**—You must learn how to get along with others and compromise. Instead of focusing on "me," this lifetime is all about "we." Guard against selfishness and a tendency to be impulsive. Past lives were spent doing your own thing. You may have been a warrior or a person who didn't need the support of others. Now you must learn to work well with your people and put others first for a change.

**North Node Scorpio/ South Node Taurus**—You must learn to let go. Possessiveness and vindictive tendencies must be relinquished. Your willpower is strong but must not be misdirected. This lifetime will allow you to uncover all the mysteries once you release your grip on control. Past lives were spent acquiring many things—including people. You're naturally good at making money—and attracting people. Guard against hoarding possessions or trying to dominate the ones you love. Let go and let the Universe take over.

**North Node Sagittarius/ South Node Gemini**—You must develop your intellect and broaden your horizons through education or travel. Seek truth and a deeper connection to spirit. Develop your own philosophy about the world and find your own relationship to faith. Past lives may have been spent dabbling in many things. The proverbial "Jack of All Trades, Master of None." You may have scattered your forces too wide, and while your life wasn't dull, in this lifetime, you must become an expert.

**North Node Capricorn/ South Node Cancer**—Your past was centered on creating a home and family. Most likely, you are loyal to your family—and perhaps lean on them too much. It's possible that your past life found you dependent on your family or vice versa. This lifetime, you must carve out your own name in the world. You must find your way without their help. Be ambitious and focus on serving the public—and you'll make your mark.

**North Node Aquarius/ South Node Leo**—You were nobility and lived a posh life in a past life. You might still possess a regal air about you. In this life, you must rise above your ego and learn how to take care of the collective. You must look to improving society rather than focusing on accumulating wealth or expecting accolades.

**North Node Pisces/ South Node Virgo**—This lifetime is about developing compassion for others. You must let go of the self and focus on healing the collective. Lean into your spirituality. Find faith in the universe without trying to micromanage the details. Past lives were spent fixing problems. You have an analytical mind and can be quite critical. Learn to detach from perfectionism. Let others be who they are without offering up your opinion.

# The Nodes in the Houses

**North Node 1st House/ South Node 7th House**—You must stand on your own two feet. You may have been codependent on others in the past—but now you must take your power. Assert your will, find your confidence, and trust that you can do this by yourself.

**North Node 2nd House/ South Node 8th House**—You can attract what you want, but you must handle resources with wisdom. Avoid relying too much on other people for financial support. You can create significant wealth if you tap into your own manifestation skills.

**North Node 3rd House/ South Node 9th House**—You must learn to develop your intellectual abilities and communication skills. Too much past life as a hermit may make you struggle to express your big ideas. Watch out for religious hypocrisy and take care of everyday matters instead of assuming it's better somewhere else.

**North Node 4th House/ South Node 10th House**—Establish home and family. Create your own traditions. Work on dismantling family of origin drama as much as possible. By that same token, you must be willing to step away from the spotlight. You had acclaim in the past life. Hand the mic to someone else.

**North Node 5th House/ South Node 11th House**—You are here to create, whether that be art, writing, or children. Express yourself boldly. Find ways to connect to your muse. Romance and parenting may be challenging if you are unwilling to let your loved ones be themselves. In the past, friends were everything. You may have been too concerned with the collective, but now you must create your own destiny and goals.

**North Node 6th House/ South Node 12th House**—You must put your energy into service. Whether it comes through work or community, this is the path that will bring out the best in you. Past lives were spent in isolation or meditation—now you must stay in the groove, connect with others, and serve in some capacity.

**North Node 7th House/ South Node 1st House**—You must learn to share and compromise without putting yourself first. Relationships will be a test. As the song goes, "One is the loneliest number." Let the ego go and take good care of others. You find meaning through your relationships.

**North Node 8th House/ South Node 2nd House**—You are here to manage other people's money. Take care of other's resources—help people recognize their values. Avoid putting your own financial interests first. Instead of asking "what's in it for me," focus on "what's best for them?" A responsible attitude to sex is crucial. Too many past lifetimes involved in sensuality could lead to a hedonistic streak, which needs to be curbed.

**North Node 9th House/ South Node 3rd House**—You are here to develop your belief system or philosophy. Broaden your horizons. Seek to find the truth. Travel as much as you can—see how the other half lives. Get away from the family and daily routines as much as possible. Watch out for a tendency to get mired in petty things or malicious gossip. Also: commit to studies. Avoid being a dilettante or dabbler.

**North Node 10th House/ South Node 4th House**—You belong to the public. As tempting as it may be, you cannot retreat to the home or family. You can make an impact on the world—and perhaps taste fame. Embrace your ambitions and seek worldly power. If you worry too much about what your parents think, you miss opportunities to be an influencer.

**North Node 11th House/ South Node 5th House**—You must develop a rich life outside of the family. Groups and friends will add much to your life. You may have spent too much time focused on children or romance in past lives. The pursuit of pleasure and romantic adventures need to be put aside while finding ways to serve a humanitarian cause or group endeavor.

**North Node 12th House/ South Node 6th House**—You must face past karmic deeds and be willing to let go. You can do this by taking on the role of helper, perhaps in a spiritual or hospital setting. Clear the subconscious, seek therapy, work on developing the strong self. Let go of tendencies to be a martyr, hypochondriac, or workaholic. Critical tendencies must also be eliminated.

## Astrocise:

Find your Lunar Nodes. What clues do they hold about your karmic mission? Are you leaning into your North Node or hiding out in the South Node? Journal your thoughts.

## Bonus Astrocise:

Write a South Node story about your past life! For example, if your South Node is in Gemini, perhaps you spent many lifetimes in libraries, keeping historical records. Let your imagination run wild and have fun with this!

# Transits: Get Time On Your Side

Alright, we've got a basic understanding of your cosmic makeup. In this section, we'll learn how to work with the astrological currents. Why? Because divine timing gives you an edge. (Psst . . . I never make a business decision without peeking at the skies.)

## TRANSIT BASICS

What is a transit? When astrologers refer to transits, they're talking about the current movement of the planets in the sky. This is a way to make predictions or to understand what's happening at the time of a particular event. When you have a working knowledge of transits, you can move with the energy rather than against it.

When astrologers want to determine where the transits are hitting your natal chart, they create a transit biwheel. The inner wheel is your natal chart, while the outer wheel shows the current transits. You can see which houses the transiting planets are traveling through and what aspects they are making with your natal chart. On page 66 is a sample of what a transit biwheel chart looks like. In order to see your transits, you'll need to use software, or order a transit chart from an online source such as astro.com--a dropdown menu will let you choose chart type: natal chart with transits.

Before we cover the transits you need to know for your career, here is a basic rundown of each of the major planetary transits:

**The Sun**—Transits of the Sun show where you can express yourself or "shine." They can also put a spotlight on a particular issue. Transits of the Sun last about thirty days. Transiting aspects of the Sun stick around for about two or three days.

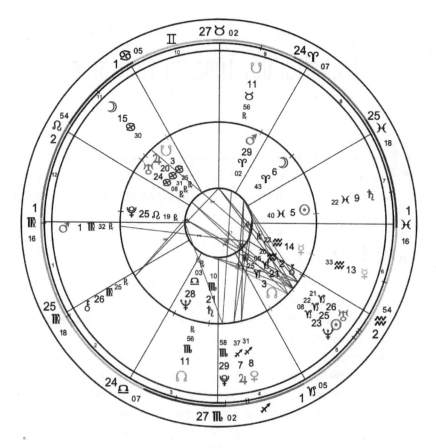

A sample transit biwheel chart. The natal chart is calculated for a birthtime of February 24, 1955, 5:30 pm PST. The inner wheel shows the transits calculated for Sunday, January 15, 1995, at 5:45 p, CST.

**The Moon**—Transits of the Moon indicate where you may experience change. It also rules emotions and relationships with the public. The Moon hangs around in a zodiac for about two days. Transiting aspects of Moon last for about two or three hours.

**Mercury**—Transits of Mercury through the natal chart indicate changes in communication, thinking, intellectual understanding, short trips, and outreach. Mercury transits are about thirty days. Mercury changes signs approximately every three weeks. If Mercury is retrograde, it could remain in one sign for much longer. Transiting aspects of Mercury last about two or three days.

**Venus**—Transits of Venus focus on finances, partnerships, creativity, and the fine arts. Venus will remain in a zodiac sign for approximately twenty days. Transiting aspects of Venus last for about two or three days.

**Mars**—Transits of Mars show where the action is taking place—or needs to. This can also have a lot to say about business activities. Mars transits bring "heat," which can lead to conflicts. Mars will inhabit a zodiac sign for about two months. If Mars is retrograde, it could drag on much longer. Transiting aspects of Mars hold down the fort for about a week.

**Jupiter**—Transits of Jupiter show where you can expand. Wherever Jupiter moves through, it can bring good fortune, too. Keep in mind that luck isn't always like winning the lottery. Sometimes luck can manifest as an ability to keep going, even when situations seem dire. Jupiter transits are associated with growth and seeking deeper meaning, too. Jupiter stays in a sign for about a year. Transiting aspects of Jupiter last for about three weeks.

**Saturn**—Transits of Saturn show where you need limitations, boundaries, or where you can experience growth if you are disciplined. This could also have a lot to say about reputation, status, and leadership. Where Saturn transits is where you mature. Saturn spends about two and half years in a zodiac sign. Transiting aspects of Saturn last for about six weeks.

**Uranus**—Transits of Uranus can bring sudden changes, goals, and support from groups or associates. It can also symbolize where you need to break free. Think of Uranus transits as your personal revolution. Uranus will visit a zodiac sign for about seven years. Transiting aspects of Uranus can linger on for about three months.

**Neptune**—Transits of Neptune can bring creative inspiration—or illusions. These mystical transits can be confusing but can also lead to spiritual enlightenment once the fog clears. Sensitivity is heightened. Neptune remains in a sign for a long time—approximately fourteen years! Transiting aspects of Neptune last for about two years.

**Pluto**—Transits of Pluto represent issues around power, transformation, and agency. Pluto transits take a long time to complete, but once they are over, they leave everything behind much better than when it started. This is the transit of destruction and regeneration. Pluto will chill in a zodiac sign anywhere from fourteen to thirty years! He's in no hurry! Transiting Aspects of Pluto can last for several years.

**Here's the deal with transits:**

Again: they are a snapshot of what's happening in the sky now. When you compare where the planets are moving through your chart, you can see what's happening and how to best show up. Look, things are constantly changing. Heck, even we are. The transits give you a personal road map—one that allows for better decision-making. As I always say: it's best to be prepared, not scared. Once you start working with the transits, you'll know when to hit the gas, pump the brakes, or make a detour. Beep!

# HOUSE INSPECTION

Now, remember our modified "houses" outline from the astrology basics section? Let's dive in a little deeper from a career/purpose/entrepreneurship lens—and then we'll cover the transits you need to know to twist your fate.

**1st**—This is your public image, how you present yourself to the world. Transits through this house might indicate a rebrand or a change in your appearance. It could also advise you to get a new headshot, update your resume or your wardrobe.

**2nd**—The second house still correlates to your financial situation but also how you can monetize your big ideas. Transits here can reveal new sources of income, promotions, and times when you need to play it cool with your cash. This house is also associated with values—as in what's really important to you. Often a transit can reveal what matters when it moves through here.

**3rd**—The communication zone is all about thinking and speaking. Transits here can indicate a change in the way you present your ideas. It can also mean writing (I wrote a slew of books when Pluto was moving through this house), public speaking, and learning new skills. Some transits can indicate a lot of short trips.

**4th**—This is your foundation, so transits here could indicate a change in your career—for example, you may be laying the bricks for a completely new business when Saturn moves through here. This could be a time when you strengthen your roots, or upgrade your working space, especially if you're working from home. If you need to move for a job, there may be a transit happening here.

**5th**—The fifth house is associated with creativity, so transits here could indicate creative works, or new ideas. It's also associated with fame—if you want to elevate your game, look at what transits might be happening here. (Psst . . . this house is also where you find true love, leisure, pleasure, and babies!)

**6th**—This is the place for work, routines, and habits. If your work life is driving you nuts, there might be a transit stirring things up in this house. Great transits can indicate new work opportunities, as well as better routines or efficiency.

**7th**—The relationship zone isn't limited to your romantic life. In a career-oriented forecast, we look at possible partnerships, joint ventures, and relations with the public. Transits here can be excellent for legal issues, contracts, and marketing campaigns.

**8th**—Taxes, biz investments, and joint resources are associated with the 8th house. Transits here can indicate new income streams or trouble with the IRS! If you need to invest in your business, you'll want to see what's happening in this house—or the 5th.

**9th**—The 9th house is associated with publishing and travel. Transits here could indicate a book deal—or a book tour! It can also have something to say about going global, traveling for work, moving to another country, living abroad, and teaching. If you're thinking about creating online classes, look at what is happening in this house.

**10th**—This is hella important. The 10th house is your career zone, but also your reputation. Transits here indicate a rise to the top or potential downfall. They can also point out times when you need to pivot or upgrade. If you're launching a new biz or website, check here first.

**11th**—Your network is in the 11th house. Transits here can indicate an uptick in networking events or community-building opportunities. If you're leading groups, this is the place to look to see how that pans out. If there is trouble in group activities (ex:

someone challenges your leadership), you'll find challenging aspects probably lurking around here.

**12th**—When you need to regroup, revamp, renovate, or rest, it's 12th house time. Transits here are most excellent for working behind the scenes, developing new top-secret products, and vacationing. If you've been feeling disconnected from your work, check out what's happening in this house. Because this is the house of enemies, you may learn about a betrayal.

Got that? Groovy.

Now it's time to consider possible interpretations.

## PUTTING THE TRANSITS TO WORK

Now, let's consider possible transits. These transits are written in a proactive way because the goal is to take charge and work with this energy. For example, Saturn is a hard taskmaster, but the rewards are significant if you're willing to do the work. This is why I don't believe there are "bad" charts or aspects (psst . . . Saturn always gets knocked!). It's what you do that matters the most.

When it comes to business or career, I focus on transits of the Sun, Moon, Mars, Jupiter, and Saturn. Why? The Sun shows where you can shine, the Moon is the public's mood, Mars is where you need to take action, Jupiter is where you can expand, and Saturn shows where you can get serious.

While the other planets can impact your career, and I do consider them, these are the transits I use the most for making decisions about work and employment. Other astrologers may emphasize Mercury or Venus. You may want to as well. It's up to you.

### Sun transits

Get ready to up your game and strut your stuff with Sun transits!

**Sun transit through the 1st house:** This is the best month for putting yourself out there. Apply for that job, debut a striking new look, grab the mic. You've got the confidence now—stand in your power and be an industry leader. If the Sun in the 1st makes challenging aspects to planets in your natal chart, keep your arrogance in check—and don't let fear gum up your game.

**Sun transit through the 2nd house:** Best time to negotiate for the money you want because you've got the gumption—and nerve. Take the lead on money matters and invest your coin wisely. This is an excellent time to spend money on social activities or get involved in business related to art. A PR campaign now might net some extra cash. If the Sun in the 2nd makes challenging aspects to planets in your natal chart, go over every single expense with care.

**Sun transit through the 3rd house:** This transit is most excellent for public speaking, writing, and learning. Express your ideas with confidence. Be the authority in your field. Want to upgrade your skillset? Sign up for a class or hit the books. Schedule short trips around this time. Also: this would be a marvelous few weeks for connecting with the locals. If the Sun in the 3rd makes challenging aspects to planets in your natal chart, you'll want to think before you speak. If you come off like a know-it-all, it could turn people off.

**Sun transit through the 4th house:** You feel rooted now. You have support from the ones who love you. This transit is fantastic for upgrading your working quarters. A fresh coat of paint, new furnishings, or a deep clean can do wonders! If you're thinking of moving your office or purchasing a building, you've got the power to make that happen. If you have a business, this is the right time to strengthen your foundation. If the Sun in the 1st makes challenging aspects to planets in your natal chart, finding the balance between home and family could be problematic. Don't neglect your loved ones!

**Sun transit through the 5th house:** Creativity is HIGH. This is a fabulous time for writing, acting, or self-expression. It's also most excellent for making social contacts with people in positions of power (it pays to network!). If you want to step into a bigger spotlight, use this time to reach out to the media. Public presentations could get you a lot of attention. If the Sun in the 5th makes challenging aspects to planets in your natal chart, do not invest in your business or the stocks without a thorough examination of the pros and cons.

**Sun transit through the 6th house:** This is a great time to apply for a new job or promotion. Also: you can express yourself creatively in your position. If you have a bold idea, bring it forward. Take the lead on work projects and speak up if you see an issue. If you're involved with a career in art, music, or entertainment, you could shine brightly now. If the Sun in the 6th makes challenging aspects to planets in your natal chart, watch out that overwork doesn't lead to burnout.

**Sun transit through the 7th house:** This is a stellar period for making connections with power players and influencers. Reach out, get to know folks, and form joint ventures. Be a mover and a shaker—and a deal maker! If you're involved in a partnership, make sure both sides get a chance to shine. Public relations, legal matters, and competition are also themes during a 7th house Sun transit. Keep your PR game tight, pitch the media, or hire a publicist. If the Sun in the 7th makes challenging aspects to planets in your natal chart, be mindful around legal issues and partnership power plays. Find ways to share the stage and responsibilities equally. You'll also want to keep an eye on your PR. If you're burning a bridge, don't put that in the public square.

**Sun transit through the 8th house:** An excellent few weeks for dealing with taxes, finances, negotiations, and business investments. Organize your resources, ask for loans, approach banks for negotiating financial issues. You're more likely to get financial help now. Business intuition is uncanny at this time. If you're getting a gut instinct about any aspect of your biz, don't ignore it. Suppose the Sun in the 8th makes challenging aspects to planets in your natal chart. In that case, you might want to go over your financials carefully. Look for outstanding bills, clean up your files, and make sure your taxes are wrangled.

**Sun transit through the 9th house:** Pitch the publishers, travel far and wide, or sign up for school when the Sun moves through the 9th house. This is a happy Sun transit, ideal for sharing or gathering knowledge. You might be moved to up-level your skills through a class, or perhaps you are ready to launch your own online classroom. You may want to consider other activities: self-publish a book, start a blog, or get a podcast up and running. Suppose the Sun in the 9th makes challenging aspects to planets in your natal chart. In that case, you'll want to watch out for extravagance, unwise travel, or promising more than you can deliver. This is NOT a good time to publish controversial stuff either!

**Sun transit through the 10th house:** This is a beautiful month for being in the public eye. You can stand tall in your work and be proud of your accomplishments. You could get recognized now. If there is a chance to grab the limelight, do not be shy. Take the mic and ROAR. If you're thinking of getting involved in politics or want to approach an authority figure for a promotion, this is your greenest light. Sometimes fame happens when the Sun saunters through this house.

If the Sun in the 10th makes challenging aspects to planets in your natal chart, you can still shine brightly, but might experience a few setbacks. Be patient. Above all, do not go into control freak mode. No one likes a dictator.

**Sun transit through the 11th house:** Ready to set some big goals? Sure you are! The Sun in the 11th is fantastic for putting your intentions together, gathering your friends, and making big things happen. It's also a super time to join organizations that support your goals. Also: your social life could end up being quite helpful now— for example, your friends may play an essential role in your success, or you may meet some influential people at a networking event. Other Sun in the 11th activities: get involved in humanitarian work, take the lead in groups (both online and off), and build your community. If the Sun in the 11th makes challenging aspects to planets in your natal chart, you might find yourself feeling restless—avoid doing something impulsive. Do NOT make significant changes at this time. If you're forced to make a change, remain graceful.

**Sun transit through the 12th house:** Rest. Hibernate. Think of this as an incubation period—research new paths or ideas. Work on top-secret projects. Leadership can happen behind the scenes. For example, you may get involved in a job that requires secrecy. Intuition is strong, so you'll definitely want to follow your gut. Take a vacation if you can. If you've lost sight of your big picture goals, a time out might be in order. If the Sun in the 12th makes challenging aspects to planets in your natal chart, you'll want to keep your feet firmly planted on the ground. Avoid escapism, daydreaming, or hiding out.

# Moon Transits

Moon transits last about 2 1/2 days. This means they don't spend a whole lotta time in your houses. It can be helpful to glance at your chart to see where the Moon is hanging out so you can be ready for the changes it often brings. The Moon can also shed light on how you're feeling—or the public's mood.

Every day, I check the phases of the Moon as well as the zodiac sign it's inhabiting. I use this knowledge to plan my business activities and make magic. More on that soon. For now, let's take a glance at what happens when the Moon moves through your chart.

**Moon transit through the 1st house:** When the Moon moves through your 1st house, you'll want to express your feelings to the outside world. Share a heartfelt blog post, release a PR statement, but watch your moods. If you're feeling some type of way, take a day off.

**Moon transit through the 2nd house:** Do not make emotional decisions around money. Wait until the Moon has left this house. You'll be clear then. Use this time to research potential expenses. This transit can be decent for making investments in real estate or your business. This can also be fab for marketing. People are in the mood to buy what you're selling.

**Moon transit through the 3rd house:** You can wear your heart on your sleeve. Express your ideas and your feelings with vulnerability. Write poetry, music, or business correspondence. Trust your gut with decisions. Intuition is sharp now. Watch that your own biases don't cloud your judgment.

**Moon transit through the 4th house:** Make changes at your home. Move, renovate, clean. What makes you feel secure? Put energy into that. Good day for working from home or dealing with family matters. Your loved ones may get on your last nerve now.

**Moon transit through the 5th house:** Artistic inspiration is possible. Great day or two for getting in front of the public eye. Invest in your business. Give a speech. Find a reason to have fun or celebrate. Connect to the bigger picture. Seek fame.

**Moon transit through the 6th house:** Emotions could create illness if you're not careful. Be sure to practice excellent self-care today. Create order in your working environment.

Engage in small tasks. Do not get into emotional arguments at work. Avoid burning the midnight oil, no matter how tempting it may be.

**Moon transit through the 7th house:** This is an excellent time for PR. Get yourself out there! Sign legal documents, honor contracts, and strengthen relationships with your team or partners. Forge new connections—and eliminate old ones.

**Moon transit through the 8th house:** Negotiate deals, ask for loans, or go over your budget with a fine-toothed comb. Get your papers in order. Make financial plans. Work on your financial strategies. If you have not dealt with your taxes, now is the time. Intuition is incredibly accurate during this transit.

**Moon transit through the 9th house:** An excellent few days for travel, especially long-distance. Seek favors from people who live far away. Go global with your business. Increase outreach as much as possible. Launch a new book. Plan travels or international trade. Upload a podcast episode. If you have a book idea, pitch it to a publisher.

**Moon transit through the 10th house:** Meet with the boss and ask for a more significant role at work. There is no better time to get your work in front of the public. You can capture their hearts—and may receive recognition. If you are having problems, do NOT make it public now—it could end up hurting your rep. If this Moon makes stressful aspects, you might receive unflattering publicity.

**Moon transit through the 11th house:** Forge connections with your community or network. Hang out with people who make you feel good. Attend a meeting or group activity. Get involved in groups, associations, or community events. Rub elbows with influencers. Hire someone for your team. This is a great time to donate to a charitable cause.

**Moon transit through the 12th house:** Rest, rest, rest. This is your self-care moment: schedule time off or time for pampering. Go on vacation if you can. Get a massage, visit your therapist, recharge your batteries.

# Mars transits

Mars transits last about 6 weeks. If Mars is retrograde, the transit can last much longer. (More on retrogrades later.) The red planet is associated with ambition, drive, and action. Where it moves is where you need to bust a move.

**Mars transit through the 1st house:** You've got the energy to slay every dragon and climb every mountain. This is your time to go for the gusto, step up your game, and BE SEEN. Ambition and confidence are in abundance, giving you the audacity to compete with the top brass. Take the initiative, and you'll go far, fast. Keep in mind the energy can go sideways—it's too easy to morph into an egomaniac or an edgelord. While it's cool to be edgy, your sharp points could end up costing you.

**Mars transit through the 2nd house:** Want to make more cash? You can do that when Mars is moving through your 2nd house. These weeks are excellent for acquiring all the things you want. You can be unapologetic in your hustle. Set your sights on the gold and then move swiftly toward it. If you're working more than one job during this time, you'll have the stamina to handle that—and it could quickly move you in a better financial direction. The hustle may be challenging, but you're hardcore now. Watch out for other people trying to muscle in on your turf. Beware of theft or impulsive spending.

**Mars transit through the 3rd house:** This is a fantastic time to go back to school. Your mind is energized, giving you the mental fortitude for studying and test-taking. You can acquire a lot of knowledge quickly, which makes this time excellent for research as well. Corporate communications can be brisk and intense. If you're in meetings, you'll need to stand your ground. Be assertive with your ideas. Mars in the 3rd is great for signing contracts and negotiating—BUT if it's retrograde, you'll want to hold off. If you're too aggressive at that time, you can blow it.

**Mars transit through the 4th house:** Mars in the 4th usually indicates physical activity around the home—or home improvement projects. If your nest is a mess, use this transit to get it up to code. If you're purchasing a building for a business, this can be a good time for that—or for renovating your space. Arguments with family could derail your focus—you'll need to keep your boundaries high if you want to avoid that.

**Mars transit through the 5th house:** This transit is associated with physical activity, especially those related to pleasure: dancing, sports, or getting outside in nature. If you're an artist or musician, this could also be an excellent time for making progress on your creative work. Your ideas are inspired—and you have the wherewithal to do something with them. Of course, suppose you use any sort of creativity in your career. In that case, you could see a larger-than-usual output, too. Mars in the 5th can be favorable for a spirited PR campaign, BUT it can also lead to trouble with public presentations if you're too aggressive.

**Mars transit through the 6th house:** If your work involves physical labor, you're in luck when Mars roars through this house. You have superhuman energy at this time, giving you the strength to power through even the most demanding assignment. Even if your work doesn't involve using your body, you've got an assertive vibe that could put you in a leadership position. You remain glued to your goals and motivate others to get behind you. This is an excellent time for starting physical-fitness programs. Watch out for injuries, conflicts on the job, fevers, and anxiety-induced illnesses if Mars is under stressful aspects. You'll also want to avoid surgery if Mars is retrograde in this house.

**Mars transit through the 7th house:** Dynamic partnerships are possible when Mars moves through the 7th. Use this transit to form connections with power players and those in positions of authority. But watch out for too much aggression. If you're coming on too strong, you'll be seen as a boor. Seek compromises and do not get too pushy. Read social cues. If you're in a lawsuit or signing a contract, the negotiations could be brisk. Some conflicts could turn litigious if Mars is under stressful aspects.

**Mars transit through the 8th house:** Business activity during this transit could be centered around joint ventures, contracts, investments, or taxes. These issues could occupy a lot of your time now. You'll need to be ready to take action in these areas in some way. It's also possible you could become embroiled in conflicts around business partnerships or taxes if Mars is making challenging aspects. Intuition is strong, and so is libido. Follow your gut . . . or your lust.

**Mars transit through the 9th house:** This is a fantastic time to travel for work or pleasure. If your business takes you to different corners of the globe, you could see an expansion. Mars in the 9th is also super for publishing or sending in proposals to publishers. If you're thinking about applying to a university, this is a green light. What to watch out for: do not push your beliefs too aggressively. Do that, and you won't seal the deal—you'll burn a bridge instead. If you are a teacher or thinking of starting an online class, this is a perfect transit.

**Mars transit through the 10th house:** When Mars breezes through your 10th house, you'll want to promote yourself and your work as much as possible. A smart PR blitz could put a lot of attention on your world. This is also the best transit for taking on a leadership role or asking for a promotion. If you want to be top dog, you can make that happen. Ambition for fame and status is strong during this transit, leading to dynamic professional actions—or interactions. Mars in the 10th is also ideal for initiating a new business, launching a new website, or doing something daring in public. If Mars is making stress aspects, you might have trouble with employers or the government.

**Mars transit through the 11th house:** Activities with groups and friends are energized. You may be more social than usual—and your social life could mix business with pleasure. This is an intense time for networking. Rub enough elbows during this transit, and you might connect with some influencers (or become one yourself). Take on leadership roles in group activities, start an online class, or join an organization. Mars in the 11th is a beautiful time to support humanitarian goals. If you want to create an organization for a good cause, this is it! You have the gumption to achieve your goals and objectives as well. In fact, plenty of people will get behind you to support your endeavors! This could also be an incredible time for raising money. If Mars is under challenging aspects, friends may be a bad influence. If you're hanging with the wrong crew, you might regret it.

**Mars transit through the 12th house:** Work on a top-secret project when Mars slips through the 12th house. If you want to engage in something out of the sight of prying eyes, there is no better time than now. But you'll also want to make sure that you carve out time for rest. While Mars doesn't usually like that, stressful aspects to this transit could find you spiraling toward burnout. Find the balance between work—and chilling. Also: if you need to get into therapy, do it now. Take the initiative on your inner work, and you could release the things that are holding you back the most.

. . . . . . . . . . . . . . . . . . . . . . . . . . . . . . . . . . . . . . . . . . . . . . . .

## Astrocise:

 Take a peek at your chart. Where is the Sun blazing hot right now? What about Mars? What might you need to be doing in the next couple of weeks to max out this fiery stuff to your advantage? How might the Moon impact your decisions?

## Jupiter Transits

Jupiter transits last about a year—and are essential for business or career astrology. This transit shows where you can expand and where opportunity is knocking. Play your stars right, and you set yourself up for success. Where Jupiter is moving through is where you need to step up your game. (This is the first thing I look for—followed by Saturn—when I'm trying to get my hustle right.)

**Jupiter transit through the 1st house:** You're optimistic, and not much can get you down when Jupiter moves through the 1st. This is a happy transit, one that gives a positive outlook that in turn inspires others. At this time, you may become interested in travel, higher education, or spiritual growth as a way to improve yourself. Jupiter transiting the 1st is a fantastic year for getting yourself out there and engaging with the public. If Jupiter makes stressful aspects, watch out for an inflated sense of self and a tendency to gain weight. Both of these give different meanings to the term "go big."

**Jupiter transit through the 2nd house:** Money is ready to grow during a 2nd house Jupiter transit. You're luckier than usual attracting the green stuff and could enjoy improved money conditions. You may receive a raise or promotion—or your biz might become profitable. A side hustle could blossom into a full-time venture if you put energy into that. If you approach authority figures for loans or wage increases, you're more likely to get it. Also: raise your rates if you haven't done it for a while. Travel during this transit could open up to new business possibilities. If Jupiter is under challenging aspects, watch out for financial extravagance. If it's coming in fast, don't blow it all in one place.

**Jupiter transit through the 3rd house:** This transit brings big, bold ideas, making it fab for writers, creatives, and anyone who seeks to broaden their knowledge base. Go back to school, write that book, and indulge in a bit of daydreaming. Brainstorm with your team at work—and you may come up with the next hot thing. Short trips during this period could expand your base—while taking an interest in your local community levels up the support at home. If you're entering politics, this is the right time to knock on some doors. Jupiter in the 3rd can be a bit impractical, though, especially when under unfavorable aspects. You'll want to avoid hare-brained schemes that lack common sense.

**Jupiter transit through the 4th house:** If you're thinking about investing in real estate, Jupiter in 4th says: let's do this! You may be able to expand your property acquisitions or make dramatic improvements on a current holding. If you're conducting business out of your home, it could lead to significant financial rewards. You could also benefit through work in building, cooking, or anything centered around the house. For some, Jupiter in the 4th opens up possibilities of living overseas. Stressful aspects could mean laziness and sloppy home environments. It might be time to hire help!

**Jupiter transit through the 5th house:** This transit brings a greater creative output. You are fertile with ideas—and many of them will turn out to be golden eggs. An expanded social circle is possible, which may include friends from the arts or spiritual community. Artists, musicians, writers, and performing artists could receive attractive new offers or recognition during this transit. It can be a good time to invest in the stock market but be careful if Jupiter makes stressful aspects—you could lose your shirt!

**Jupiter transit through the 6th house:** Jupiter in the 6th brings abundant (and lucky) work opportunities. If you're looking for a new job, this transit boosts your chances of finding suitable work. Heck, you might even find your higher calling this year! A career in publishing, teaching, travel, or spiritual fields could be rewarding now. You can improve your working conditions as well. If your current working conditions have been a drag, Jupiter will open possibilities to create a better environment. Health is good at this time, but you'll want to watch your eating habits. Too much celebrating your wins could lead to an expanded waistline. If Jupiter is under challenging aspects, you may lose interest in your work or start to take your situation for granted.

**Jupiter transit through the 7th house:** You'll have good fortune in partnerships of all kinds. You can expand your network and form new business alliances. Plus: the public loves you, so get your beak in front of the camera as much as you can. An inspired PR campaign will pay off. If you've made any PR errors, this transit is ideal for a redemption tour. If you're an artist, teacher, PR agent, lawyer, or relationship expert, Jupiter in the 7th brings accolades and inspiration. This transit is favorable for signing contracts or dealing with legal matters too. If Jupiter is under challenging aspects, you may not appreciate the support around you.

**Jupiter transit through the 8th house:** You can attract more money during this transit, which means it's favorable for asking for loans, raises, or promotions. It's also great for increasing your rates. If you haven't done that in a while, now is the time. If you're running your enterprise, you might make a lot of cash—you'll want to keep an eye on your taxes, because they might expand too. Intuition is elevated—trust your gut 100 percent. If something smells fishy, it's probably a fish. If Jupiter is experiencing challenging aspects, you might experience issues around taxes or litigation. Be sure to cross every T and dot every I if you wish to avoid problems.

**Jupiter transit through the 9th house:** This transit feels excellent on many levels because Jupiter rules this house. It's a good year for travel, education, and publishing. Put out a book during this transit, and you may achieve success. If you're a teacher or a student, Jupiter in the 9th broadens knowledge and leads to academic achievements. It's also an excellent time for expanding your empire into a global brand. However, if Jupiter is under unfavorable aspects, there can be a tendency to be narrow-minded. You don't always need to be correct.

**Jupiter transit through the 10th house:** Jupiter in the 10th is the time to claim your fame! If you want to get known, this is your year! Seek the media and be ready to say yes if they approach you. People in positions of power want to help you—you might receive plenty of exciting offers during this transit. Travel could take your name to new corners of the world. If Jupiter makes challenging aspects during this transit, watch that you don't abuse your power and status. If you start acting like a prima donna, you could lose your crown..

**Jupiter transit through the 11th house:** Your network can expand significantly during this transit. As the old saying goes, "it's who you know," so get out there and know new people. Influencers may enter your social circle, and you could enjoy friendships with people in exciting groups. Those could be primarily spiritual, humanitarian, or intellectual. Many opportunities to realize your large-scale goals and objectives can manifest during this time. Think big—the sky is the limit—and you've got plenty of folks willing to help you. If Jupiter is under stressful aspects, your friends may take advantage of you—or vice versa.

**Jupiter transit through the 12th house:** You've got a guardian angel protecting you all year long. Even if you pull a boneheaded maneuver, your guides will keep you safe. Take vacations, spend time in retreats, seek inner harmony during this period. If you've lost touch with your spiritual life, this year will help you reconnect to it. Prayer, therapy, and meditation will benefit you greatly. Revisit your bigger vision and refine it. Watch out for escapism, self-pity, and addiction during this transit. If you're overdoing any of that, seek support. If Jupiter is experiencing stress, you may need to pull back and get help.

## Saturn Transits

Okay, I admit it: I adore Saturn. Sure, it gets a rep for being full of lessons and limitations. But Saturn, if handled properly, is the secret sauce to all things awesome. Here's the gist: structure and discipline are Saturn's BFFs. Wherever Saturn transits in your chart, you must knuckle down and fly right. If you do that, you'll build a more robust structure that will support you, possibly for life.

While Jupiter is the first transit I explore in a chart, Saturn is next. These two are my main guidelines for making intelligent choices. The Moon handles my daily stuff—but Jupiter and Saturn are themes of opportunity and structure. Use them well, and you'll achieve your goals in the best way possible.

Saturn transits last about two and half years. We'll talk about the Jupiter and Saturn return in a bit. For now, let's focus on Saturn transits from a business, career, and life improvement lens.

**Saturn transit through the 1st house:** It's time to get serious about who you are—and how you're presenting yourself to the world. No more goofing off. You need to straighten out your pants, tuck in your shirt, and tame those cowlicks! You don't have to look perfect, but you can't walk through the world like a gadabout if you want to rise. Saturn in the 1st says: get your act together and present a mature front to the world. This will create opportunities for you. That doesn't mean you have to be some dullard. You can have fun. But staying up all night, refusing to pay the bills, and showing up to work hungover? Those days are done. This is the time when you can create new directions in your life. You've had two years to ask, "who am I?" Now you can take the information and start building your personal brand, perhaps from scratch. New cycles are possible, and you may have to work harder than usual. But it's all worth it. Once Saturn leaves this house, you'll feel more capable and respected. If Saturn is under stress aspects, you may lack confidence or fall back on old habits.

**Saturn transit through the 2nd house:** If you want to grow wealth, start here. Create structures and budgets. Set financial goals. Then: get to work and don't screw it up. Try not to incur too much debt during this transit. Instead, you'll want to put your energy into getting debt-free. You can develop greater organizational skills with your money—and if you do, you'll come out of this period in better shape for the future. Get your affairs in order and stick to the budget. You may encounter a few issues at work, especially around sales. It's also possible that there may be legal issues around money (ex: you have to go bankrupt or may get some bad news from the IRS). Or you may simply have more anxiety than usual around your financial situation. If that's the case, speak to an expert. You can turn it around. Some people lose money or their jobs during this transit—but if you prepare for that well in advance, you can sail through that and onto the next thing. In fact, you could end up in a better job. (Fun fact: before Saturn entered this house, I set a major goal to pay off my mortgage early. Once the ringed planet began moving through this sector, I busted my hump, stuck to the budget, and stayed focused on the goal. I paid off my mortgage fourteen years early! BAM! It wasn't easy . . . but I did it!)

**Saturn transit through the 3rd house:** Serious study may be your jam when Saturn transits your 3rd house. This is the house of mind, and hitting the books is the right thing to do during this time. It's especially favorable for formal education. Enroll in a university, go for that degree, or seek continuing ed courses to up-level your skills. It's also most excellent for writing (I wrote three books when Saturn went through my 3rd house!). There may be more professional communication at this time, primarily if you work as a writer in some capacity. You'll want to be uber-careful signing contracts now, especially during the periods where Mercury is retrograde. You could end up in agreements that hurt you—and could be stuck with them for a long time to come. Sometimes this transit can bring mental stress or a cynical attitude. If you're fixated on the dark side, you'll want to seek support.

**Saturn transit through the 4th house:** Now is the time to work on your foundation. That could be your home life, the structure of your business, or old family of origin drama. There may be greater responsibilities with the family or home life. So, you'll need a vigorous routine to avoid overwhelm (or resentment). If you're trying to buy a property or want to renovate your current crib, this is your green light, provided you're ready to handle what comes with that. If you have a business built on an unstable base, it may be time to tear it down and start over. Likewise, it's an incredible period for crafting a whole new business. You can build from the ground up during this transit. Other good biz moves: update policies, refine your biz principles or manifesto, become firm about what you stand for (or don't). If you're carrying around old family stories that are making it difficult to live your present life, now is the time to get therapy and let that stuff go. Revisit those stories, forgive, release them, and create a new storyline for the future you want, not the one imposed on you. What to watch out for: oppressive family situations, mother guilt trips, depression, burdensome home expenses, or ignoring business structures that are beginning to fall apart (ex: your website is outdated).

**Saturn transit through the 5th house:** Get cracking on your creative projects during this transit. If you are an artist, musician, or performer, this is a beautiful transit for growing your skills. You have the discipline now to perfect your craft. Practice hard, and you could attain a new level of mastery. This is also a fantastic time for business or professional development for anything related to the entertainment industry, theatre, teaching, education, or careers related to children. Investments could bring financial gain—but you'll want to be mindful about speculation during stressful aspects—you could lose your shirt. This transit isn't considered favorable for romance or having children—BUT I've found it can be if you're approaching either with a serious, grounded mindset. For example: getting married because your spouse is putting pressure on you—nope. But getting married because you're in it for the long haul and it makes good sense (ex: combining your income elevates your living standards), yep.

**Saturn transit through the 6th house:** There is no better transit for getting your working life in order. You can clean up your environment from the ground up. Create divine order in your schedule, habits, routines, and surroundings. Hate your job? Use this transit to plan your exit. Start taking classes that might open the door for something new—or consider advanced training in your current work. Streamline workflow and look for ways to upgrade policies or general conditions. This transit is fab for getting your health back on track too. If you've allowed your regimens to slide, there is no better transit for changing your habits. On the downside, this transit can bring stress-related health issues due to overwork. If you've been burning the candle at both ends, you need to dial it back. Sometimes this transit can indicate job loss—but if you use this time to focus on what you want to do, you can build something better. Saturn in the sixth can also mean a lack of opportunities—so create your own! I've also seen some people strapped with two jobs for financial reasons during this transit—or building a side hustle while working a day job for the insurance. The work may be hard now—but there is a payoff later.

**Saturn transit through the 7th house:** While Saturn in the 7th could indicate increased responsibilities toward other people, it can also be a good time for establishing partnerships, especially in business. Look for possible partners for joint ventures. Build your network by making connections to older, established pros in your industry. Professional partnerships or organizations could take your career to new heights—or new directions. You can gain support from hot shots and influencers if you position yourself well at work. This transit is also fab for public relations. If you want to establish a stronger presence, use this time to amplify your PR. You'll want to watch out for contract issues and legal problems during this transit. Get your legal affairs in order if you're anticipating a change and read contracts over with great care. Better yet, have an attorney do that for you. Also: you could experience negative PR during this transit if Saturn makes stressful aspects. If that happens, work on damage control. My advice: don't do anything that could mar your rep when Saturn is hanging around here!

**Saturn transit through the 8th house:** This transit is excellent for getting your financial affairs in order. If you've neglected to set up a retirement account, will, or insurance, you'll want to put that together now. Also: budget, especially for your business. Saturn can bring nasty surprises in the form of tax bills or unexpected expenses. If you've been ignoring your money situation, it will get your attention now. Another possibility: you may be managing other peoples' finances during this time. If that is so, you'll want to handle it with great care. For example, you may be in charge of an estate. If you are in that position, be mindful of the decisions you're making. (Psst . . . I've also known a few folks who got stuck taking care of an estate without a will! They got tangled up in probate, which was stressful!) Be careful about losses through joint finances and business investments. While Saturn in the 8th could be favorable in strengthening your biz foundation through prudent investing, if you're not meticulous, you could end up losing money. Interestingly, this transit is ideal for developing your intuition.

**Saturn transit through the 9th house:** This transit is fantastic for higher education. If you want an advanced degree, this is one of the best times to apply to a university. Fields of interest could include religious history, literature, publishing, philosophy, or law. (One of my clients entered a seminary during this transit!) Also: if you wish to work in academia, start plotting out your strategies now. You could land a position in a coveted educational institution. This transit can also bring a heavy academic load—or problems with travels. If you desire to see the world, you will need to exercise patience and plan wisely. A trip for business or professional reasons is acceptable during this transit, provided you are flexible should things go awry. Saturn in the 9th is also suitable for getting a book done or published, BUT it can also bring difficulties with getting your writing off the ground or finding a publisher if there are stressful aspects.

**Saturn transit through the 10th house:** Saturn in the 10th is my favorite transit of all. Why? Saturn rules the 10th house, so it's at home here. When Saturn moves through your 10th, this can be your glow-up. You're primed for the top position, ready to soar, and can go for the gold. Want a promotion? It can happen now. Want to build your online rep? Do it. Thinking of unveiling a website or new biz? Yes, please. Recognition is possible, as well as advancement. You can get superiors and industry shot callers on your side—be sure to keep those relationships on speed dial. Saturn in the 10th is for leaders—if you want to take on a lead role at work or in your industry, use this time to step up your game. Also: this transit bodes well for anyone interested in serving the public or politics. It often brings responsibility and fame. You'll want to take your public image seriously during this transit. If Saturn makes stressful aspects, you could experience a significant backlash or fall out of favor with your superiors. Personal scandals could become public and harm your rep. Saturn in the 10th negatively aspected signals the fall of the dictator—or a career that gets sabotaged in some way (ex: haters). Rise up—but watch your step.

**Saturn transit through the 11th house:** This is another good transit for Saturn, because Saturn is the traditional ruler of Aquarius, so it's dignified in this house. You can strengthen your community as well as your associations. This is a fantastic time to join groups that further your goals. Friends and colleagues will be helpful during this period. Serious or professional organizations could assist you as well. If you're involved in humanitarian groups, you could see many of your ambitions being realized. Want to lead a group? Go for it! Establish friendships with serious-minded individuals. Seek a mentor. Reconnect with old friends, too. Stressful aspects to Saturn could bring problems with groups, friends, or goals. Be ready to revise your big vision plans and ditch the low-energy people. Watch out that you're not the one using old pals to get your way.

**Saturn transit through the 12th house:** When Saturn slips into your 12th house, it's like going into a cocoon. This is your time for INNER WORK. Go within, get into therapy, spend time in retreat. There is no better period to start a meditation or yoga practice. If you wish to deepen your connection to spirit or your inner wisdom, Saturn transits in the 12th can help with that. Most importantly, you're shedding the old you to make way for a new life. Look at the parts of yourself that need healing. Explore modalities that help you understand yourself better. Let go of the things that no longer define you—or the person you're becoming. Shed the old limiting beliefs, identities, or stories you've outgrown. Suppose you're interested in working in charities, hospitals, asylums, or in a therapeutic setting. In that case, this is a fantastic transit for pursuing those paths. If Saturn makes unfavorable aspects, elevate your self-care. It's too easy during those times to go down a dark spiral of regret and rumination. Put your needs first, seek support, and you'll avoid that.

## Astrocise

Grab your chart and find out where Jupiter and Saturn are currently transiting. What do you need to expand (Jupiter) and where do you need to get to work (Saturn)?

# From Retrograde Madness to Retrograde Badass

If you've dabbled in astrology for any time, you've probably heard a horror story or two about Mercury retrograde. Computers crashing, travel drama, and all sortsa communication gaffes. It's not a myth! I've had my own brushes with this pesky transit—including losing a 60,000-word manuscript.

I can assure you: that was the last time I ever brushed it off!

### What does it mean to be retrograde?

Retrograde means the planet's orbit has slowed down. To the human eye, it almost appears as if that heavenly body is moving backward. Don't worry—it's not! (Although that would be freaky!) *This signals a time when you need to slow your roll, too.*

All of the planets, except the Sun and Moon, will be retrograde at various times. The outer planets spend months in retrograde motion, and their effects are subtle at best. Although Mercury, Venus, and Mars hang about in this slo-mo vibe for shorter periods, they can cause a lot of chaos.

However, if you know when these funky transits are stirring up trouble, you can use them to your benefit—especially in your career. Here's the scoop:

## MERCURY RETROGRADE

The messenger planet stations retrograde approximately three times a year for three weeks at a time. During this period, you might experience messy communication, travel problems, and tech disasters. Aggravating? Yes. But if you prep beforehand, you can sail through this astrological anarchy with a minimum of fuss.

Begin by backing up your computer, phone, and other technology well before the retrograde kicks in. If you're smart, you're doing this on the regular automatically in multiple places! You'll also want to back up your website. (Yes, websites can crash and burn during this transit—I've seen it happen!) This will give you peace of mind should something happen to your tech gear.

If you need to travel, make sure you've carved in extra time. I recommend adding in an extra day before and after just in case you miss a flight or get stuck in the traffic jam from hell. You'll also want to organize your plans well in advance and double-check your flight info before you head out the door. Also, bring an extra pair of underwear and a small toiletry set on the plane. If your luggage gets lost, at least you can brush your teeth. Pack a snack, bring something to read, and keep your cool, no matter what.

Because Mercury is associated with communication, you'll want to observe your words. If you don't, they can be used against you. One wrong social media meme, and you're toast! If you're in the middle of important meetings or negotiations, this is the right time to listen more than you speak.

If you're applying for a job, make sure you are ultra-clear on details. Ask all the questions, so you know exactly what you're getting into. Better yet—wait until Mercury is direct before starting a new position.

Entrepreneurs need to be mindful around launches at this time. I've seen my share of business fails when the grand opening or product launch happened during a Mercury retrograde. If you make the mistake of going ahead anyway, you might want to consider a relaunch at a more auspicious time. Speaking of which: while this transit isn't favorable for launching new things, I've found it's pretty good for relaunching a product or program. For example, if you're opening the doors on a yearly offering, that's perfectly legit. As long as your initial launch happened during Mercury direct, you're in great shape.

For students, Mercury retrograde brings additional mental stress. Instead of cramming for exams at the last minute, start your studies well before this begins. Pace yourself well in advance so you can keep your tension low and ace every test!

Trying to make a decision at this time? Give yourself plenty of room to research your options. Do not rush to a conclusion. The more space you have to ponder, the more likely you will make happy choices.

Sometimes Mercury retrograde proves to be revelatory. Some of my biggest "aha" moments arrived during this transit. It can show you where you've taken a wrong turn—and possible paths you've never noticed.

I also recommend using this period to tie up loose ends. If you have any old project (or situation) still lingering around, finish it now. Get it out of your hair so you'll be free to work on new things once Mercury stations direct.

If it's possible, take time off. Put as much effort as you can into self-care. You'll be glad you did.

Always remember this rule: put "re" before every action. Rethink, renovate, redo, reuse, recycle, release . . . you get the picture.

## VENUS RETROGRADE

Unlike Mercury, Venus retrograde occurs only every 18 months.

While Venus is often associated with romantic relationships, it also covers client care, public relations, art, beauty, and spending. When retrograde, these areas can be impacted. I've found some of my most significant client issues have happened around Venus retrograde. It always seems to bring out the high-maintenance types and boundary-pushers.

This means you'll want to be firm with boundaries at work. Not just for clients but also for coworkers. Reinforce your policies when needed. It may be tempting to make exceptions as a way to keep the peace, but I've found this backfires during this transit. Instead, you'll want to uphold your rules and use the word "no" as often as necessary.

Keep a close eye on business expenditures and risky speculation. You may be tempted to waste your cash on things you don't need. Instead, put your wallet away and stick to your budget. This is actually an excellent transit for collecting money owed to you. If you have an outstanding client bill, hit them up. If they refuse to pay, it may be time to visit a collection agency.

If you follow these simple guidelines, you'll keep the peace at work—and your piggy bank will thank you.

# MARS RETROGRADE

Mars retrograde motion happens once every two years and lingers for about ten weeks.

Like Mercury retrograde, you do not want to launch a new business or product during this period. If you decide to go ahead and do it anyway, don't say I didn't warn you. A launch of anything new during this transit usually fails or doesn't live up to its full potential.

I cannot tell you how many times I've seen new businesses open during a Mars or Mercury retrograde only to shutter their doors two years later or less. It's a bummer when that happens!

This transit is also unfavorable for starting a fight. Whoever begins the war loses. A few years back, I had someone start some drama with me during a Mars retrograde. I immediately contacted my lawyer, who penned off a letter. I never heard from that person again.

Mars retrograde can amplify tempers. Keep your stress levels low, try not to lose your cool, and above all, take no aggressive action until the red planet is direct. Find constructive ways to work with your anger (ex: exercise it out!).

Lastly, avoid doing anything impulsive. Sure, it might seem exciting to say yes to that new position that popped up suddenly . . . until you actually start and see it's a total drag. Look before every leap, and you'll clear every hurdle like a gazelle.

Psst . . . you'll want to avoid elective surgeries during these three retrogrades. Trust me: your lip injections can wait.

These are the three biggies you'll need to master for your career . . . and life. Once you learn how to roll with the retrograde punches, you'll be ready to knock 'em out!

. . . . . . . . . . . . . . . . . . . . . . . . . . . . . . . . . . . . . . . . . . .

## Astrocise:

Are any of these planets retrograde now? If so, what are you noticing? Journal your observations.

## Common Sixth Sense:

Do not freak out if there are some things on your calendar that happen to fall during a retrograde. People can and do travel all the time when Mercury is retrograde—and some folks buy luxury villas when Venus is in slo-mo. Look, sometimes things happen when they do and there is no way to put it off until the timing is better. If you have something scheduled during one of these retrogrades and cannot shift things around, take a deep breath, examine every detail as closely as you can, and ask for support. You can't stop living just because the planets are gnarly. Bring a little more mindfulness into your game during these periods, and you can find your safe spaces and detours.

# Return the Beat Around

Astrology is a language of symbols and patterns. One pattern astrologers look for is known as a "return." A planetary return refers to when a transiting planet is in the same sign and degree as it was in the natal chart. For example, let's say your Jupiter is in Taurus. When transiting Jupiter enters the sign of the Bull, this would be your "Jupiter return." A return indicates a new planetary cycle or a chance to revisit the issues associated with the planet. To find your own returns, you can use the same chart you created for transits--just look at where the transiting planets match up with your natal chart. When they hit on top of each other, that's a return.

Each planetary cycle is on a different timeline. The inner planets are closer to the Sun and will transit more quickly than the outer planets. Ladies of a certain age--that Lunar transit? Once a month. Solar returns? Once a year—happy birthday!

Here's a list of the approximate length of time each planet takes to return to the place it was at the time of your birth:

**Inner planets:**
> **Moon: Once a month.**
> **Sun: Once a year.**
> **Mercury: About a year.**
> **Venus: About a year.**
> **Mars: Two years.**

**Outer planets:**
> **Jupiter: Twelve years.**
> **Saturn: Twenty-nine years.**
> **Uranus: Eighty-four years.**

**(And not-in-your-lifetime planets:)**
   **Neptune: One hundred sixty-five years.**
   **Pluto: Two hundred forty years.**

You will experience *many* returns of your inner planets. Most of the planets (except Neptune and Pluto) will return to the same sign in your natal chart during your lifetime, but the slower-moving ones (the outer planets) have a more significant impact. Jupiter, Saturn, and Uranus returns are substantial. Each one brings a new chapter and a chance to reassess your life, particularly around the planetary theme.

Using our Jupiter return in Taurus example, let's say it falls in your 5th house, which could happen around age 36. This could indicate expansion and opportunity in the areas of love, creativity, or children. Perhaps you're considering expanding your family, or maybe you're an artist and experiencing new opportunities to showcase your work. Whatever the case may be, the doors are wide open—it's up to you to go through the ones you want.

See how that works?

I pay close attention to Jupiter, Saturn, and Uranus returns (as well as the midway point for Uranus, which often correlates to the "mid-life crisis"). I'm also a fan of Nodal returns when the Lunar Nodes conjoin with the ones in the natal chart.

Here's what you need to know about each of these important astrological happenings.

## JUPITER RETURN

The Jupiter return occurs once every twelve years. Like I mentioned above, it happens when transiting Jupiter enters the same sign as the one in your natal chart. It signifies a year of luck, growth, and opportunity. Some of my luckiest breaks happened during my Jupiter returns.

When you are in your Jupiter return, you have what I call "dumb luck." You seem to be in the right place at the right time. Doors that seemed closed are suddenly open for you. You've got more choices—and chances. Even if you don't experience any major life upgrades, you will likely avoid or minimize drama. For example, you might not receive a new job, but you remain employed while the company goes through a downsize.

During a Jupiter return, you'll want to keep an eye out for opportunities—and be ready to say YES. You can expand your horizons in many ways. Look at the sign and the house it occupies for clues. This will show where you're lucky—every twelve years, you'll get another shot to max it out. The biggest key to this transit is remaining open, willing to learn, and ready to take a few risks.

For example, my natal Jupiter is in Gemini, and it's in my 8th house of joint finances, taxes, and investments. During my Jupiter returns, I always focus on securing my finances. I might invest in my business, create new income streams, or schedule an appointment with my financial advisor. During my last Jupiter return, I got serious about developing my writing career by taking classes and working with mentors. A few years later, I received my first book deal—and I haven't stopped writing since then. This also created a new source of income, as in book deals and royalties. Because I knew it was my return, I looked for opportunities to grow my revenue in new ways—and also started laying the groundwork for my legacy as a writer (8th house can indicate legacy).

During this period, I also successfully closed the door on family of origin financial matters. I settled my parent's estate and paid their bills off. Because of my ability to see opportunities, I also found a way to create a small inheritance for my siblings well before this transit kicked in. This is the perfect example of a conscious Jupiter return.

When you lean into your Jupiter return like that, you're planting seeds for bigger things. Of course, it's perfectly fine to move through it without overthinking about what's up. Either way, this is your lucky year, and if you want to see your life improve, use this transit for making bold moves and saying yes to opportunity. At the very least, count your blessings, no matter how humble they may be.

**Good activities to do during a Jupiter return:**
- Take classes in anything that interests you.
- Go back to school.
- Travel the world.
- Publish a book.
- Up-level your skillset by working with a mentor.
- Start a spiritual practice.
- Expand your social circle by networking.
- Be grateful for every opportunity.

- Get physical.
- Feng shui your living quarters.
- Start a new side hustle.
- Open your mind.
- Trust the Universe.
- Create a vision board for the future.
- If you don't like your career, pivot!
- Say yes to opportunities (and stay alert for them).

## Astrocise

How old are you now? Note the house where Jupiter will make (or made) its return—at 12, 24, 36, 48, 60, 72. . . . What insights can you glean? What should you be doing? Where should you be paying attention? What should you expand? Where should you place your focus?

## SATURN RETURN

I'm the first to admit that I'm a Saturn lover. Maybe it's because I have Capricorn intercepted in my 3rd house. Or perhaps I just like underdogs. Saturn is the dark horse of astrology. It's associated with limitations, restrictions, and hard work. But it delivers many gifts to those who are willing to do the job it demands. It brings maturity, capability, and wisdom.

The Saturn return occurs when Saturn conjoins with your natal Saturn. This period lasts for about two and a half years.

One of the best times to grok Saturn's stern vibe is during the Saturn return. This transit happens every 27 years or so. In my opinion, the first one is the most important. It signals the end of childhood and the beginning of adulting. This is the time in your life when you need to stop goofing off and get real. Pay your bills, commit to a school, lay the groundwork for your career, get married, start a family—all of those things are common during the first.

But this transit can also bring a crisis or two. Suddenly, you're on your own without the support you need. You have to learn to handle your business instead of relying on dear old mom and dad. While that seems scary, once you cut those apron strings, you're free to go . . . and to grow.

Here's something to know: many people "fail" their Saturn return. I mean that some folks are simply not ready to step up their game at the magical age of 27. This can lead to some stumbles along the way or Peter Pan syndrome. Later on, when the second Saturn return comes along, it's time to knuckle down and get serious.

If you find that you're around the age of your first Saturn return, this is your chance to grow up and glow up. You might go back to school or be in the final leg of finishing your degree. Get serious about your career (psst . . . you can always pivot later!) and prepare for the future you want. Above all, start taking responsibility for yourself. Rather than leaning on others, find your footing and do the work. If you start handling your business now, you're setting yourself up for future success.

Be sure to look to the area on your chart where Saturn lies. This will give you a hint on where you need to restructure and build stability in your life. For example, if Saturn sits in your natal 2nd house, you may need to create a budget and start saving for the future. I've found the Saturn return can break old patterns if you are willing to look at them critically—and do the work.

The second Saturn return is like a review of sorts. This one happens around the age of 57 and allows you to see how far you've come—and where you might go from here. Many people reach the pinnacle in their career at this time. Their best earning years happen now as well. You can begin to see retirement looming—and start planning for the "golden years." If you've messed up or feel lost, don't worry—you can reboot your life now. Many people use this period to pivot to the life they REALLY want.

For example, one of my clients was unhappily married and "stuck" in a miserable high-level job. She admitted she had been too afraid to get a divorce because they had children. But now the kids were on their own, the nest was empty, and there was no reason to stay in a relationship that wasn't growing or a job that created anxiety.

During her second Saturn return, she began taking classes in the work she really wanted to do: photography. She also started putting together a small portfolio and website. She went to her boss and talked about a demotion, which would reduce her stress while she figured out retirement options. Lastly, she began divorce proceedings, which wasn't easy, but both she and her partner knew it didn't make sense to carry on any longer.

A few years later, she's still at her job, but now enjoys the low-stress position. Instead of dreading her work, she looks forward to going into the office. Her photography career is still in the early stages, but she's excited about it becoming her work after retirement. She's single and enjoying her time alone. Her ex is in a new relationship and has moved to a bigger city, which suits him.

The biggest lesson in her second Saturn return? To stop putting everyone else first. Her Saturn sits in her 7th house of partnerships—so no surprise to see this is where she needed to do some work. Now she is living her best life—HER life, on HER terms. Proof that it's always possible to find a new path.

If you are fortunate enough to live to a ripe old age, you may experience the third Saturn return, which begins around 84. This is a beautiful transit to release anything that no longer serves you as you prepare for the "ultimate journey," which is death. You have time to reflect on your life—and where you need to forgive and forget. Mend the relationships that matter, delete the ones that don't. Your health may be a little more fragile now, so don't hesitate to reach out for assistance. Your health should be a priority. Do what you can to take good care of your body. If you're alone, this might be the right time to find a community or reconnect to old friends. Above all, this is your period for reckoning, to settle outstanding debts, especially the karmic kind. Take stock of your life and look where some lingering lessons remain. From there, continue your inner work, and you'll be setting the stage for a peaceful, contented end.

Every Saturn return is a transition of sorts. The first is the transition into adulthood, the second into the role of the wise elder, and the third is the transition to the other side.

**Good activities to do during a Saturn return:**
- Commit to or finish your education.
- Apply to grad school.
- Create a budget and stick to it.
- Purchase a home.

- Start your own business.
- Settle down.
- Clean up your act.
- Assess your life—and make necessary changes.
- Schedule appointments with your doctor, dentist, and financial advisor.
- Let go of old relationships, limiting beliefs, and habits.
- Make your health a priority.
- Get involved in work you love.
- Tie up loose ends.
- Take responsibility.
- Forgive and forget.

## Astrocise

 If you've picked up this book, chances are you're in or around your first Saturn return. You're interested in making a change, a fresh start, getting rid of the old and bringing in the new. In other words, the time is ripe to manifest your best destiny. Note the house where Saturn will make (or made) its return—at 27, 54, 81. . . . What insights can you glean? Where do you need to kick it up a notch? What should you make your priorities?

# URANUS

## Return, squares, and the midway midlife crisis point

Uranus transits can stir things up and crash your party—especially when it creates challenging aspects to your natal Uranus. That's not shocking since it is the "rebel planet." But here's something you need to know: those tough Uranus transits create the perfect conditions for reinvention. I always call this the David Bowie planet—he was a master of reinvention. Bowie constantly changed his look and the game. He kept us guessing and interested to see what's coming next.

This is the way to approach the four significant Uranus transits. Instead of looking at them with dread, start seeing them as your opportunity to make ch-ch-changes.

There are four primary Uranus cycles you'll experience in your lifetime: two squares, one opposition, and if you're lucky, the Uranus return. When these aspects show up, get ready to blow up, throw up, and GLOW UP.

## The first Uranus square—age 21

I remember when I was 21. My life seemed to explode into a million glass shards with plenty of collateral damage. Suddenly, I was ready to throw everything into the bonfire and burn it down to a crisp. I had enough of my parents, my first husband, and every authority figure in my life trying to tell me who to be. I made some extreme choices (some regrettable at the time), but ultimately, this was when I began finding out who I was.

Many people hit age 21 and are finally able to drink. Some are in college—or getting ready to leave the nest. It is a pivotal age. There are many firsts and milestones to experience around this age. The square marks your time to ditch the comfort zones, break the rules, sow your wildest oats, and become your own person. You're ready to enter adult life—and the realities and consequences that come with that.

Although this square can shake things up, it can also help you to find your independence. Think of this as the beginning of YOUR story. What family of origin beliefs are you ready to release, and what chapters will you write?

## The Uranus Opposition—age 42

This transit was the beginning of one of the most difficult periods in my life (see a theme here with Uranus transits?). My mother passed away, and suddenly I was caring for my 90-year-old father. Worse yet, her spendaholic ways left behind a mountain of debt—and my squabbling siblings decided to make my life a living hell. Needless to say, I had to put my foot down, handle dad's business, and get him safely to the finish line.

Although my Uranus opposition was challenging, it allowed me to finally break free of harmful family dynamics. In a way, it broke the wheel once and for all.

When Uranus opposes your natal Uranus, it feels like the lights go on, and suddenly you realize your life is half over. The question becomes, "did I miss out on something?" This is the midway point for Uranus—and the so-called "midlife crisis."

For some, this could be a period where you're saddled with too many responsibilities and feeling more pressure than ever to fit a mold. You might wonder if the grass is greener, the sex better, and if the glory days are truly gone. Some people get that seven-year itch, cheat on their spouses, and do other outrageous stunts. Others get a facelift or some other drastic thing to recapture their youth. (I know of one woman who started drinking for the first time in her life when the Uranus opposition began. Suddenly, she was going out every weekend and leaving her partner home to deal with the kids!)

The mid-life crisis point looks different for everybody but know this: the Uranus opposition is your chance to look under the hood of your life and examine what's working and where you need to reboot. If something no longer fits the person you're becoming (or want to become), you can drop it like it's hot.

The only thing I recommend is that you examine your life and the impact your decisions might have on the other people in your life. While there's nothing wrong with a little midlife rebellion, if you're suddenly playing Peter Pan and ditching out on your child support . . . that's not cool.

## The second Uranus square—Age 63

During this square, you're about to taste freedom again. How? This is the age when most people exit the workplace. You might choose to retire at this time. If that's not an option, or if you enjoy your work, the aspect might signal other changes in your life. For example, you may feel like downsizing or moving to someplace warmer. Or maybe you'll purchase an RV and plan to roam the country without a care in the world. Friendships may shift, and you could discover a whole new social circle.

Since this comes on the heels after the second Saturn return, it could be a wonderful time of rediscovery. "What do I want to do next? What stones can I turn over?" Start thinking of all the things you can do once you've bid your job adieu. Heck, you might even begin a whole new career! You're reclaiming your time, getting back to yourself, and maybe living La Vida Loca. Yeah, baby!

Or something like that. For some, this can be a hard time, especially if you're alone or unable to retire. If you feel lonely, there is no better time to get involved in your community. That could be through social activities or getting involved in a good cause (so

Uranian!). Look for meaningful ways you can contribute to the collective—and you'll never feel alone. Find interests, hobbies, and all sorts of ways to be involved in the world. You've got the time.

## The Uranus return—Age 84

Suppose you're fortunate enough to live this long, which many people do these days. In that case, you get to experience the Uranus return! This means you get to do your thing, period. If you have the well-being and means, think about how you want to express yourself or what you want to contribute. For example, former president Jimmy Carter kept busy with humanitarian work, building homes for the needy. Perhaps you'll feel called to get involved in your community or a worthy cause too.

For some, the Uranus return is a permission slip to develop a new style. If you've always wanted to lounge around in a pink boa and a fez, go for it! Friends will be necessary during this cycle, so be sure to keep up with your social activities. Many of your old pals may be gone now, so cultivating new friendships will add excitement and companionship (psst . . . a few younger buddies will keep things interesting!).

Because Uranus is associated with freedom, you may also be in that strange place where you desire independence . . . but need more assistance. If you're experiencing health issues, you may need to accept help. If you can live on your own, enjoy that—but don't forget to invite other folks over to keep things fun.

I also recommend having plenty of hobbies and keeping tabs on current events. Uranus loves mental stimulation, so don't allow yourself to get stuck in the same-old-same-old. Shake up your days, learn something new, and stay on top of tech.

The Uranus return could also be a meaningful time in your life when you're able to reflect on where you've been and where you're about to go. If you've lived your life well, on your terms, you could be planning your exit, also on your terms.

. . . . . . . . . . . . . . . . . . . . . . . . . . . . . . . . . . . . . . . . . . . . . . . . . . .

## Astrocise

Take a look at your chart. Are you in the middle of a Uranus aspect? If so, what's shaking up and how are you waking up? Are you a cool rebel or acting like a brat?

## NODAL RETURNS

I would be remiss if I didn't mention the importance of the Nodal Return. This is another return you'll want to keep an eye on. There are two.

The Nodal Return occurs when the transiting North Node aligns with your natal North Node. This signals a time when karmic debts are coming due—and some of your latent gifts are available for you to use. It feels like a "cosmic graduation," with the potential for tremendous growth, especially if you've been leaning into your North Node lessons. It's also possible that specific themes or patterns are getting your attention. There may be a few events that push your buttons. But, if you've avoided or misused the lessons, you can get a karmic smack down!

**The Nodal Return happens around ages 18, 37, 56, and 74.**

Both Donald Trump and Kamala Harris experienced their Nodal Return when they were running for election in 2020. In a way, their fates were intertwined, and there was something about that election that had karmic undertones for both.

The Reversed Nodal Return happens when the transiting North Node is conjunct your natal South Node. This signals a time when you can release the old gifts that have served you for too long. You can step firmly out of your comfort zone and into a new future. This transit can be tricky. It's not easy to move past the things that make you feel secure. But this allows for growth. Use your Reversed Nodal Return to explore the things and situations which kept you safe but haven't done much for spiritual growth. From my own experience, my Reversed Nodal Returns were more significant than my Nodal Returns. The Reversed forced me to take charge and make bold moves. My second one was when I began my business.

**The Reversed Nodal Return happens around ages 9, 27, 46, 65, and 83.**

. . . . . . . . . . . . . . . . . . . . . . . . . . . . . . . . . . . . . . . . . . . . . . . . .

## Astrocise

 Grab your chart! Are you currently in the middle of one of these " nodal returns?" If so, what is releasing? Where can you reinvent yourself? How are you growing? Ponder these questions and journal about them.

Psst . . . there are other big transits astrologers may consider, such as Neptune squares or oppositions. I didn't include them because I wanted to focus on returns, which in my opinion, are way more important, not to mention more relevant to this book's topic. Of course, I encourage you to explore other astrologer's work around this topic for additional insights and other perspectives. Don't just rely on me!

By the way, I'm not totally done with this return business! I've got two more specific charts I use to determine yearly and monthly themes. Read on, astro-cats:

# SOLAR RETURN CHARTS

The Solar Return chart is an annual chart that shows the themes for your year. It's calculated to the exact degree the Sun was in when you were born. Which means it could land directly on your birthday or not.

One important thing to keep in mind: to calculate it, you'll need to be aware of where you'll be **at the time of your birthday.** For example, suppose you're going to be in Chicago on your next birthday. In that case, you'll use that as your location when you plug in the info on your astrology software.

Here's why that's important: your Solar Return chart will be radically different depending on your location. And one place may be better than another.

Astrologer Bob Marks wrote the book on this topic with *How to Get More Love, Money, and Success by Traveling on Your Birthday*. His theory: if you don't like how the planets are stacking up for your upcoming Solar Return, change your location on your birthday.

This may sound weird, but it works.

For example, one year, my Solar Return chart was dicey. The planets were not well-placed, and it looked like I was heading into a year of challenges. So not my cup of astro-tea! Another astrologer suggested I visit Los Angeles on my birthday as I would have a better astrological setup. Skeptical yet intrigued, off I went. My birthday was spent in a cozy Italian restaurant in Silver Lake. That year turned out to be one of the best I've ever had, especially career-wise.

Since that time, I've become a total convert—and I check my Solar Return from multiple locations to find the best chart for my year. Keep in mind, sometimes travel is impossible. In that case, you'll want to scrutinize your Solar Return to see where you can max things out or ask for support.

Let's see how this works on a sample chart for an individual born in San Francisco (see page 108)

This individual was born in San Francisco (chart **A**), but no longer lives there. Currently, she's in Dallas, Texas. Overall, the chart is balanced and shows a sensitive, intelligent nature. She's happily married and runs her own business.

Next, look at the Solar Return, in Dallas, for 2019 (chart **B**). You can see a lot of planetary action in her 7th house of partnerships. This tells me that there may be important things happening with her significant relationships and her 6th house of work. Both areas will take up more of her attention. Her career might be taking off (Jupiter in the 6th conjunct Venus), and she may be loaded with more responsibilities (Saturn). At the same time, the Sun in the 7th means she may want to focus more on her relationship. Mercury conjunct Pluto shows powerful conversations—and that conjunction is in a square with Uranus, which lends unpredictable energy to the year. Relationships may be challenged by her growing fame or by sudden opportunities. Also: Saturn is square Mars, another troubling aspect that implies hits to her public rep.

In my opinion, that wasn't going to wash.

We poked around and found a few places she wanted to travel to for her birthday and settled on New York (see sample chart **C**, on page 109). The 6th house is full, giving her a ton of career-boosting vibes. Also: Uranus is conjunct her natal Midheaven, excellent for making a pivot (something she was considering). Mars in her 9th puts many travel possibilities on the horizon and makes it easier for her to focus on publishing a book, something she's keen to do. But my fave: that Venus-Jupiter conjunction in her 5th house of romance is so sweet. She can have her cake and eat it too. Traveling to NY for her birthday looks like a better decision (PS she agreed—her year was successful, and she's still married).

· · ·

Once you've cast your Solar Return, here's what to look at: where is the Sun? That will show you where a lot of your energy is going to be focused for the year. For example, if the Sun is in your fourth house for your Solar Return, your home or family may be the main focal point.

Next, look at the Ascendant. Yes, you get a different Ascendant for your Solar Return! This will give you information on how you're projecting yourself to the world.

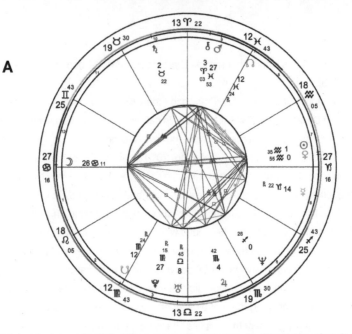

**A**

Natal chart for January 21.1970, 4:55 pm, born in San Francisco, CA. Cancer Ascendant, Cancer Moon, Aquarius Sun.

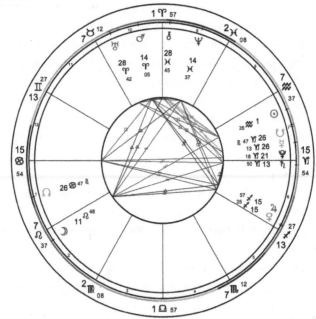

**B**

Solar return chart for same individual, now calculated for her 2019 solar return (i.e., birthday): January 21.2019, 5:30 pm, Dallas, TX.. Cancer Ascendant, Leo Moon, Aquarius Sun.

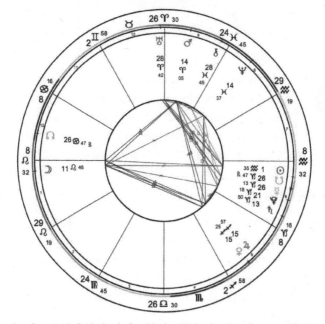

**C**

Solar return chart for same individual, calculated for her 2019 solar return, but now with a birthday trip to New York in mind: January 21.2019, 6:30 pm, New York, NY. Leo Ascendant, Leo Moon, Aquarius Sun.

What's the ruling planet for the year? You'll find that here too—and want to consider which house it lands in. Say your Solar Return Ascendant is in Taurus. You might be more grounded and stable—or at least, that's how you'll appear. Your ruling planet for the year will be Venus. If Venus is in the 5th house of your Solar Return chart, love is in the air!

Take a gander at the Moon and you'll get a clue to your emotional life and how you're handling the events of the year.

Pivot around and see what Jupiter and Saturn are doing. This can show you the areas where expansion and growth are happening.

Are any planets conjunct? Is there a stellium (a cluster of three or more planets in the same sign)? Pay attention to these because that part of your chart is amplified.

You can consider other planets and aspects too—but these are the main players I like to look at, especially when I'm considering interpretations around career.

Your turn!

## Astrocise:

Open your astrology software and find the setting for Solar Return Charts. Plug in your info and see what your "birthday chart" looks like. What themes are amplified? Are the planets friendly? Do you see possibilities that excite you—or bum you out? Now: try a different location. Is it better . . . or not? Try other places until you find one you like. Then: book your trip!

## LUNAR RETURNS

There's one more chart you might want to check out: the Lunar Return.

The Lunar Return chart can help you understand the emotional impact of the planets for the upcoming month. You can see which themes are operating—and that information will help you remain centered, no matter what. Think of it this way: when you know what's coming, you're prepared, not scared. Instead of being caught off guard, you're emotionally ready.

Keep in mind that all this astrology cannot predict every single thing down to the wire—but it's still better to have a general idea of the state of your emotional affairs, in my humble opinion.

Like a Solar Return chart, a Lunar Return is simply a chart cast from the moment the Moon returns to the position in your natal chart. You can calculate your Lunar Return with astrology software. You'll need to put in the exact place you'll be for the month to get an accurate chart.

Once you've run your Lunar Return chart, check where the Moon is hanging out (it will always be in the same sign of your natal chart—but everything else will change). Are there any aspects to the Moon? Are those aspects challenging or supportive?

Next, look at the Ascendant. You'll notice it's different than your natal chart. This will give you an idea of what image you're projecting for the month.

Check to see if the Lunar Return Ascendant is making aspects to your natal chart. For example, recently, the Ascendant for my Lunar Return chart was making a square with my natal Sun and Mercury. This indicates tension about how I feel about myself—or my work. I may be having issues with self-expression. With a Virgo Ascendant for the Lunar Return, we can guess that the month ahead will have my mind on details and perfectionism—that's pretty nifty since I'm in the middle of heavy editing.

Because Virgo is rising at the time of this Lunar Return, Mercury is the ruler—and it's sitting in my 6th house of work and routines. Seeing that I'm deeply involved in Mercury-ruled activities such as writing and teaching, it makes sense.

The Moon was hanging out in my 3rd house, which is quite lovely for plugging into my emotions, which can also be helpful for writers. Imagination is strong for that particular month, another thing I need. Additionally, it was supported by happy angles with Mercury, Neptune, and Pluto, which set the perfect conditions for imaginative writing. Needless to say, I got a tremendous amount of writing completed—and although there was tension, I knew I could move past it if I shut out distractions.

Results: I was productive as can be—and moving through my writing deadlines like a boss!

Doing a monthly Lunar Return chart will give you information for excellent decision-making. Also, remember: if your chart for the month is challenging, you'll get a fresh one every month! Yay!

· · · · · · · · · · · · · · · · · · · · · · · · · · · · · · · · · · · · · · · · · · · · · · · · ·

## Astrocise

 Get out your trusty astrology software and click on Lunar Return. Create a chart for the previous month. What did it say about your month—and moods? Now, do another chart for the upcoming Lunar Return cycle. What do you need to pay attention to? Make notes—then check back at the end of the month and see how things panned out!

# Reach for the Moon

Since the time humans were able to stand upright, they've been fascinated with the Moon. It looms large in our imaginations—and in the night sky. Legends of werewolves and other supernatural beings continue to spook folks to this day. But the Moon isn't as scary as you think. Farmers and magical types know this. They also know how to work with it to create abundance, weed out problems, and more.

I'm a "Moon-centered" person. I follow it closely and have seen the results. Even though I didn't inherit the green thumb of my ancestors, I have planted other seeds in my life according to the phases of the Moon—and they have flourished.

While the other planets show yearly or monthly themes, La Luna dictates the daily energy. The Moon moves through signs every 2 1/2 days, so you must pay attention because the vibe is different when it enters a new sign.

When you set up your day-to-day routines around the lunar rhythms, you become way more present. This awareness leads to intentional living. The more conscious you are of every choice, action, and intention, the more likely you're carving out the future you want. This is how you twist your fate.

A reminder: the Moon rules changes, emotional states, and your home. It shows how you express your feelings and respond to other people's emotions. It's also associated with maternal feelings.

It's especially helpful in business. Here's why: the Moon also indicates financial fluctuations and the mood of the public. Suppose the general population isn't feeling spendy. In that case, you certainly don't want to put out a major marketing effort on that day!

It might be because I have three planets in Virgo or I'm a planner by nature, but when it comes to Lunar Living, I'm highly detailed.

Every month, I take stock of the Moon phases (New Moon, Full Moon) and create plans around those events. Each morning, I check the Moon's sign, and this information helps me put my energy where it's going to have the most impact. This high level of attention allows me to move through my days productively and with a minimum of fuss.

## MOON PHASES

Even though there are eight Moon phases, the ones you need to know are the New Moon and the Full Moon when you're setting up your monthly goals.

The New Moon represents a time of possibility. This is your monthly spot to plant the seeds for future growth. Every New Moon is an opportunity to set goals and start fresh. You can launch a new business or product now, provided Mercury and Mars are not retrograde.

But one of the most important habits you'll want to establish is setting New Moon intentions. This is something I've done for many years—and it's fantastic to witness how many of my wishes have manifested. I highly recommended you check out **New Moon Astrology** by Jan Spiller; it has been my "bible" for setting New Moon intentions.

It doesn't require anything special other than a journal you love and a pen. Set aside quiet time around the New Moon where you will not be disturbed. Light a candle if you'd like or burn a little incense. Then jot down ten wishes in your journal. You might want to check which sign the Moon is in to guide you in your intention setting.

When the Full Moon arrives, take stock of where you are. Have your seeds begun to show signs of life? If so, rejoice—and carry on! If you're not seeing any growth, it may be a sign that you've got work to do—or may need to revisit your goals. Full Moons are also times for releasing. You're creating space for the things you want to arrive. Tie up loose ends, finish outstanding work, and find something to celebrate. Above all, count your blessings and give thanks. A grateful pocket will always attract more riches.

As I mentioned in my book *Astrology For Real Life*, the formula for manifesting with the Moon goes something like this:

**Dark Moon** (the period before the New Moon): Prepare the soil (meditate on what you want—declutter your life to prepare)

**New Moon:** Plant the seed (write your intentions).

**Waxing Moon** (the Moon is getting bigger—your "seed" is growing): Nurture the seed (take divine action on your goal).

**Full Moon**: Reap your reward and celebrate!

**Waning Moon** (the Moon is getting smaller): Weed the garden (get rid of anything that isn't contributing to growth).

Ta da! Manifest your best!

# Moon through the Signs

Next, let's consider the Moon through the signs. This shows the energy operating and where you need to focus. By engaging in activities aligned with each zodiac sign, you're kicking ass and not wasting your precious energy.

Much like a weatherman, I check the transits of the Moon every morning. The Moon remains in a sign for about two and a half days. While I consider where it is in my natal chart, I'm more concerned with the zodiac sign. When I align my day with the areas associated with that particular sign, I'm going with the flow rather than swimming upstream (fish that swim upstream to mate die shortly after!).

**Moon in Aries**—This fiery Moon isn't sitting around—and neither should you. This is your time to take the risk and make bold moves. Initiate projects, apply for that job, assert yourself, and go after your passions. Situations require bravery and leadership. Don't wait for someone else to take command—grab the reins and sally forth! The energy is high now, giving you the ability to get many things started. BLAZE TRAILS. You'll need to pace yourself because it's too easy to burn out if you push it too hard. This is also a fab time to change your habits or turn over a new leaf. The Aries Moon is a reminder it's never too late to start fresh. Watch out for impulse, rudeness, and a tendency to be selfish. There's nothing wrong with putting yourself first, provided you're not a brute.

**Moon in Taurus**—The Moon is exalted in Taurus, which means it's happy as a bull in a pasture full of flowers. This day moves slowly, and so should you. Unlike the Aries Moon, this is a chill vibe. Slow your roll, take your time, and approach every situation with practicality. Because Taurus is ruled by Venus, this is a lovely lunation for indulging in things that make you feel good: a hearty meal, long soaks in the tub, massages, and lovemaking. It's also a positive few days for getting your finances in order. Balance the checkbook, pay bills, apply for a loan, ask for a raise, or engage in new money-making activities. This is also a fabulous time for art or anything creative. If you're an artist or want to create new content for your business, here's your best spot in the month! Be careful with stubbornness now. If you become unreasonable, you could end up smashing the china shop for no reason at all.

**Moon in Gemini**—This Moon brings opportunities to learn new things. It's the perfect time to take a class, enroll in school, or read all the books. You can update your skillset, which could lead to opportunities down the road. Communication matters need your attention as well, both conversation and writing. Send off letters, clean out your inbox, and talk it out. Schedule important meetings and negotiations on these days. You'll have a greater ability to find the right words—and seal the deal. Curiosity is piqued, and you want variety, which could lead to restlessness. Therefore, you'll want to limit your distractions as much as possible if you wish to get anything done. The Moon in Gemini is also marvelous for taking care of your daily errands. Write out your shopping list and get stocked up. You might also want to take short trips or get involved in your community in some way. What you don't want to do: sit around. How can you be bored when there are so many exciting things to do these days?

**Moon in Cancer**—The Moon in Cancer is right at home since the Moon is in its domicile. The Moon rules Cancer, making this your best few days to center your energy on activities associated with the Crab. Clean your house, create order in your surroundings (including your desk at work), pay the household bills, and spend time with your family. Emotions run high, and intuition is elevated. Be sensitive to your own feelings as well as the feelings of other people. If you need to have a conversation around a delicate topic, this might be a good day for that. The Moon in Cancer is kind-hearted, so it's easier to understand how the other person feels. If you're working from home during this lunation, make sure you keep the door closed, so your loved ones don't barge in. This Moon makes people a bit needy—you'll want to keep your boundaries high while remaining as gracious as possible. Sometimes people want to dredge up the past at this time. If there is no good reason for it, let it go. Also: watch out for drama. A few touchy types might be spoiling for an argument. Put your shell up and stay out of the line of fire.

**Moon in Leo**—The Moon in Leo wants all the flash, so be prepared to put on a show today. You'll want to stand in your glory, adorn yourself, and toot your horn. All the world's a stage—get up there, express yourself, and be proud of your accomplishments.

This is a good day for creative work—if you have a project tugging at your heart, begin working on it now. It's also one of the best times to step into a leadership role. This noble Moon favors leading with the heart and encouraging others to be their best. Take on that role in your work, community, or family—and everyone will benefit. Because Leo rules children, this lunation is ideal for spending time with kids—or indulging your inner child. Whatever you decide to do today, just remember to be generous and think big.

**Moon in Virgo**—There is no better time to clean up your act than when the Moon moves into Virgo. Create divine order in any area of your life. Clean your surroundings, declutter your possessions, file papers, take out the trash, and sort out every detail. If you're a writer, this is a fabulous few days for editing your work. Because Virgo is associated with health, you might want to schedule appointments with your health-care providers, including your dentist. The love language of this Moon is "acts of service," making this an excellent time for taking care of others. If you see someone in need, offer to help. Sometimes, this lunation brings out the inner and outer critic. While there's nothing wrong with pointing out the problems, if you can't be nice about it, it might be wiser to mind your own business. Ask yourself this: is my criticism necessary . . . and is it kind?

**Moon in Libra**—Relationships matter during this Moon. Focus on your most important connections and see where you can strengthen them. Cut ties with toxic people, set boundaries, and watch out for passive-aggressive tendencies in yourself or others. Above all, be diplomatic wherever possible. Even if the other side chooses rudeness, remain a class act. Because this Moon is ruled by Venus, you'll want to create beauty and harmony wherever you go. Upgrade your surroundings with new art, hire a Feng Shui consultant, or straighten up anything out of order. For business, this lunation is stellar for meetings, signing contracts, or taking care of legal matters. It's also the perfect time to launch a spirited PR campaign. Lastly, this is your time to speak up about injustice. Although every day should be devoted to social justice, this day, in particular, offers a chance to fight for what's right. As Spike Lee says: "Do the right thing."

**Moon in Scorpio**—This is the most psychic of all the Moons, which means you'll want to trust your gut today. Follow your instincts and do not ignore red flags . . . or green lights. You're more likely to make significant decisions if you do. If you need to get to the bottom of a matter, this is your best time. Do your research, dig deep, and you'll uncover the truth. Scorpio is associated with finances—balance your checkbook, file taxes, and schedule an appointment with a financial advisor. If you need a loan, this is a good day to apply. It's also the best day for a tarot or astrology reading! This Moon can bring out a tendency to brood. If you feel moody, ask yourself what's up with that. Do not take your problems out on the wrong person. The Scorpio Moon loves a little mystery—and is perfect for sharing secrets (provided you know the other person is trustworthy). Because Scorpio rules the reproductive organs, intimacy is IN.

**Moon in Sagittarius**—This Moon is happy-go-lucky. Positivity radiates now—tap into that optimism and enjoy your day. You can motivate others through your inspiring example. Stand up, speak the truth, and shine bright! This is an excellent time to travel—or to book plans. Plot out your next adventure, hit the road, and see where it takes you! Roam where you want to—and enjoy the view along the way. You can also broaden your horizons through education. This would be an excellent time to apply to a university or sign up for an online class. For writers: send in that book proposal, hit up a publisher, or finish your manuscript. Also, if you've neglected your spiritual practices, this is the time to reconnect. The Moon in Sagittarius loves nature and physical activity. Get outside, move your body, and breathe in the fresh air! A few things to watch out for: self-righteousness, hypocrisy, and a tendency to shove your opinion around like it's the gospel. NOPE.

**Moon in Capricorn**—I call this the "CEO Moon," the best one for business and leadership. You can tap into your deepest ambitions—and find your way to the top. Discipline is on tap during this lunation, giving you the grit to overcome odds and reach the top. Take the lead in every situation, speak up, share your bold ideas, and make boss decisions (not just for work—but life!). When the Moon is in Capricorn, focus on the long-term results. Take your time, lay out the steps, and keep going. Create structures, and do not hesitate to tear down any that don't work. No matter how big the mountain, this Moon gives you the power to reach your goals. Above all, be unapologetically ambitious. There is no shame in getting your hustle on hard when the Moon is in the sign of the Goat. (Psst . . . if you want that promotion or a new job, here's your green light to throw your hat in the ring.) One thing to be mindful of: overwork. It's easy to commit to too many things. Delegate or risk burnout!

**Moon in Aquarius**—This is the humanitarian Moon, and it's ideal for getting involved in your community. You can organize other people, join groups, and inspire others to do good things. Focus on worthy causes and shake up the status quo. What can you do for the collective? How can you promote equity? This future-oriented Moon wants seats at the table for everyone. Do your part to make room—and make noise if you see injustice. There is also no better time to check in on friends. If you've been too busy for your besties, schedule a catch-up date around this time. Also: networking during a Moon in Aquarius can open you up to dynamic new relationships. That person you rubbed elbows with at an industry meet-up may turn out to be instrumental in your rise later on. It's also my fave Moon for updating computer gear, learning new tech skills, and online classes. Upgrade your mind with some high-level learning, and you'll be ready for the future, no matter what it looks like. Also: idealism is strong, so create your big-vision goals now. With a bit of help from your friends, anything is possible. This Moon can bring a cold vibe. If you've checked out emotionally, watch that you don't cause harm along the way.

**Moon in Pisces**—This is a sensitive Moon, so self-care needs to be a priority. Emotions are heightened—for both good and bad. You may be weepy one minute, joyful the next. Boundaries get blurred, and people can be needy. If you're taking on everyone's problems, your spirit could feel wilted. Try not to absorb every person's situation and avoid fixating on the news. Instead, meditate, rest, reflect, take a salt bath, go on a retreat, pray, heal, or write poetry. Forgive the past while you dream of the future. Intuition is sharp for the days the Moon travels through this sign. If you're getting a sense of any situation, trust it. You'll want to keep your feet on the ground during these few days, especially if you're dealing with some unpleasant matters. Avoid turning to substances or running away. While there is nothing wrong with wanting an escape, it could be problematic now.

. . . . . . . . . . . . . . . . . . . . . . . . . . . . . . . . . . . . . . . . . . . . .

## Astrocise

 Begin paying attention to the daily lunar cycles for a month. Check the sign the Moon is in and plan your activities around that. Every evening, journal about your day. How did it go? Did the suggested activities move you forward? Did you do something entirely different? If so, how did that work out for you?

## Common Sixth Sense

While it's lovely to be able to attune your life to the Moon, keep in mind it's not always possible to hyper-manage your days like this. For example, you may be knee-deep in a project during a Pisces Moon and unable to rest. In that case, be mindful of the energy, stay on your hustle, but find those small moments for a sacred pause.

# LUNAR ECLIPSES

An astrologer once said that eclipses are like New or Full Moons on "steroids." I wish I knew who that astrologer was so I could give them full credit, because I've never heard a better way of describing eclipses.

These lunar happenings are intense, jacked up, and unpredictable. When they show up, you know something is about to blow up (not always in a bad way, mind you). It's no wonder eclipses strike fear!

But hear this: they are not all doom 'n gloom. Nope. When they arrive, it's a sign that change is on the way. Something or someone is about to get "eclipsed" out of your life. Usually, these are things that need to go. It's best to go with the flow—and trust the Universe is sorting it out.

Eclipses always arrive in pairs, so you'll hear astrologers refer to this as "eclipse season."

According to some, eclipse season is not the time to set intentions or do magical work. The unpredictability could backfire, leading to the opposite results. (Note: I'm born near an eclipse and have never experienced this when setting intentions or any other sort of thing.) Just to be on the safe side, you might want to hold off on those activities until a few days later.

So what does this have to do with your life purpose or vocation? How can you work with eclipses to twist them in your favor?

Simple. When eclipse season kicks in, know that change is on the way. An eclipse can shed light on what needs to go—and what's possible. If you want to make a career pivot, the information or nudge you need might arrive around this time. The best thing you can do is remain open and adaptable.

## Dos and Don'ts for Eclipses:

- Don't freak out. There is no need to fear an eclipse.
- Do not rush to make decisions around eclipse season. Instead, allow a few days to pass. You'll have the information you need to make excellent choices.
- If situations are dicey, this is not the time to push. Instead, allow. Wait and see. Trust the Universe.
- Do be alert for changes. A situation may reach a boiling point—or a new opportunity may appear. You'll want to be awake at the wheel so you can make the right turn.
- That being said, don't force significant changes until you are crystal clear. It's too easy to make assumptions on the day of the eclipse. Again: hang tight for a few days. Let any dust settle before initiating something new.
- If you can, take time off for self-care. Stay hydrated, rest up, and don't over-book yourself.
- Emotions are elevated, both yours and other peoples. Be tender with yourself and give others room to be with their feelings, too.
- If the eclipse falls near your birthday or on a planet in your chart, pay attention. This signals an important shift for you. (Two of my most significant career changes happened when an eclipse landed on my Ascendant—and the day before my birthday.) According to astrologer Susan Miller, if an eclipse happens around your birthday, you also need to take care of your health—something may occur around this time that gets your attention (I got a massive tooth infection around a recent eclipse that landed a day before my birthday!).

**Fun astro-fact:** if you're born on or near an eclipse, you're here to shake things up. Tradition won't mean much to you. You're a catalyst and possess unique gifts, which, if used wisely, can help other people evolve. But if you choose to use your gifts negatively, you could wreak havoc. You'll either create chaos or find yourself in the middle of intense situations that feel karmic in nature. Life will not be dull!

## Astrocise

Check out NASA's eclipse website: **eclipse.gsfc.nasa.gov** and see where the eclipses were the year you were born. What themes were getting a shake-up then?

# VOID-OF-COURSE MOONS

The void-of-course Moon occurs when the Moon makes its last aspect to a planet before heading into the next sign. This is a cosmic "time out," a period to chill or finish tasks. Sometimes the void Moon lasts only a few minutes; other times, it can linger for many hours—or almost a day.

Your ephemeris or astrology software will show when these void Moons happen.

## Dos and Don'ts for the Void Moon:

- This is another time when you don't want to overdo or overcommit. Instead, take time off if you can. If you cannot, be mindful of your energy.
- Avoid making major decisions such as signing contracts. It's better to wait until the Moon is no longer void. You'll have more clarity then.
- Do not start new projects or anything new under the void-of-course Moon. Instead, put your energy into taking care of tasks already in motion. Finish up projects, tie up loose ends, and put every duck in a row. Then you'll be ready to take action when the Moon is in the next sign.
- While this may sound like a lot to remember, it's really not that hard. Once you start rolling in the deep with the Moon, you'll see how it illuminates the possibilities while keeping you centered on your right path.

# MOON IN THE WORKPLACE

Want to know how to hire the perfect person? Want to make sure you're putting people in the correct positions for their temperament? Here's the deal: look at their natal Moon. The Moon can explain someone's emotional makeup, but also what they need to be happy. (Psst . . . some folks might think you're weird if you begin nosing around asking about birthdates and such. If you sense they're not down with giving you the deets, don't push it!)

Here's what you need to know about the Moon—and how to keep your hired guns happy:

**Aries Moon**—These folks want to be where the action is. They are willing to take chances and are excellent at handling last-minute drama. They can be great leaders because they inspire others to act. However, they can be impatient and hot-tempered, especially if things don't go their way.

*Best jobs:* management, team leadership, anything that requires physical movement, risky industries. Do NOT stick this person behind a desk. They will make your life hell.

**Taurus Moon**—Taurus Moon folks are gentle, slow-moving, and reliable. They are naturals at design or handling money. They don't like to take risks and can be stick in the muds about some things.

*Best jobs:* payroll, money, financial management, art, writing, music, design, anything that requires concentration. Do not put them in a situation that changes rapidly. They need time to process changes.

**Gemini Moon**—Quick-witted and curious, these are people-people. They can talk to just about anybody—and are excellent at teaching. They get bored quickly, so tedious stuff is not for them. Also, they can be gossipy, so probably not the person to trust with your brand secrets.

*Best jobs:* teaching, sales, human resources, customer service, data entry, writing. Gemini Moon people need to be around others—stuck in an office in the back, alone, will make them miserable.

**Cancer Moon**—Cancer Moons are natural caretakers. They are loyal workers and possess excellent memories. Because they are kind-natured, they're most excellent in customer care. Put them in charge of any services that require a human touch, and they soar!

*Best jobs:* customer care, team leader, counselor, human resources, personal assistant. They don't like to be criticized—if you do it, you'll need to be sensitive on how you deliver the info.

**Leo Moon**—This is the "star employee," the one who wants to shine. They're loyal as can be and need plenty of praise. At times, they can be dramatic—but they're also passionate and fun. Most of them are extroverts, which makes them great at the front end of a business. They want to lead, so you'll want to give them responsibility.

*Best jobs:* creative work, artist, leader, performer, entrepreneur, CEO. NEVER humiliate them in front of other teammates. Do that once, and you'll regret it.

**Virgo Moon**—If you need details handled, a Virgo moon is your person. These people like to analyze and find the most efficient way to get things done. They are organizing experts—and they aim to please when it comes to service. Virgo Moons make wonderful teachers and managers, but they have a tendency to nag.

*Best jobs:* teaching, writing, editing, organizing, analysis, computers, planning, data entry, anything that requires expertise and patience. Keep in mind they enjoy fixing. Don't be insulted if they have a few suggestions for you to do your job better!

**Libra Moon**—Libra Moons need harmony—and they will do what they can to bring that to the work environment. They're great at smoothing over conflict and enjoy any sort of creative work. Fairness is important to them—they'll want to make sure everyone is getting the same treatment. Because Libra rules justice, they tend to understand rules and laws well.

*Best jobs:* design, diplomacy, sales, art, team leader, any work that requires teamwork, human resources, legal affairs. They can be passive-aggressive, so watch what they say—and don't be afraid to call them on their shit.

**Scorpio Moon**—Scorpio Moons like to dig deep to get to the bottom of things. They have a robust bullshit detector and can be counted on to get to the truth of the matter. They're private and enjoy working alone. You can trust them to get the job done without having to watch over their shoulders. Most of them have a keen interest in financial matters. (Psst . . . I almost always hire Scorpio Moons, because they are loyal.)

*Best jobs:* intuitive work, insurance, financial advisor, payroll, money management, research, strategizing. They don't like to be around people 24/7. Give them privacy, and don't take it personally if they're reserved.

**Sagittarius Moon**—These are truth seekers and tellers. They demand honesty and are never afraid to tell it like it is. They're also easily bored, which means you certainly don't want to put them in a job where they have to fib—or sit still. Travel makes them happy, and they're fabulous at making connections with other people. Sag Moons are enthusiastic by nature—making them perfect for marketing or sales.

*Best jobs:* presentations, thought leader, public speaker, sales, publishing, advertisement, marketing. Like Aries Moons, they don't like being chained to a desk. It makes them fidgety.

**Capricorn Moon**—This is my favorite Moon for entrepreneurs, bosses, and leaders. Capricorn Moon people are born to rule the roost. You can trust them in positions of power and responsibility. They bring gifts of organization to the work environment. Every single one is a pro—and expect you to be one, too.

*Best jobs:* management, entrepreneur, developer, organizing, CEO, CFO, leader. Even if they start at the bottom, their eyes are always on the top position. Make sure you reward their hard work.

**Aquarius Moon**—Aquarius Moon people are dynamic in group interactions. They are also highly innovative. Which means you'll want them by your side when you're brainstorming new ideas. They love variety and network with ease. In meetings, they are the ones with the aha moments and best ideas. Every one of them is a natural with tech. They can understand abstract concepts and turn them into tangible goods.

*Best jobs:* networking, the humanitarian aspect of your biz, ideas person, group leader, outreach. Aquarius Moons are friendly but can seem aloof at times. Don't worry about that. They're probably busy conjuring up new ideas.

**Pisces Moon**—Pisces Moon folks are wonderful working behind the scenes. They are spiritual by nature and love to help. They are great with counseling, but they are also highly artistic. Put them in any job that allows them to serve, create, or heal.

*Best jobs:* client care, art, creativity, healing, fundraising, teaching, intuition. Their feelings are easily hurt, and they don't do well in any work that is too structured. Ironically, structure helps them stay on track.

# The God of War at Work

G ot an enemy at work? Wondering if your new boss is going to be helpful . . . or problematic? Always look at their Mars first before planning an interaction or confrontation. Mars shows a person's drive, ambition, leadership capability, but also how they fight.

Knowing someone's Mars can keep you out of trouble—or give you the edge. Also, your own Mars can show you how to lead in the best way possible.

A few stories. Many years ago, someone I knew was in a legal battle with an ex-employee. Accusations were flying, lawsuits were threatened, and the damage to the company's rep was growing. I looked at the astrology chart of the former employee. I knew right away the owner of the company was in a losing battle.

Why? That former employee had Mars in Scorpio. That showed a tenacious personality with a vindictive streak. Mars is at home in Scorpio—and the owner of the business had Mars in Cancer, which was a more timid expression of the red planet. I knew he would lose, especially when I witnessed how he was trying to lead the fight (super emotional, telling everyone under the sun about it).

My advice to the employer: pay the employee to get her out of your hair. Which he didn't follow, and the war kept going for a few years until his business folded. Her accusations hurt his rep, his words fell flat in the community, and any attempt he made to jab at her made him look like a bully.

Another story: a client was getting a new boss. She was worried because the last one made her life a living hell—and she didn't want to go through that again. Once she learned the new boss's birthdate, she asked me to take a peek. They had Mars in Capricorn, which was exalted. This told me the boss would be a stickler for details, highly organized, and a total pro. All she had to do was be an excellent employee, and they'd get along fine. Sure enough, the new woman was fair, professional, and able to turn the company around through her shrewd management. The client found the working environment tolerable at last—and without office politics, she was able to excel at her job.

Again, it may be odd to ask someone their birthdate—especially a boss. You might seem like the office super freak if you do! You'll have to be stealthy—my suggestion: wait until an office birthday party. Shazam!

Alrighty then—let's look at Mars at work:

# Mars through the Signs

**Mars in Aries**—Mars loves being in the sign of the Ram because it rules Aries. Here, the energy becomes bold, passionate, and pioneering. People with this placement are capable of getting big things started—and inspiring other people into action. They can be impatient and selfish—and god help those who don't move as fast as they do. This makes them angry, and when they get mad, they burn every bridge down. If you're an Aries Mars, look to inspire people with your courage and willingness to take risks. Keep your temper in check. If your boss has this placement, you'll need to be a go-getter. Be willing to speak up and work unsupervised. If you have problems with a Mars in Aries person: they can be nasty, so it's best not to get on their wrong side. But if you do, try to cool the fires down as quickly as possible before they burn out of control. Mars in Aries people can get red-hot angry, but they chill out fast. In some cases, they can be bullies. If you lock horns with them, you'll need to hold your ground—or get the hell out of the way as soon as possible.

**Mars in Taurus**—This is a mindful, steady placement for Mars. Instead of rushing to the top, Mars in Taurus folks prefer to take it one step at a time. They are thoughtful, reliable leaders—and good to turn to for problem-solving. They keep the team going but can be extremely stubborn. Have you ever tried to push a bull around? Ain't gonna happen. Which means they can become obstinate when fixated on a particular thing. When that happens, they shut down—and don't listen. If you've got Mars in Taurus, your reliability is your asset. People naturally trust you—which allows you to get people on your side. Encourage your team to be mindful—and be an example of grace under pressure. If you have trouble with a Mars in Taurus person, you can really get their goat by being flaky. That will probably get you fired, though. A better bet: take a few deep breaths and follow their pace.

**Mars in Gemini**—This is not the best placement for Mars. It does give a sharp wit, intellectual gifts, and the ability to talk your way in and out of any situation. Bosses with this placement can be strong orators and gifted communicators. Expect long meetings, lots of emails, and conversations over drinks after work. If you have this placement, you can win people over with your words. Use them to motivate and watch your tendency to be sarcastic when you don't like something. If you're dealing with a Mars in Gemini enemy, they can be malicious gossips. You'll need to be ready to defend your rep. I recommend keeping a paper trail in case they make false accusations.

**Mars in Cancer**—This is the weakest placement of Mars and produces leaders who wear their hearts on their sleeves, for better or worse. Their emotions can get in the way. However, at their best, they are nurturers who care about developing other people's talents. Get on their wrong side and expect a whole lotta emotional drama. However, you can quickly get the upper hand with impeccable logic. Use that to your advantage, and you'll win every time. If you have this placement, your kindness can be your blessing—or a curse. You'll need to learn how to protect yourself from people who might take advantage of your soft side.

**Mars in Leo**—Leo Mars are noble leaders. They are big-hearted and generous—and great to work for. Unless they go to the shadow side of Leo, which is the ego. Once they go that route, it's all about them. They want the spotlight, the credit, and plenty of butt kissing. If they don't like you, they will look for ways to make you look small, so they can feel big. Best way to deal with these types: flattery will get you everywhere. If you can't stomach that, the next step is to mess with their fragile egos. A bit of public humiliation, and that should seal the deal. If you are a Leo Mars, treat everyone like a star. Show others how to shine. Bring out the best in your team, and they'll deliver the gold every time.

**Mars in Virgo**—A person with a Virgo Mars tends to be strategic. They are detail-oriented and demand perfection. You need to show up on time, do a great job, and not make excuses. If you mess up, be quick to fix things or risk their wrath. No one works as hard as they do—so know that they make a god out of work. They expect you to, too. I'm a Mars in Virgo, and I work no matter what. What pisses me off: incompetence. I hired someone once who ran everything down to the wire and did such a crap job that I had to accept what they gave me and then hire someone else to fix everything to my exacting standards. We ended on a sour note, and any chance of working together again was done. How to deal with Mars in Virgo people: do a great job. Period. If you get on their bad side, you will be dismissed. Better to move on and leave these prickly types alone. If you have this placement, you can inspire others through your perfectionist ways. But you'll also need to be ready to micro-manage if you don't like the way things are going. While you may not like to do this, you're good at it. Just make sure you don't nag everyone to death or you'll get a reputation for being "difficult."

**Mars in Libra**—Libra Mars leaders are fair, diplomatic, and easy to work with. That is until they need to make a decision. When they are in the hot seat, they will go to everyone to ask which is the best way, which means deals can be left dangling, and meetings could quickly go long. Once they've made up their minds, they stick with those decisions. When they go bad, they become passive-aggressive. Always be upfront with them, especially if they are not with you. Call them on their shit. They don't like conflict, so they will be fast to fix it. If you have this placement, be honest, try not to people-please, and be candid when you're not happy.

**Mars in Scorpio**—If you're working for a Mars in Scorpio boss, they will reward loyalty and expect you to work hard. They can be intense, brooding, and exacting. If they're in a bad mood, the silent treatment is their weapon. Do NOT go to war with them. They will get revenge. If you're dealing with a Scorpio Mars person who doesn't like you, it's better to get out of the way. I never mess with one. If this is your placement, you'll expect fealty. People will get behind you because they know you can move mountains. A few timid types might be on your side because, face it, you can be terrifying.

**Mars in Sagittarius**—Mars in Sagittarius people are fun to work with. They are truth seekers, fiery, passionate, and willing to go where no one else can go. You can expect lots of excitement at the office. They love to travel—and are great at public speaking. They will pat you on the back, encourage you to do your best because, by golly, they believe in you! If you're a Sag Mars, you're at your best when you're cheering on the team and getting folks to stand up and tell the truth. If Mars in Sagittarius goes rogue, you must be ready to blow the whistle, no matter what. Truth is their weapon, and it's yours, too. Use it wisely.

**Mars in Capricorn**—Mars in Capricorn people make great bosses. Mars is exalted here, which means it's at its best. Expect total professionalism, great managerial tactics, and an ability to organize. They inspire confidence. Lucky you if you have a boss with this placement—or if you're a leader with Mars here. If they go wrong, they can be dicta-tors. Once they've gone in that direction, it's game over. You must always be a pro with them—no matter how they act. Keep notes on bad behavior. Don't let them one-up you. If they pull a power play on you, they could win. You must be able to outsmart them.

**Mars in Aquarius**—Aquarius Mars bosses are excellent in group leadership positions. They network well and are "one for all, all for one" types . . . every single one of them a humanitarian with a bleeding heart. But they can be aloof and stubborn. If you don't get along with them, you'll be wise to keep it under your hat, because most people will like them. They can be vindictive when angered—and have a way of getting everyone else on their side. I find it's best to keep them at arm's length if that is the case. You'll be better off as a lone wolf.

**Mars in Pisces**—Pisces Mars bosses are kindly, sensitive souls. This is not the best placement for Mars, because they want to escape when the pressure is on. They can be moved to tears, which can come across as a weakness. If they are your enemy, you can best them by hurting their feelings. Be unreliable. Keep them guessing. BUT if you have this placement, you'll need to toughen up, or you'll be eaten alive.

# Vocations and Life Callings

**O**kay, we've covered some of the basic info you need to use astrology for discovering your life purpose and tricking out your career. This section on astrology has given many tips and suggestions, as well as possible career options. You might look through those lists and think: "none of this applies to me." Here's the deal: these are simply suggestions. Although your chart may point to politics, you might be happier as a stay-at-home parent (which is a calling too). Or you may have circumstances which prevent you from working, such as an injury. Your life purpose may have zero to do with work. Instead, you may be called to serve the world in a different way.

Also, keep in mind that life changes, and we do too. Depending on your circumstances, you may have many paths. I've been a waitress, office worker, bartender, tarot reader, and author. You may wear many hats. Each one is valid, and you should always be proud of what you've done, are doing, and may do next.

I'd also like to add that the list of possible professions is small. There are many types of jobs—too many to include. If you don't see something you like or that fits your description, no worries. Simply look for the different energies and see how that fits with what you love to do or are doing at the moment. It's all good!

The purpose of this first section has been to show you how to use your natal chart and astrology to take a deep dive into learning who you are: your strengths, weaknesses, dreams, and desires. You will want to return to the first half of this book many times; what I've presented here is easy to accomplish, but it's as complicated as juggling balls. You're keeping track of your planets, your elements, your signs, your houses, your transits, your returns . . . it's a lot to digest, and you'll want to check it out frequently, particularly since this is a book about growth and future goals and success—things that are always in flux. The cosmos never stands still!

# WHAT I TELL MY CLIENTS

My process for helping a client understand their purpose and best vocation is simple:

**1** Look at the Big Three. This will give you an idea of what you need to be fulfilled. The Sun is what you're here to do, the Ascendant shows the best way to do the work of your Sun Sign, and the Moon represents what your soul needs.

**2** Find the Midheaven. This is your potential. The Midheaven indicates how you need to share yourself and your gifts with the world.

**3** Elemental Makeup. The Elements shows the "weather patterns" in your chart. Lots of Fire says you're full of passion but you can quickly turn into a raging inferno, while an abundance of Water says you're emo and can get quickly drowned in the "monsoon" of your feelings.

**4** Check to see if there are planets in your 10th house. If there are, they could impact how the world sees you—and possible career options . . . or problems.

**5** Lastly, check the Nodes for karmic lessons and patterns.

This is a simplified process that gives enough information to begin plotting a fulfilling path. Keep in mind, there are many interpretations—which means you're never limited. Once you know what your soul is here to do and what makes it happy, you can choose many options. The possibilities are endless!

Once you've got these basics down, you dive deeper by looking at other points in the chart, such as Chiron or Saturn. You might also want to explore your other vocation houses, the second and sixth.

Let's look at a sample chart. I picked Dolly Parton.

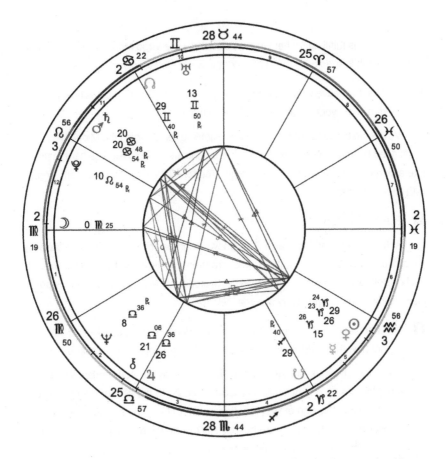

Natal chart for Dolly Parton, January 19, 1946, 8:25 pm EST, Locust Ridge, TN. Virgo Ascendant, Virgo Moon, Capricorn Sun..

## Using my outline:

**1** Look at the Big Three. This will give you an idea of what you need to be fulfilled. The Sun is what you're here to do, the Ascendant shows the best way to do the work of your Sun Sign, and the Moon represents what your soul needs.

Dolly is a Capricorn Sun, Virgo Moon, and Virgo Ascendant. Capricorns are born CEOs. They are brilliant businesspeople and are here to build empires. We can certainly agree that she's done that! The Virgo Ascendant shows she does this through acts of service, which is fulfilling for her when you consider the Virgo Moon. Dolly is "down to earth" even while she's busy trying to make the world a better place.

 **Find the Midheaven.** This is your potential. The Midheaven indicates how you need to share yourself and your gifts with the world.

Moving up to the top of her chart, we've got Taurus sitting on the Midheaven. Taurus is ruled by Venus, which means Dolly is artistic and here to express her creativity. Interestingly, Taurus rules the throat—many Taurus Midheavens are excellent singers with distinct voices!

**3** Element makeup.

WHOA. Look at all that Earth! This shows an imbalance. While Dolly is certainly grounded as can be, she might get stuck from time to time. And stubborn? Nobody pushes Dolly around! I would encourage her to step away from work as much as possible to enjoy fun, play, and plenty of romance!

**4** Check to see if there are planets in your 10th house. If there are, they could impact how the world sees you—and possible career options . . . or problems.

She's got rebellious Uranus and the North Node in her 10th house. We can all agree that there is no one quite like her. Dolly marches to the beat of her own glittery drum. With both in the sign of Gemini, she's meant to be in the spotlight, inspiring us with her words. From time to time, she may say things that makes people uncomfortable. But that's when she's at her karmic best.

**5** Lastly, check the Nodes for karmic lessons and patterns.

With the North Node in the 10th house in wordsmith Gemini, we can agree she's living fully in that Node. The South Node in Sagittarius sits in her 4th house, which makes me wonder if she was yearning to be free from an early age.

Okay, your turn!

Fill in the blank chart on page 137 with your birth info. I've provided a "cheat sheet" of the symbols for the signs and planets.

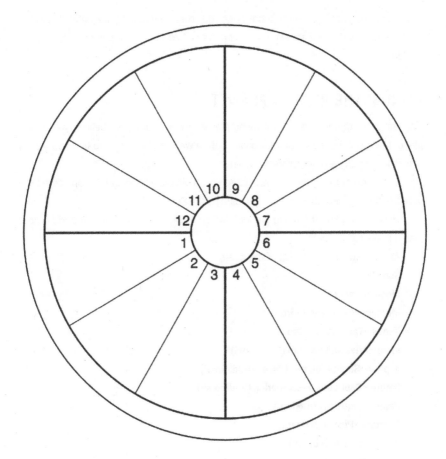

| Signs | | Planets | |
|---|---|---|---|
| ♈ Aries | ♎ Libra | ☉ Sun | ♃ Jupiter |
| ♉ Taurus | ♏ Scorpio | ☽ Moon | ♄ Saturn |
| ♊ Gemini | ♐ Sagittarius | ☿ Mercury | ♅ Uranus |
| ♋ Cancer | ♑ Capricorn | ♀ Venus | ♆ Neptune |
| ♌ Leo | ♒ Aquarius | ♂ Mars | ♇ Pluto |
| ♍ Virgo | ♓ Pisces | | |

Using the same five steps, what does your chart say about you? What does your soul need? How do you best express your purpose? What karmic lessons might you be working on?

# BONUS! THE RULING PLANET

One last point to consider is your ruling planet. Some astrologers believe your ruling planet to be like the "boss" of your chart. Before we talk about how to find your ruling planet, let's briefly go over rulership again.

Each sign of the zodiac is associated with a planet. That planet is considered the "ruler" of the sign. For example, Leo is ruled by the Sun.

How do you find the ruling planet? Simple. Look at your Ascendant and find the planet that rules it. That's it.

As a reminder, here's a list of the rulers::

**Sun—Leo**

**Moon—Cancer**

**Mercury—Gemini and Virgo**

**Venus—Taurus and Libra**

**Mars—Aries and Scorpio (traditional)**

**Jupiter—Sagittarius and Pisces (traditional)**

**Saturn—Capricorn and Aquarius (traditional)**

**Uranus—Aquarius (modern)**

**Neptune—Pisces (modern)**

**Pluto—Scorpio (modern)**

You'll notice I've listed both modern and traditional rulers for some signs. Once Uranus, Neptune, and Pluto were discovered, astrologers pinned those planets on Aquarius, Pisces, and Scorpio. When I work with a client, I use modern rulers—but I'll also acknowledge the traditional (Geminis like to have it both ways!).

Now here's where it gets fun. Once you've ascertained your ruling planet, notice where that planet sits in your chart. This will tell you a lot about your potential or where to focus your energy. For example, my Ascendant is Libra. The ruler of Libra is Venus, which means my ruling planet is Venus.

Venus is sitting pretty in my ninth house of travel, higher education, spirituality, and publishing. I love writing and have written many books (this is number seven). I've also traveled extensively and never tire of learning new things. Considering I spend most of my time teaching about spiritual matters, you can say I'm letting my ruling planet do its thing.

One more example! Dolly Parton's ruling planet is Mercury—and it's hanging out in her natal 5th house of creativity and romance along with Venus and the Sun. I would probably say this is the ideal placement for a glammed-up country music singer!

. . . . . . . . . . . . . . . . . . . . . . . . . . . . . . . . . . . . . . . . . . . . . . . . .

## Astrocise:

 Find your ruling planet. Where is it in your chart? What clues does it hold for you? Journal your thoughts.

Psst . . . you can also play around with the rulers of other houses too. For example, as I mentioned before, the 2nd and 6th houses are career houses too. Find the sign on the cusp of those houses and determine the ruling planet. What clues does the ruling planet give about that house? Where is that planet hanging around? What might that tell you? Example: let's say the planet on your 2nd house is Virgo. It's ruled by Mercury. That shows you make your money through analytical work. If Mercury is in your 9th house, perhaps you write technical manuals or teach calculus at a college. Have fun with this!

### Common Sixth Sense

Although astrology can provide many clues to your best path, sometimes it's wise to speak to a mentor or career counselor. Always seek the advice of a pro when in doubt!

Up next: tarot.

PART TWO:

# Tarot—
# Your New
# Business Cards

# The Tarot Lowdown

've been reading tarot professionally for about thirty years at the time of this writing. Although many people come to the tarot table to inquire about love, many want to know about career, success, business, and life purpose. Frankly, those are the readings I enjoy the most.

There's something about looking at tarot through a business lens—and looking at business through a tarot lens—that satisfies both sides of my brain.

I've used tarot and astrology for my own career. Like I've said before in this book, it's helped me move my work forward in a fulfilling, successful direction. While astrology created the map, the tarot has helped me find the detours.

You might be wondering: how on earth can tarot help you succeed?

Long story short: tarot is a tool for conscious decision-making. When you begin working with the cards, you'll start to connect with your own inner wisdom. The cards serve as a method for accessing that information. This will help you make better decisions and move your future in an empowered direction.

The images in the cards are universal prompts with symbols and archetypes everyone can recognize. Like a picture book or a Rorschach inkblot test, you gaze at the images and start to put together a story. You don't need to be "tarot fluent" to do this. Even children can find the meanings in the cards.

In this section of *Twist Your Fate*, we'll start with interpretations for each tarot card with a business or success slant. No romance here—we're squarely looking at getting your working life in working order. Next, I've got a list of questions to ask for business, purpose, and career, along with what NOT to ask.

Then the good part: a section of spreads for every type of situation you might encounter. Client Avatars. Comparing options. Quick decision-making. The yearly overview. Problem-solving. Your annual card for life purpose and upcoming trends. I've got a spread for everything!

You're getting a peek at my tarot business brain and the methods I use for my own career.

Ready? Let's go to tarot town and make it rain!

. . .

When I'm reading tarot for business or career, my brain is in a different place than a "general reading." My interpretations take on a distinct flair—especially the cards that are traditionally associated with romance.

In this section, I'm sharing some of my favorite biz or career interpretations for each tarot card. Since the focus of this book is on manifesting your best destiny, charting your best path to success, this section will help you begin to look at the cards through the proper lens for business or life purpose-related tarot readings.

Today, tarot is having a hot moment. A recent surge in popularity has brought tarot out of the closet once and for all. Many well-known people rely on this ancient tool to live their best lives—and an intentional one at that. Even designers such as Dior have been influenced by the cards!

Alrighty—let's break down the deck!

There are 78 cards in a traditional tarot deck. Some modern ones have extra cards, which you may enjoy. Frankly, I'm a traditionalist and don't see a reason for additional cards. Everything you need is pictured in the original 78.

You might want to begin with the *Rider Waite Smith* deck because it is a classic—and many contemporary decks are based on the imagery. If you start with the RWS, you'll be able to read any deck. That being said, you might prefer a different one, and I strongly recommend *The Weiser Tarot*—a new version of Smith's classic art, repainted for diversity and inclusion. And, as I mentioned earlier in this book, the *Modern Witch Tarot*, which is a modern-style deck still centered on the RWS symbolism, is also diverse and inclusive. Many readers and clients want to see themselves in the deck, something the RWS doesn't deliver (those images are white, cis-gendered heteronormative). Frankly, my all-time favorite deck is the *Baroque Bohemian Cats' Tarot*, which is a bunch of kitties in Victorian clothing! (The future is super cute!) Always pick something that sings to you!

There are variations on tarot cards. Some decks use the term Coins instead of Pentacles, and you'll also find that Strength and Justice (cards 8 and 11) are reversed in some. While the original tarot had Justice as 8 and Strength as 11, Waite decided to switch them around to keep the astrological correspondences flowing in order. This makes sense to me. Hence, it's why I prefer RWS inspired decks (astrological background . . . duh).

Tarot is divided into two sections: the Major Arcana and the Minor Arcana. The Majors represent the big themes, lessons, and karmic patterns at play. The Minors correlate to day-to-day living. It's the stuff we have control over—and the people involved in the situations. Got that? It may seem like a lot to remember, but the more you practice, the more this info will stick. I promise!

# The Major Arcana

There are 22 cards in the Majors. The Majors have astrological correspondences, which I'll include here, and this will be handy for you to really tie them into what you've just learned about yourself astrologically.

## The Fool—0

### Uranus ♅

The Fool symbolizes the first steps on the path. This is where you take the leap of faith—or need to. Sure, you're stepping off into the unknown and perhaps have a lot to learn, but nothing happens if you don't start somewhere. This card can indicate a new career, line of study, or opportunity. A few folks might think you're being reckless now, but you must follow the call, regardless of what they may say. Trust the Universe. You're about to embark on a magical journey. Sometimes, the Fool indicates a significant change must be made to pursue your dream. You might have to move, travel abroad, or go back to school.

*Reversed*—When the Fool is reversed, it says, "you're not ready . . . yet." You need more time to study the lay of the land before making your move. You don't have enough information or skills at this time. Take a step back, give yourself more time. It's better to play it safe than do something foolhardy.

## The Magician—1

### Mercury ☿

This is a card of skill and talent. When the Magician shows up in your reading, you've got every resource available to manifest the destiny you want. Recognition may be coming your way—or a sweet opportunity. This is your time to shine brightly, show off your prowess, and take control. No matter what challenges await, you've got the mad skills to pull off miracles. This is a fab card to see if you're in the public eye. If you're stepping on a stage, grab the mic and own it. Sometimes the Magician may suggest you need to stand in your power. If someone is throwing shade your way, flex.

**Reversed**—If the Magician shows up reversed in your reading, it's a warning that you are lacking the tools needed to achieve your goal. You may have the dream and the willpower, but you must polish your skills further. Go back to school, get support from a mentor, or take a step back to ponder if this is really your right path. This reversal can also indicate an abuse of power or being a charlatan. If you're heading in that direction, pull back and change course. If you're dealing with someone who fits that bill, be ready to call them out.

## The High Priestess—2

### Moon ☽

You may not have all the facts, but your instincts are singing loudly. Follow your gut in every decision. Soon enough, you'll have the information needed to support your feelings. The High Priestess can also indicate working behind the scenes or gathering more information on a topic. Instead of taking outward action, this card suggests inner action. It can also mean seeking guidance from a spiritual person you trust.

*Reversed*—It might be hard to access your inner guidance at this time. You may have a feeling about something, but it's too cloudy to see if there is any truth in it. Sometimes this can indicate a secret being revealed or a time when you're out of your personal bat cave and working in groups. The reversed High Priestess is more active, which can also mean you're more involved with a specific project . . . or need to be.

THE EMPRESS.

## The Empress—3

### Venus ♀

The Empress is maternal, nurturing, and in control. She follows her passions and leads with her heart. You have these qualities at this time, which can put you in the role of a beloved leader. If you're in the boss role, take good care of your people. If you're working under someone else, do your part to ensure that everyone is getting what they need to succeed. You can attract great prosperity and clout if you plant your seeds right. The ground is fertile, and abundance is on the way. Everything is possible at this time; you're growing and glowing.

*Reversed*—This symbolizes a lack of nurturing or passion. Perhaps you're not getting the support you need to succeed. You may need to reach out to an authority figure, teacher, or mentor for assistance. It's also possible that you may have planted your seeds on infertile soil. That doesn't mean you must give up your dream—you simply need to go back to the basics, clear out the things that aren't working, and begin plotting new goals for your future. Sometimes a setback leads to a better foundation.

## The Emperor—4

### Aries ♈

Lucky you if you're an entrepreneur or boss and pull the Emperor card! This says you've got it going on. The structures are sound, your leadership is strong, and you're confident. Others are looking up to you—and you have the power to achieve every one of your ambitious goals. You are the authority—or ready to be soon enough. This is your time to stand out in your industry and show what you know. This card can also indicate stability after a long, hard slog. In some cases, this can represent an authority figure. If so, they are a no-nonsense type who expects you to follow the rules.

*Reversed*—If you've ever done a sloppy job, you know the Emperor reversed. This is the card of the slacker or the person who isn't serious about reaching their goals. Sure, they have big dreams, but nothing can materialize if they're not doing the work. In some cases, this can warn of a downfall. The best way to avoid that: get on top of your game. Find your discipline and your passion. Take pride in your work. Another interpretation is an abuse of power. Suppose you're in a situation where you're being mistreated. In that case, you may need to take it up with a higher power—or be ready to leave that environment.

## The Hierophant—5

### Taurus ♉

This is the card of the teacher. It can represent a time when you're teaching—or learning new skills. If you are the one in that role, you can shine brightly now. Share your knowledge and support your students. If you're the one getting schooled, you're getting all the correct information to help you succeed. This is a fabulous card if you're thinking about going back to school. Sometimes the Hierophant can indicate a need to seek guidance.

Perhaps you need to work with a career coach or a mentor. The other side of this tarot card is rules and conformity. Which means it's not the time to buck the system. You must go along with the status quo, even if you don't like it.

*Reversed*—Sick of the way things are? Go ahead and shake up the system, you bold rebel! The Hierophant reversed is ready to tear down the old traditions and form new, modern rules. Or perhaps they simply want to break every established structure without any idea of what to do next. This is innovation, rebellion, and a chance to thumb your nose at the sacred cows. Sometimes this card can warn of hypocrisy or hanging on to the old far past its due date. If you're busy telling everyone else what to do, but still clinging to the past, it may be due to a lack of faith or cowardice.

## The Lovers—6

### Gemini Ⅱ

If you're starting a business partnership, this is a welcome card to see. It can symbolize the perfect union, a dynamic duo ready to take on the world. Even if you have different points of view, you can make it work. This can also symbolize the blending of talents. Perhaps you and your team are each doing your part to reach a goal. Yay team! The Lovers can also mean an important decision is ahead, one that may change your destiny. Trust your higher guidance to lead the way. If you're making a choice, you may be choosing between something predictable versus an exciting unknown. Your heart knows which way to go. In some cases, this card can also indicate approaching an authority figure about a problem at work.

*Reversed*—Partnership fails. A business relationship falls apart—or never gets off the ground. Squabbles at work lead to a hostile working environment. The powers that be are turning a blind eye to the problems. It's also possible you may be unable to make a decision at this time. You need to gather more facts before you can say yay or nay.

## The Chariot–7

### Cancer ♋

You are on the right path. You've found the perfect vehicle to realize your goals. Look ahead, take command, and keep going. It won't be long before you score an important victory. Progress is assured, and success is yours for the taking. The key is to remain disciplined. Limit distractions and let your willpower take the wheel. This could also indicate a time when you must balance your head with your heart. Situations require some sort of compromise on your part. In some cases, this card suggests moving on, leaving behind the old to make way for something entirely new.

*Reversed*—You're losing control, lost, or stuck. Nothing is moving. Goals are out of your sight. Perhaps you're not focused, or you've encountered an obstacle. You must gather your forces, reroute your plans, or look for a new direction altogether. Consider this a pit stop on your journey. It's frustrating but maybe precisely what you need to slow your roll . . . and give you more time to assess what you really want.

## Strength–8

### Leo ♌

You're finding your power. After a significant test, you're getting on top of your game. Proving yourself to the doubters. No matter how big the obstacles, you will prevail. Believe in yourself—you can do this! Passion may guide your decisions—if you're feeling some type of way about anything, let that lead the way. At work, you may be forced to take control of a beastly situation. Tap into your courage, persevere, and you'll succeed. This can also symbolize loving your work so much that you're willing to put up with the challenges that come with the territory.

*Reversed*—You're losing control or faith. Everything is falling apart. You may not be suited for the position—or may not have the skills just yet. You need more training or support. This could also indicate a time when you're overwhelmed. You've got too much work or too many decisions. Or perhaps life is handing you a complicated set of circumstances. Ask for help; don't go it alone.

THE HERMIT.

## The Hermit—9

### Virgo ♍

This is an ideal card to see if you're seeking knowledge. For example, if you're in school or working closely with a mentor, the Hermit says you'll be acquiring the wisdom you need to master a skill. Of course, this could also symbolize a time out—or a period of working in solitude. Perhaps your career is in research or some other solo industry. The Hermit can represent a teacher, mentor, counselor, or guru who guides you through problems. Take a step back, and you'll be better able to see what your next move needs to be.

*Reversed*—You're coming back into a social time after a period away. If you were sequestered due to work or illness, now you're ready to mingle. This marks an excellent period for networking or returning to the job. The Hermit reversed could indicate trouble with a teacher, mentor, counselor, or other trusted authority figure in a negative reading.

## The Wheel of Fortune—10

### Jupiter ♃

Fate turns the wheel. What goes down is about to go up. Lady Luck points the way forward. Your destiny is calling—be ready to heed that call and see where it takes you. Of course, you could be creating your own luck. The consequences of past actions are coming due—and the laws of karma are showing you what's up next. Changes may be happening at this time, and you may feel like you have no choice but to roll with them. In some cases, this card can symbolize a stroke of luck or fortunate opportunity.

*Reversed*—Instability and unpredictability. The wheel moves off course, and suddenly, you don't know where you're going. Direction is lost, luck runs out, and you have to fly by the seat of your pants. This is not a good time to start a business or a new job. It's too unstable. Wait until things settle down. You'll be in better shape to see what to do then. This can also represent a blockage that comes up out of the blue. It may cause anxiety, especially if you were set on a particular goal. Get ready to find a new path.

## Justice—11

### Libra ♎

On one level, this card can indicate legal matters. You might be signing a contract or negotiating a deal. Or you're seeking a loan. In general, this is a positive card for that sort of thing. It's also a card of decision-making. You may have to make some sort of choice—and there may be significant consequences. You'll want to gather all facts and look at every side of the coin before making your move. Put things on hold if you need to. Take nothing for granted and be serious. You may also be playing a balancing act between more than one thing (ex: a day job and a side hustle).

*Reversed*—Life isn't always fair. When Justice is upside-down, it indicates injustice. Perhaps you get passed over for a promotion even though you worked your ass off. Or maybe you're accused of something you didn't do. It sucks when that happens, but you'll need to do whatever it takes to clear your name or prove you have what it takes. On a mundane note, this reversal can indicate legal trouble—or it can warn you not to sign a contract without an attorney present.

THE HANGED MAN.

## The Hanged Man—12

### Neptune ♆

Before taking action, pause. Things are not happening . . . for now. Instead, you're in incubation mode, which requires great patience. It may seem as if you are going nowhere. You are actually gearing up for a rebirth. Soon, you'll get the nudge to begin pushing. But until that time comes, hold on. Rest. Look at things in different ways. Take an unconventional approach, and you may discover a whole new perspective. Sometimes the Hanged Man can indicate putting goals on hold until a later time. You may not be ready or in a position to go for the gold just yet.

*Reversed*—No more hanging around in limbo—it's go time! All systems are gearing up for major movement. You are ready to implement your ideas, make bold moves, and get unstuck. This is the moment of rebirth, the time where you can see exactly which end is up. Soon enough, your feet will be firmly on the right path—and you'll be on your way. Sometimes this can warn of procrastination. If you're putting things off today, you might be doing more work tomorrow.

## Death–13

### Scorpio ♏

A major transformation is at hand. An ending is happening, but you need not fear it. You are letting go of all the unnecessary things. Let go of the old and embrace change. Liberate yourself from anything no longer aligned with your journey. Declutter your life to make way for the new one just over the horizon. Something is taking shape. You may not be sure what it is, but soon enough, you'll know. Death can indicate the end of a job or graduation from school. It can also suggest other life changes that propel you in new directions: a move or the end of a significant relationship. You're getting down to the bare bones and what really matters. This is the pivot your soul needs. Straight ahead is the new day, and it's golden.

*Reversed*—Are you resisting change? Are you holding on to something because you're afraid? Choosing what you know versus what you don't? If so, you're experiencing the Death card reversed. You cannot grow if you do not let go. Find the willpower and courage to take those first big steps. Your rebirth is waiting for you. This reversal can also indicate an unwanted change. For example, you get fired, or your business can't seem to get off the ground. In cases like that, great patience is needed until things settle down.

## Temperance–14

### Sagittarius ♐

You are in the midst of extraordinary alchemy. Temperance marks a time when you can blend many things together to create something entirely original. You may be consolidating some aspect of your business or bringing two things together in a whole new way. Bit by bit, you're finding perfect harmony. Experiment with new things, test the waters, learn new skills—try it all out. Throw the spaghetti at the wall and see what sticks.

Soon, you'll be on the right path—and a unique one at that. This is also a reminder to slow down and find your balance. Create divine order in your life or schedule. If you're making a significant decision, weigh all options with care. Do not rush until you turn over every stone.

*Reversed*—Imbalance. Something isn't coming together. You may be trying to pound a square peg into a round hole. Or perhaps you're being impatient, which could create a tendency to push too hard. Give it time. Go with the flow. Allow space for things to come together in their own way. It's also okay to give up if it doesn't seem to be assimilating the way you want.

## The Devil—15

### Capricorn—♑

If you've ever gotten yourself stuck in a situation that felt impossible, that's the Devil in action. Picture being at a soul-sucking job or under the iron fist of a power-hungry boss. The energy is dark, negative, and it feels like there is no way out. There is, but it's hard to see or change right now. This is oppression, bondage, or greed. It's the abuse of power by others—or yourself. In some cases, the Devil represents temptation—or choosing between the Devil you know and the one you don't. Choose wisely—and understand what you're getting yourself into. I've sometimes seen this card represent an offer with "strings attached."

*Reversed*—You're free! You leave that job, move on, and release yourself from whatever is holding you back. That could be another person, financial circumstances, or your own stinking thinking. Fate is about to shift. You see the light at the end of a dark tunnel and find the truth. This could also represent a time when you are in recovery. Perhaps you've left an abusive situation and are rebuilding your life. In that case, know the most challenging part is behind you, and better days await.

**THE TOWER.**

## The Tower—16

### Mars ♂

The Tower symbolizes a break-up, a shake-up, and a wake-up. Everything is crashing down around you, which may feel scary. You may experience a blow to the ego or some sort of downfall. It's an intense, chaotic, and unpredictable time. You must take the leap of faith—or be prepared to leave a situation. In some way, this signals your liberation. You're getting free—and starting to see why change is necessary. The lightning bolt signals enlightenment—the kind that comes after destruction. Later on, you may realize the foundation was faulty all along. Soon, you'll be rebuilding something better. This card can indicate a hostile takeover or downsizing. You're fired, or you quit. There's a mutiny or walk-out: chaos, a shocking turnaround, a revolution, or rebellion. While the Tower isn't a happy card, it certainly lays the groundwork for a better way.

*Reversed*—The drama happened, everything got blown up to smithereens, and now you can begin anew. The danger is behind you. You've escaped the oppressor and are free to go. Rebuild your life, start fresh, and create a better foundation from what is left. If nothing remains, you can start looking for different resources. If you're still clinging to the old, another aftershock will help you to let go once and for all.

**THE STAR.**

## The Star—17

### Aquarius ♒

A healing is taking place. Hope returns, and you can see the way forward. This is the calm after the storm. This could symbolize a wish fulfilled in a career or a chance to be in the spotlight. You're getting much-deserved recognition for your efforts. For entrepreneurs, this is a nudge to get into the public eye more. Be visible, and your Star can rise! The Star can also symbolize a career in healing or humanitarian concerns. Suppose you've been involved in metaphysical or consciousness-raising. In that case, this card says your work will be of great benefit to the collective.

*Reversed*—Are you losing hope? Does it seem like nothing you do produces results? Or are you putting yourself out there . . . to crickets? That's the Star reversed. This can indicate a period where you're unable to receive recognition or reach your goals. You might feel cynical. "What's the use of trying?" While it's easy to feel that way when the rewards are not forthcoming, you must remain focused on the work without worry of the glory for now. Do not lose faith—or your dream. If you've been hiding out, this reversal says, "Get out into the public eye." Don't dim your light!

THE MOON.

## The Moon—18

### Pisces ♓

The Moon is a tricky card. It shows a path, but that path is shrouded in darkness, guarded by wolves. This signals a time when nothing is straightforward or easy. While there are options and the right track, it's hard to see which way to go. You'll need to trust your instincts. They will lead the way. Intuition is queen and serves you well now. Your subconscious may send you strong messages—follow them and see what happens. You might be surprised to find where you end up. This card can also warn of enemies, frenemies, and backstabbers. You may be in the company of wolves—watch your back.

*Reversed*—Instead of instinct, logic rules. You can see the most effective path. Nothing is hidden. The most obvious way is straight ahead. The choices are clear as day. Go forth and trust that the obstacles are minimal or removed. Something is about to come out in the open—and it may be shocking. Ultimately, it will illuminate a situation to your benefit.

## The Sun—19

### Sun ☉

Success is yours for the taking! You can follow your bliss with all your heart. You see what you want and know how to get it. The Sun signals rebirth, an awakening, or a time when everything is possible. Luck is on your side—and opportunity is knocking. Everything you've been working toward comes together beautifully. This is also the joy you feel when everything is going well. You're making your way in the world, doing the work you love, and prospering. Abundance is yours for the taking, and you can create whatever you want. You're free to go and grow.

*Reversed*—It's still positivity, but the joy is muted. Perhaps you still have things to finish, or you reached your goal, and it's not as exciting as you thought it would be. You may be ready to move on to something bigger. This can also symbolize naivety. Maybe you thought you were prepared . . . but you weren't. Or you say yes to a deal only to discover it's not all that. The Sun reversed can also indicate dimming your light—or the opposite of that, which is being a braggart.

## Judgement—20

### Pluto ♇

A rebirth or awakening. You receive the call and are ready to answer it. This could be your life's calling or a wake-up call. Either way, you can rise and shine! You're shedding the old, coming to terms with the past, and starting a new chapter. You may have a reckoning if you've been on the wrong path. It's never too late to turn the beat around and start fresh. This is your memo to unzip the old suit and be reborn into a new state of higher consciousness. Sometimes this is a card of judgement—as in getting judged. Maybe you're getting a review at work or being slammed in the media. You might be in front of a group of peers and experiencing a "call out." Stand up, take it, and learn from it. For entrepreneurs, this card says: toot your horn and make some noise.

*Reversed*—You're not ready for the transformation that this card offers. You're still working on old stuff and need to process that. This could be feelings of unworthiness, fear of success, relying on the old—even when it's not to your benefit. Rebirth can be painful and scary—but so is refusing the call. Push past your resistance, and you'll rise up to the next level. Watch that you don't make a poor judgment at this time. Wait until you have more information before making a move. In some cases, this could indicate getting judged harshly and unfairly—or being the one who is doing that to someone else.

## The World—21

### Saturn ♄

You've learned your lesson, passed the test, and graduated! Yay! This signals your success. Life is coming together—you've arrived! The chapter closes perfectly, and you're ready for your next adventure. Be proud of what you've accomplished. The World could also indicate worldly success or traveling the world. Maybe you're going on a book tour or studying abroad. Or you're taking your business in a global direction. Whatever the case may be, horizons are about to broaden in amazing ways. Go big!

*Reversed*—You're almost there . . . but not quite. There is still work to be done before you can collect your reward. You may not receive the compensation you want, or perhaps it's delayed. It's also possible that you don't want to be in the public eye. Maybe you're retiring or prefer your privacy. Rather than touting your success, you're celebrating quietly. This can also indicate issues around travel—or an inability to see the bigger picture. For some, the World reversed can also symbolize a lack of boundaries.

# The Minor Arcana

The Minor Arcana symbolizes the day-to-day things we have some control over. These are the people and events we deal with regularly. Unlike the Major Arcana, which can feel fated and laden with "big" lessons, the Minors bring awareness to all the things that make up our daily life. This section will cover them from a perspective on work, vocation, and purpose. There are 56 cards in the Minors. Within this section of the deck, you'll find four suits: Wands, Cups, Swords, and Pentacles—these relate to the four elements Fire, Water, Air, and Earth (again, tying everything back to astrology). There are also four characters in each suit: Pages, Knights, Queens, and Kings. They are referred to as the Court Cards and represent the people in the situation—or different facets of ourselves.

**Here is a brief description of each suit and court card character::**

**Wands:** Fire, Passion, Creativity, Work, Entrepreneurship

**Cups:** Water, Emotions, Relationships

**Swords:** Air, Thoughts, Ideas, Conflicts

**Pentacles:** Earth, Money, Values

**Pages:** New Beginnings, Students

**Knights:** Action, Young People, Energy

**Queens:** Nurturing, Leadership, Mature Folks

**Kings:** Mastery, Leadership, Grown Folks

# WANDS △

Wands are the fire element. They symbolize passion, creativity, entrepreneurship, and work. This is what drives us, our motivation.

**Ace of Wands**—The Ace of Wands can indicate a new job, creative venture—or the launch of a new business. When this card shows up, it says: let's go! You can take action on your big ideas or say yes to that opportunity. This is your sign that everything is ready for you. No holding back—let your passion lead the way!

*Reversed*—Perhaps the opportunity didn't show up. Or you were passed over for someone else. It's also possible you don't have every duck in a row to launch your next big thing. Hold your fire, give yourself time, go back to the drawing board if need be. Trying to push something out now may be premature. Let it incubate longer.

**Two of Wands**—All plans are coming together brilliantly. You've scored a win or two—and are in the position to go as far as you want. Take a look at where you stand—and visualize what is possible. Create an organized plan for your next big step—and then go for it! This card is excellent for business travel. It can also indicate graduation. All in all, you're going places! This card can suggest "going global" as in a big PR campaign or outreach to other countries for business. For some, it can also mean studying abroad or working remotely.

*Reversed*—Nothing seems to be coming together at the moment. Do you have a plan B in place? Did you remember to cross every T and dot every I? Or do you need to tear it down to the root and start over? The Two of Wands reversed shows a lack of success or planning. Don't despair—go back, look for what went wrong, and start again.

**Three of Wands**—This card always indicates success—and more to come. There are three ships on the horizon, a sign of expansion and opportunity. You are in the winning position and can expand your work into new territory. If you are seeking opportunities abroad, this is a welcome card to see. If you're looking for a new career, the Three of Wands means many options are coming your way. For entrepreneurs, this is your time to shine as a leader. Be visible, make your voice heard, and stand for something. Create your big vision for the future you want—and trust everything is coming together in divine order.

*Reversed*—Like the Two of Wands reversed, this card suggests plans have gone awry. You can't get things off the ground. Or maybe you're blocked—you can't seem to pull your ideas together cohesively. Do not let these setbacks deter you. Take a step back and look at where you need to tweak things. Seek support if needed. If your plan is too grand, trim it down. If you're traveling, this could warn of delays. If you're waiting for an offer, it's on the way but might not look the way you envisioned.

**Four of Wands**—Celebration time! You've graduated and are ready to make your way in the world. Or maybe you've landed that killer job. Whatever the case may be, put your hands up in the air and strike a pose! The Four of Wands is always a good card to see in a reading. This is the touchdown, the moment where everything comes together in the best way. For some, this is the successful launch of a business. You're opening your doors to the public and welcoming people in.

*Reversed*—It's still a good omen, but the joy is muted. Instead of a blow-out celebration, this could be a small gathering of people. Your team might be working on a project behind the scenes. Conflicts could be coming to an end. You're moving on to a new job or taking a leave of absence. In some cases, this card could be "welcome back," like when you return to a job you loved. For business, this symbolizes an opportunity to reach out to old clients or partners.

**Five of Wands**—The Five of Wands signals a competition is ON. You may be in the running with other qualified candidates for a position. Throw your hat in the ring and bring your A-game. Do not play shy—show what sets you apart from the rest. In business, this card could indicate a need to market hard. The competition is stiff, which means you do not get to be idle with your messaging. Conflict in the workplace is another possible interpretation. The office politics could get ugly if everyone is trying to take the lead— the proverbial "too many cooks in the kitchen" scenario.

 *Reversed*—Giving up. The conflict comes to an end, or you decide to opt out. Dirty tricks take office politics in a nastier direction. Someone throws the game and puts the entire dynamic into a tailspin. In business, this could either indicate the competition fails—or you're slacking on your hustle, giving them the edge. Sometimes this reversal can mean an internal conflict. For example, you may want one thing but go after another due to peer pressure.

**Six of Wands**—Success at last! This is the card of victory, teamwork, and leadership. You made it to the finish line, and the prizes are yours. Be sure to acknowledge the people who have helped you achieve your goals—you did not do this alone. This could also be a sign that you finally have the right team in place. If you're in a position of leadership, you can inspire people to get behind your mission. Sometimes this card can indicate a message is on the way—and it's a good one.

 *Reversed*—You may experience a letdown with a member of your team. Perhaps they don't follow through on their duties—or they're a saboteur. I've seen this reversal come up when espionage by a rival infiltrated the company. This is also a card that says "losing." The victory isn't happening. You might not be prepared, or you were bested. Back to the drawing board. Sometimes this reversal can symbolize the problematic leader. Sure, you were happy to get behind them until they turned out to be full of it.

**Seven of Wands**—There are many challenges in front of you, but bit by bit, you'll overcome the odds. Keep holding on to your dream—and pushing forward. You may be in a situation where you have to defend yourself—or your work. For example, the boss may give you a bad review, or you're accused of something you didn't do. Be ready to hold your ground. In some cases, this card can indicate a hard-won success.

*Reversed*—The challenges ease up, and finally, you have room to breathe. Things were not as complicated as you thought they were—or you got help. Of course, this could also indicate giving up. You didn't have the stomach for the fight, or there was too much working against you. The competition takes over. You lose your position—or walk away. This can also indicate a need to set strict boundaries. If you lack them, you'll come to regret it soon.

**Eight of Wands**—Good news is on the way! Everything is progressing swiftly. Projects are coming to a hasty solution, and hard work is pushing you toward a swift victory. If you've been stalled, this card shows sudden movement. It's an excellent card to see if you're nearing a goal, traveling, or moving for a job. It's also "moving on up," like into a higher position. Business is brisk, and many opportunities are coming soon. Expansion, business abroad, internet or global interactions—these are all possible.

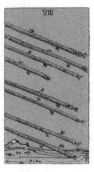

*Reversed*—Nothing is happening. Everything is on hold. Or you're going in the wrong direction. You may need to assess where you're heading. Stalled out. Bad news. You've jumped the gun. In business, this card indicates a slowdown or period where not much seems to be progressing. It's not a good time to launch or travel for biz. Moving forward without a plan isn't wise.

**Nine of Wands**—You're almost to the end of a goal, but you still have a ways to go. Do not give up. Keep going! You need to persevere as much as you can. Seek support if you're overwhelmed. Sometimes this card warns of a setback or a distraction. Get back on track, even if that means having to redo a few things. In business, this warns of competitors or boundary issues with clients. You'll need to assert yourself. This is not the time to shrink. Go forward, even if you don't feel ready.

*Reversed*—You drop your guard and wish you hadn't. A client pushes past your boundaries, or a superior tries to pile on more work than you can handle. Assert yourself. Learn to say no. If you don't stick up for yourself, you can't expect others to do it for you. In some cases, this reversal says to let your guard down. Allow others to help you. You don't have to go it alone. The reversed Nine of Wands could also mean paranoia—or making assumptions . . . that turn out to be true.

**Ten of Wands**—The pressure is intense, but you're nearing the finish line. Soon, the hardest part is over, and you'll be celebrating a remarkable win. Give yourself credit for how far you've come—and keep going. This card can also indicate a time when you've taken on too many responsibilities. You're feeling oppressed or trapped. There is no getting away from it. Suck it up, keep going, or ask for help. The one-person show. Pressure from outside sources. Trying to hide your light.

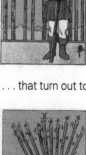

*Reversed*—The reversal shows the pressure is released. Relief at last! The proper support is present, which means you don't have to go it alone. You've got a great team. You can delegate the load rather than trying to carry it alone. The goal is complete; let it go, move on. In some cases, this could indicate giving up the power position to someone else because you don't want the responsibility any longer.

**Page of Wands**—A new idea, venture, or creative outlet. You're heading off in a new direction, ready to explore things you've never done before. Growth is possible. An adventure. This could also symbolize good news, as in the job you've been waiting for. For students, this card indicates being engrossed in a topic you're passionate about.

PAGE ⚜ WANDS.

*Reversed*—You've lost your fire. You're bored and no longer interested in a particular goal or line of study. Or you're being forced to learn something for the job and don't want to. Either way, your attention is elsewhere. This could also indicate being a dabbler. Just because you love your hobby doesn't mean you should monetize it. Keep it a hobby.

**Knight of Wands**—This is a time for taking risks. Be ready to go for the gold, even if you're not sure how to get there. Make a bold move, take action, and see where it gets you. You might be pleasantly surprised. The Knight of Wands brings enthusiasm to every project or prospect. If this is you, you're keeping everyone on their toes with your energy. If this is a teammate or employee, they'll hustle hard for you.

*Reversed*—The Knight of Wands reversed is reckless, thoughtless, and a bit careless. They come off the wrong way,

turn people off, and are generally pushy. If you're acting like that, sales may fall flat—or you may not get the job. If you're dealing with someone like this, you'll need to assert boundaries or report them to HR. Sometimes this reversal indicates temper tantrums and burning bridges. YIKES.

**Queen of Wands**—You're regal, powerful, and confident. You can inspire others through your generous leadership. Let your passions lead the way—and be ready to encourage other people. If you're an entrepreneur, this is a fabulous card. It represents an exciting business, one people are talking about. You have creative ideas, and every single one brings growth. You can see the future—and know what to do to inspire a big harvest. This card can also indicate a creative thinker who leads with passion.

*Reversed*—The negative sides of this card are weakness, timidity, or bitchiness. You may be playing the 'devil wears Prada' at work and alienating your team or peers. Or you're unable to set boundaries, which allows people to walk all over you. In some cases, this could indicate you've lost interest or feel defeated. If you can't feel the fire any longer, why bother? It's also possible you're working with a spiteful, envious person.

**King of Wands**—The ultimate leader. You're bold, benevolent, and able to inspire action. When you say go, people listen. Your intuition guides you into making snap decisions. This may be when you must take command of a situation and be ready to push others. You can express your ideas with confidence. The mastery of a problem or a creative venture coming to full bloom.

KING ♂ WANDS.

*Reversed*—Instead of generous, you're all about you. You want to hog the spotlight and are unwilling to give credit where credit is due. If this is you, you'll undoubtedly lose favor soon. If you're working for someone like that, it may be impossible to deal with them for long. This is the emperor without clothing, the all talk no action, the blowhard or dictator. They think they've got it going on . . . but they don't. A rude awakening is on the way. This may also be a time when you're not ready to boss up. If you're not up for the job, don't say yes.

# CUPS ▽

Cups are the water element. They represent our feelings, relationships, and deeper longings. For work or purpose, they reveal what the heart wants.

**Ace of Cups**—This is the beginning of something you love. At work, that could be the ideal job or position. It could also symbolize the opportunity or offer you've been hoping for. If you're thinking of starting a business, the Ace of Cups says: go for it! Create something people will love. This is a big "yes" to any question. It's "follow your heart and see what flows." The opportunities are limitless at this time.

*Reversed*—The offer doesn't materialize or is rescinded. You've overplayed your hand and squandered an opportunity. Instead of following your heart, you choose the safe route. Settling. If you're not sure what you really want to do, that's the Ace of Cups reversed too. Your heart isn't in it.

**Two of Cups**—An important meeting or negotiation. This could be a job offer or a new partnership. A toast to a new partnership. Relationships are helpful to your goals at this time. Expand your network, rub elbows with hotshots and influencers—and you will benefit. Your social contacts could lead to an exciting opportunity. In some cases, this could indicate cooperation or a merger.

*Reversed*—A stalemate. You can't seem to meet eye-to-eye. One person refuses to budge, creating a standoff. This could be a conflict of interest or disagreement that sours a partnership. You're at a disadvantage. In some cases, this might mean inappropriate conduct at work or sexual harassment. You may have trouble attracting what you want—or negotiating a deal.

**Three of Cups**—This card can indicate a support system or circle of helpful friends. You've got the right people cheering you on. With their help, you can achieve all of your biggest goals. The Three of Cups can also suggest having fun at work. Maybe there is an office party or some reason to celebrate (ex: a major campaign goes well). Or perhaps it's simply drinks after work with your coworkers. Meetings with your team for a brainstorming session. Graduation from school or retirement.

*Reversed*—When the Three of Cups is upside-down, it can indicate a lack of support. It can also mean treachery amongst peers. There may be a troublemaker in your orbit. Watch out who you share info with—they may use what you say for gain. Office gossip. A premature celebration. There are times when you want to work alone, and this reversal may indicate you're doing your own thing.

**Four of Cups**—A lack of motivation. Nothing is inspiring you at this time. You're bored with the work or losing interest fast. The options available don't meet your standards. This might be a time of inaction, perhaps better suited to meditating or brainstorming. Taking a time-out might generate new ideas. Until then, hold off and wait. Something else is on the way soon.

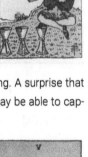

*Reversed*—A new opportunity shows up. This could be the one you've been waiting for. The options are better at this time, and you're excited to begin exploring them. Returning to work after a leave of absence. Having a hard time committing to one thing. A surprise that captures your attention. If you're running your own business, you may be able to capture the attention of a bored public.

**Five of Cups**—A partial loss. Something you were working on doesn't come together. You're disappointed, but there's enough left to move on. Don't let this get you down for too long. You can rebuild something from what remains. This can also indicate regrets. Perhaps you turned down an offer and now wish you hadn't. Or maybe you let fear get in the way—and you realize too late that it was a golden opportunity after all.

*Reversed*—The mood shifts, hope returns, and you're moving on to something new. Rebuilding a bridge you thought was burnt. New beginnings. You're creating something new out of old materials. Recycling. Getting fresh eyes on your work. In some cases, this might be a time for olive branches. If you've goofed up, make amends.

**Six of Cups**—The Six of Cups can indicate a blast from the past. An old client or boss comes back into the picture with an offer. An opportunity is presented—and it's sweet. You may be receiving a job offer or some sort of gift. A friend may return home—or you may decide to revisit your roots. For some, this card could mean getting involved in the family business. This is a great time to give

back to your community or to reward your team. The seeds you planted long ago are beginning to blossom.

*Reversed*—Mistakes from the past come back to haunt you. Regrets. You can't let go of the old and refuse to embrace the new way of doing things. If you're hung up on "the good old days" or "glory days," you may be unable to move to the future. Sometimes this reversal indicates starting fresh, rejecting the old ways, and blazing a few trails. Taking chances and breaking free from security.

**Seven of Cups**—So many opportunities. Which one to take? It's hard to say because there are many good ones in front of you at this time. Explore each one in depth before committing. This is also the card of creative thinking. You may be solving problems through an imaginative approach. Or maybe you're conjuring up new ideas for products. Your imagination is unlimited! Of course, all that glitters isn't gold. Watch out for get-rich-quick schemes or anything that seems too good to be true.

*Reversed*—The choice is clear. You know exactly what's up and what you want. Your heart is showing you which decision is best. Follow that, and you'll be happy. Instead of imagination, this reversal indicates practical thinking. Going with what's tried and true. It can also symbolize a creative block or lack of vision. The inability to see the bigger picture.

**Eight of Cups**—Moving on. You may be exiting a job, moving out, or leaving your current location, searching for something better. Even if you've enjoyed your work, you're on your way to something else. This could indicate a job search or soul-searching. If you're unfulfilled, a spiritual quest could give you the answers to build a better life. Sometimes this card could mean getting fired or forced out. On a happy note, the Eight of Cups might suggest a vacation.

*Reversed*—You're going back to the familiar. You might be returning to a job or going back to school. There is a sense of getting back on track after a time away. It might even mean moving back to your old hood to rebuild your life. If you're trying to travel, this could indicate a delay. This reversal could also say you are not sure where you're going. So, you go in circles and hope something sticks.

**Nine of Cups**—You're getting the thing you want the most! This is the wish card, a good omen overall. The Universe is helping you manifest one of your biggest goals. The Nine of Cups is the satisfaction that comes after a job well done. You're feeling proud of your accomplishments—as you should. Rewards. Getting the ultimate prize.

*Reversed*—You may not get what you want. Instead, you get what you need. Sure, it sucks when something you desire doesn't materialize. But you're not in a terrible position—you're just not in the one you want. This could also indicate a time of overdoing it to the point where it affects your work. If you're spending too much time in party mode, it may cause problems for your career.

**Ten of Cups**—You made it! This is the happy ending—a sign that everything is coming together in divine order. You're winning—and everyone is here for it! Expect a celebration . . . or two. You've realized one of your biggest goals. The support you need is there. For some, this card suggests settling down and creating security. For entrepreneurs, the Ten of Cups puts the focus on building community or networking. Be inclusive—welcome folks into your biz.

*Reversed*—You're shutting people out. People do not feel welcome in your world. A toxic work environment. Failure due to arguments and lack of cooperation. The security is threatened. Outside influences impact the working environment. A team is broken up. The dream dies or is taken away.

**Page of Cups**—That feeling when you're doing something you love? It's the Page of Cups! If you're engaged in a creative project, starting a dream job, or following your big vision, this is an excellent card to see. Intuition is strong—and it may compel you to take a few risks. Let your heart lead the way. This card can also indicate art school or a creative person who plays an important role in events.

PAGE *f* CUPS.

*Reversed*—Instead of going after your dream, you're allowing fear to hold you back. You're sitting at the starting line, waiting for validation or reassurance. You must get out of your own way. Sometimes this card can indicate a lack of interest in a particular line of study—or immaturity. There's nothing wrong with admitting you're not ready.

**Knight of Cups**—Knights take action, and the Knight of Cups moves toward their bigger vision. Their heart is wide open, allowing for self-expression. You have this energy at your disposal. Go for your dreams, follow your heart, and make bold moves. This card can also symbolize an offer—or a helpful person who brings you good news.

KNIGHT *f* CUPS.

*Reversed*—This warns of deception and get-rich-quick schemes. If someone is approaching you with a multi-level marketing scheme, for example, RUN. Do not be naive. Do your homework. A lack of opportunity—or a lack of follow-through. Receiving an offer you don't love. A duplicitous person enters the arena. Getting lost in sorrows or escapism. Running away from the truth. Any and all of these things are possible now.

**Queen of Cups**—Nurture your creativity, and it will yield rich rewards. Intuition is queen at this time, follow it, and it will steer you right. Emotions also run strong—this could lead to compassion or drama. It's up to you how that manifests. If you're in business, this is a smart time to cast your net wide—you'll catch more fish that way. If you're trying to up-level your sales, connect with people's hearts. This could also represent a nurturing person who helps guide your career.

QUEEN *f* CUPS.

*Reversed*—The drama is real. Emotions run amok, clouding your vision. This may get in the way of making wise decisions. You'll need to ground and center yourself. If you're feeling too emotional, hold off on making a move. Other people around you may be moody. If that is the case, work on your boundaries. This reversal could symbolize a manipulative person who uses guilt trips and gaslighting to get what they want. It's also the smothering type who "love bombs" you.

**King of Cups**—Leading with love. The benevolent boss or mentor. You may be in a role where you can influence people by touching their hearts—or listening to their concerns. Kindness will work in your favor if you're in that position. This could also be the care-taker, counselor, or human resources person who proves to be helpful when you need it most.

KING ⚜ CUPS.

*Reversed*—In some cases, this could warn of heartless vibes—as in the cruel boss who lacks empathy. It can also be a person who puts on a false front of caring when they are looking out for number one in reality. If you're working with someone like that, you'll want to be on guard for manipulation. It's also possible you're having a hard time getting in touch with your feelings. There is a coldness to this reversal, but in some cases, it could speak of an overly emotional sort who can't stand up for what's right. It can also represent deception as in the con artist.

# SWORDS

The Swords are the air element. They represent thoughts and conflict. In work or purpose, they can reveal problems, breakthroughs, and breakdowns.

**Ace of Swords**—A new, mentally stimulating opportunity. A job or promotion that allows you to up your game. Your mental focus is sharp, giving you the ability to cut through the fog and gain traction on projects. This can also be a new idea or a new perspective. You can see where to go and what moves will get you to the finish line. Strategic thinking. A mental breakthrough. Signing documents. In some cases, this Ace could say "cut ties." Start fresh—and on your own.

*Reversed*—Someone stabs you in the back. You're the victim of malicious gossip and lies. Or this reversal could mean an inability to see what's ahead. Mental blocks or lethargy. Lack of solutions to problems. Communication failure. A contract that doesn't come through—or is rescinded. Someone ignites a war—and it might not be a battle worth fighting.

**Two of Swords**—If you're choosing between more than one option, it might be best to slow your roll. Sit on it. Put all judgment on hold until you've had more time to weigh the pros and cons. Taking a time out. A leave of absence. In some cases, this card could warn of someone trying to drag you into the middle of a situation. Best to play neutral or avoid getting involved altogether. Finding balance. An inability to form an opinion. You're not open to new ideas or input.

*Reversed*—The time to hesitate is over. You must take action. Be decisive. No more waffling—get moving! Or maybe you're losing your sense of balance. In some cases, this reversal means ripping off the blindfold and facing the truth. Feeling uncertain about which side to take. Trying to play both sides of the coin—and it ends up hurting you. You might find out that someone isn't who they said they were.

**Three of Swords**—A situation doesn't work out the way you want. 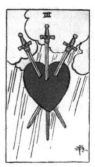 Disappointment. The job doesn't come through, or someone sabotages you. This could be the stab in the back—or the public faux pas—that creates an ending. It's also possible that you fail at something, which strikes a blow in your confidence. The Three of Swords could also suggest a toxic work environment with plenty of drama.

*Reversed*—The healing begins. After a challenging period, you're moving forward again. The chaos is over; you see the light and are well-supported on the next leg of your journey. An apology. Cease and desist. The end or beginning of a battle (depending on the context of the reading). You might need to make a difficult, but necessary, decision.

**Four of Swords**—This card is traditionally associated with rest  and recovery. But it can also indicate planning or strategizing—as well as contemplation. You may be taking time out to ponder your next big move. Dreaming instead of doing. For some, this card could indicate burying the hatchet. It's also a card of retirement or leave of absence. In some cases, it might mean a test of faith.

*Reversed*—Back in action after time away. You've returned from vacation or a leave of absence. You're ready to get back in the game. However, this could also be Rip Van Winkle—you come back and see everything is different. It can also mean implementing ideas and strategies. Feeling healed from a challenging situation.

**Five of Swords**—When this card arrives, it indicates a hollow  victory. Winning through deceptive means. Instead of one for all, someone is grabbing all the goodies for themselves. A hostile takeover. Sowing the seeds of division. Corporate espionage. Deception or theft. It's rarely a good omen—be ready for drama if it shows up.

*Reversed*—All lies are out in the open. The situation is revealed. Getting caught in the act. If you've had a beef with someone, this reversal could mark the end of a feud. Apologies and restoring what was taken. Admitting wrongdoing. A company gets bought out—and a new team is taking their place.

**Six of Swords**—Moving on after a difficult situation. You're done, it's over, and you're off in search of something better. You might feel a twinge of regret, but soon enough, you'll be glad you made this decision. Everything is about to get a lot more peaceful. There is help and support. Getting fired or laid off from your job. Retirement. Travel overseas. Getting away from it all.

*Reversed*—You're unable to move at this time. You must sit tight until you get the green light. Situations may require you to wait. Or you could be holding back because you're afraid to make a change. Being forced to move for your job. Leaving the nest and feeling scared. Returning from vacation or a leave of absence. Going back to your old job. The plans didn't work out the way you wanted.

**Seven of Swords**—This card can play out as a theft—or a time when you need to fly under the radar. If it's the former, that theft could be embezzlement, a Ponzi scheme, or someone using dubious methods to score a victory. If it's the latter, it could mean you need to be stealthy until the coast is clear. For example, if you're thinking about leaving your job, you might have to wait until you get another one—and you may need to keep it secret from your current boss.

*Reversed*—Getting caught in the act. The cat is out of the bag, the thief is detected, and the goods are returned. A hostile takeover is averted. The plan fails. Someone blabs. A whistleblower. This could also indicate a time when you need to come clean about a situation or your motives. Lay it on the line.

**Eight of Swords**—The Eight of Swords is usually associated with feeling trapped. You might be stuck in a job or situation with no way out. There may be a contract that needs to be fulfilled or a lack of apparent opportunities. You are stuck because of an agreement—or you simply cannot see a way forward at this time. Feeling isolated. A lack of support. You're on your own.

*Reversed*—You're free to go! The binds are off, the blindfold removed, and liberation time has arrived. There are no limits to how far you can go now. You've passed the test and are ready to expand your horizons. Obstacles are gone. Everything is wide open. Where will you go next?

**Nine of Swords**—Mental stress and anguish. Doubt. A situation is getting under your skin and causing sleepless nights. You cannot see how to get out. So, you suffer in silence or assume things are never going to change. This card can also represent an ending. There is pain involved, but it won't last forever. Accept things are coming to a close and seek support.

*Reversed*—The depression ends, and you're clear. No more sleepless nights! You can rest easy. If you've been struggling with depression or anxiety, this could indicate relief. A problem is solved. You get the help you need and can start over.

**Ten of Swords**—An ending and a new beginning. Something comes to a grand finale. This may be bittersweet. On the one hand, there is relief when some conclusions arrive. Even if the situation was beneficial, the ending might be emotional. On the other hand, there might be fear of a new beginning. Ultimately this card spells the end of a situation that has passed the expiration date a long time ago. A new day is dawning. Resigning from a job. Getting stabbed in the back.

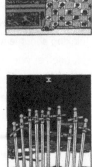

*Reversed*—An inability to let go and move on. Something is pinning you down. Or the swords fall out—if you're feeling stuck, it may be in your head.

The relief is here—accept the ending. The sabotage is revealed, and you know who to trust . . . or not. Healing. The worst is behind you—and there is so much potential in front of you.

**Page of Swords**—A new way of looking at things. A mentally stimulating subject that captures your attention. Communication is bold and clear as a bell. The air is cleared, and you can see which way to pivot. Important professional news. A young person or student with a strong point of view. New ideas. Innovation.

*Reversed*—You don't have the information needed to make a move just yet. You must gather more facts. You're in a vulnerable position—watch your back. Lacking skills. A flawed plan creates an inability to get things off the ground. Lots of ideas but zero practicality. Distractions galore. Sometimes this card symbolizes an immature troublemaker.

**Knight of Swords**—You're hitting the ground running. This is a time of movement and challenge. Everything is coming at you at once. Be ready for a few battles. You can make your point now. Lead with your truth—it is an effective weapon. A person enters the scene quickly and turns over every apple cart. Fighting the good fight. Take a stand against injustice. This card could signal a time when you need to speak out.

*Reversed*—A lack of truth. Fighting a useless battle of wits. Dropping your defenses, getting put into a disadvantageous position. The backstabber or thief is revealed. Sometimes this reversal can symbolize a "blowhard" personality—someone who likes to run their mouth. The office gossip.

**Queen of Swords**—Logic will help you see the clear path to victory. Let your head rule over your heart. Make decisions from a rational point of view. You may be conjuring up new ideas and seeing the bigger picture. Sometimes this card is about speaking the truth plainly. Deliver the facts and let the chips fall where they may. For people, the Queen of Swords could be a professional person, a strict boss who expects everyone to follow the rules, or a critic.

*Reversed*—This reversal can indicate treachery or sabotage from a superior or coworker. The stab in the back, or scathing critique. A gossip that spreads malicious rumors. Or you lose your temper because you feel frustrated by a current situation. Not able to see the forest for the trees. Losing your direction—or allowing someone to bully you. Emotions cloud the facts. Like the reversed Queen of Wands, this card can also symbolize a *Devil Wears Prada* type.

**King of Swords**—This is the thought leader, the person who sees the future—and guides others brilliantly. The expert or mentor. You may be ready to take on that role—or to receive support from someone like that. You can convey your thoughts clearly and express yourself well. The mastery of thinking or ideas (I've seen this card symbolize getting an advanced degree!). The King of Swords is a sharp person who can cut to the chase in any situation. They seek the truth and never mince words.

*Reversed*—The abusive boss. A harsh critic who has zero sympathies for how their words land. A lack of empathy. The incompetent or corrupt leader. The thought leader who turns out to be a hypocrite or fraud. They experience a fall from grace. In some cases, this reversal means criminal elements or activities. For example, white-collar crime. This could lead to legal problems. Sometimes this card indicates words coming back to haunt you.

# PENTACLES

Pentacles are the earth element. They symbolize money, values, and resources.

**Ace of Pentacles**—This is always a welcome card to see, for it symbolizes a new job or source of income. This could be the position you've been waiting for or a long-overdue raise. If you're starting your own business or side hustle, this is a YES. A project that pays off. Getting on the right path once and for all. Financial aid. If you're wondering if you should raise your rates, this is your sign to do it!

*Reversed*—Living large. Making a down payment on a home or business. Investing in school. In some cases, this could indicate losing money or hoarding it. It can also suggest making money through illegal means—or under the table. Or you get a raise, but it's minuscule (ex: the cost of living). Charging too little for your services. Not valuing your own skills. This reversal could mean someone is trying to haggle with you.

**Two of Pentacles**—You're doing a juggling act. Working two jobs at the same time—or work and school. A time when you must be adaptable and able to multitask. Doing the job of two people. Trying to do too many things at once. You'll need to do some fancy footwork to pull it off. This could also indicate a choice between two offers. You'll need to weigh the pros and cons, especially the salary and benefits. Financial instability. Sometimes, this card means travel or working bicoastal.

*Reversed*—Dropping the ball. Losing your financial security. Getting hung up on an idea and unable to let go. Dealing with legal issues or endless red tape. Problems with bureaucracy. Going from one job to another. Career instability. Not being able to find your footing in a situation. You might be in over your head.

**Three of Pentacles**—This card could indicate building a career or your reputation. You're stepping up your game and finding new success. If you're working with a team, this is a great card to see. It indicates a capable crew—and great results. Plans are coming together. For some, the Three of Pentacles means skill development, usually through an apprenticeship or internship. Highly skilled work. Recognition for a job well done.

    *Reversed*—Sloppy work or lack of work. You may be struggling to find a job that pays well, or that fits your skillset. Or you get a job, and you're not qualified. It might be wise to go back to school to develop new skills. Sometimes this reversal means trouble with coworkers. A project falls apart, a business relationship turns sour, the team does nothing but argue. You're building on a faulty foundation. A lack of recognition—or someone else tries to take credit for your work.

**Four of Pentacles**—Financial security. You've achieved success on your terms and are in complete control of your future. The Four of Pentacles represents steady employment or income. It can also suggest you're ready to take on a more significant role of responsibility. You know what you're worth and are not going to accept less. For entrepreneurs, it might be time to raise your rates—and set new boundaries. Keep out the troublemakers. Take control of your finances. Prepare for the future. Buy property, invest in your retirement account, or put money in the bank. It's good to be king.

    *Reversed*—A loss of control. You lose your job or your source of income. You take a risk and lose your shirt. Perhaps you're gambling on the wrong things or spending like a maniac. Living beyond your means. Not thinking of the future—living for today. Sometimes, this card could indicate investing in a business that goes belly up. You may be forced to let go of your assets or your position.

**Five of Pentacles**—This card warns of financial hardship. You may lose a job or your security. Bankruptcy. Mental strain over money. Or perhaps you choose to live simply and give up your high-paying job for a spiritual cause or meaningful work. This can also indicate a friend who helps you when the going gets rough. There is help around the corner—keep going! If you're not fitting into the company culture or some other situation, you know the feeling of this card.

*Reversed*—You're out of the cold and back on track financially. Help has arrived, or you have found a new opportunity. Debts are paid, and you can begin to accumulate money again. The problems come to an end. You find your peers or a group that welcomes you. Sometimes the Five of Pentacles reversed signals the end of a relationship. For example, you go your separate ways from a business partnership. Divvying up the assets or selling off a business.

**Six of Pentacles**—When this card arrives, it can indicate charity. Perhaps you're involved in a good cause—or you may be drawn to humanitarian work. You're sharing what you have, not just money, but also skills or experience. You have a lot to give. This could indicate having a charitable part to your business—or receiving help from an investor. The scales represent justice or legal issues. This could also mean loans for business or school. You may be receiving financial aid or paying it back. In a negative light, this could indicate being in a situation where the energy exchange is not equal.

You're receiving crumbs for your efforts. Servitude. Being reduced to begging while others are flaunting power or wealth (or vice versa).

*Reversed*—Wanting something for nothing. Deal seekers. Guilt trippers. Not valuing your skills or talents. Undercharging for your services (time to raise those rates!). Refusing to pay a loan—or you apply, and your loan is denied. Lack of capital. Legal drama. Ingrates. MLMs or other get-rich schemes. In short: be mindful, set boundaries, and handle your business.

**Seven of Pentacles**—There is growth, but it is slow. This may make you wonder if your efforts will ever pay off. They will—in due time. You must continue to do the work and not obsess over the rewards. Everything is growing in its own way and own time. Be patient. There may be a few obstacles. "Weeding" the garden. Take a step back to assess what needs to be done. Rethink your plan of action.

    *Reversed*—Nothing is happening. You're busting your hump but have little to show for it. So now you're getting impatient. You're ready to throw in the towel. Low wages. Digging for gold. This could also indicate laziness, procrastination, or slacking on the job. If you're not trying, don't expect a pat on the back.

**Eight of Pentacles**—The Eight of Pentacles symbolizes a time when you're happy on the job. You like the work you're doing, you're good at it, and paid well. Recognition comes for your talents. This could be a pat on the back, a new position, or a raise. This is also a card of craftsmanship. You take your work seriously, maybe you're a perfectionist, and you bring your best self to the job. In some cases, this card could mean growing your skills under the eye of a mentor—or through consistent practice. Overall, it's a productive time in your career.

    *Reversed*—You may need to polish your skills. Go back to school, get on-the-job training, or perhaps get trained for a new position. It's also possible you lack talent—in that case, you need more practice. Sometimes this card can indicate a lack of work—or work that is beneath your skillset. It might also mean a bridge job that pays the bills until you find your dream job. A crappy employee who doesn't follow orders. Work that isn't worth it. The workaholic who has no time for a personal life.

**Nine of Pentacles**—Living large! The self-made success story. You've created incredible abundance. Goals have been reached. Financial success is yours. Now you can collect the fruits of your hard labor. Treat yourself! Celebrate your success! You're moving on up. This card could mean success in real estate—you might want to buy property at this time—or if you're an agent, it might be a seller's market. Living in a gated community. Having all the creature comforts around you. Huzzah!

*Reversed*—You're almost there—but not quite. Keep going. The hard work will yield sweet fruit when the time is right. What are you trying to grow? Does it make sense? You may be bored with your current situation or seeking an escape. Or perhaps you're staying in a job just for the benefits. You're trapped due to financial issues aka the "golden handcuffs." Sometimes this reversal could mean living beyond your means. Unable to get out of debt. Living with the parents. In some cases, this could warn of a rip-off.

**Ten of Pentacles**—The Ten of Pentacles symbolizes security. You've built a strong foundation and can take care of your loved ones. You've created a legacy—or are on your way. Prosperity is here. The seeds you've planted have grown. You might own a beautiful home or be investing in real estate. For students, this card means attending a respected university. Scholarship or windfall. Going home to visit the family.

*Reversed*—Family drama or financial issues impact you. You're feeling stressed from the responsibility—or lack of support. Or you may be estranged from your loved ones, so now you're going it alone. Unable to care for your family. Returning to the parent's home after a job loss or other misfortune. Doing what your family wants rather than what you want. Entering the family business and resenting it.

**Page of Pentacles**—This is the card of the excellent student. If it shows up, it means you're on the right track in school. You're learning valuable skills that will help your future goals. Seeking knowledge and experience. Getting accepted into your school of choice. Financially, this card could indicate a new opportunity or venture. Good money news. Investing in the future. Planting financial seeds. Learning how to stand on your own two feet. The first job. An internship.

*Reversed*—Bad money news. A loss. You don't get the job, or your application gets rejected. A loan doesn't come through. Or perhaps you're having trouble with your studies. Learning difficulties or too many distractions. Wanting the rewards without the work or skill. Under-qualified. Making foolish money moves. Investing in a losing situation.

**Knight of Pentacles**—This is the only Knight that isn't moving. It is a sign to pause and examine the land's current lay before taking your next big step. Take your time. The energy is steady and stable—but also stubborn. Maybe you're not giving up your goals, or perhaps you see the possibilities when others don't. Whatever the case may be, you're primed for greatness and abundance. Stay the course, be practical, and keep the faith. This card can also represent someone who offers solid support.

KNIGHT ⚜ PENTACLES

*Reversed*—You're hanging on but for what? There is little growth to show for past efforts. You're stuck and unwilling to let go. Or it's the opposite: you're giving up before you've had time to see the rewards. Losing your patience—or losing your job. Investing in something that doesn't pay off. Depending on others. A lazy, impractical person who ends up costing you.

**Queen of Pentacles**—The Queen of Pentacles is patient, creative, and practical. Everything they touch turns to gold. They are abundant and kindly. You can rely on them. This may be qualities you're expressing at this time—or it may be someone who is a source of help. A trusted ally or close confidant. Everything is growing. You're conserving for the future and feeling secure.

QUEEN ⚜ PENTACLES

*Reversed*—Laziness. Instead of practicality, this card lacks warmth and trust. A person who cannot seem to get it together. Infertile. Planting seeds that will not grow. A refusal to take care of your responsibilities. The control freak or damsel in distress. Perhaps you're depending on others—or trying to make others dependent on you.

**King of Pentacles**—This is the protector of the realm. The King of Pentacles creates security for all. They are productive, pragmatic, and caring. You can count on them to be a reliable leader. You may possess these qualities at this time. You're the caring boss, the kind leader, the nurturing coach. People trust you because they know you will get the job done right. Cultivating abundance. I also call this my "King Midas: card. What you touch turns to gold.

KING 4 PENTACLES

**Reversed**—This is the miser, gambler, show-off, or deadbeat. It can also be an abusive, corrupt boss. If it comes up, it's a warning to take responsibility for your loved ones or your debts. Job loss. The overbearing coach or difficult to please parent. Financial problems, most likely caused by living beyond your means. Not able to attain security. You may need to look for new work. Getting downsized at work. Demotion.

You might be wondering: how the heck do I remember all of this? Here's the deal: you don't have to memorize all of those interpretations. The tarot is a visual aid—even if you draw a blank, the pictures provide clues. Feel free to use the book—or to simply follow the flow of the images and allow your intuition to fill in those blanks.

. . . . . . . . . . . . . . . . . . . . . . . . . . . . . . . . . . . . . . . . . . . . . . . . .

## Tarotcise:

Let's put that into practice right now. Grab your journal and your favorite deck. Shuffle your cards and draw one from the deck. Without thinking too much or looking up the meanings, journal whatever you feel. Let the image inspire you! How did that feel? Were you nervous? Did you find the words flowing . . . or not? Now, find the card in this book. How close was your interpretation? Did you find a whole new way of looking at the card? Have fun with this exploration!

### Common Sixth Sense:

Sometimes you'll get a reading that makes no sense to you or your situation. It may be tempting to reshuffle. My advice: don't. If you keep on shuffling to get the answer you want, you'll end up with mixed messages. Instead, put the cards aside and revisit your reading later. It may make sense then. Or not. Everyone has an "off" tarot day.

In the next section, I'm sharing some tarot spreads and other ways to work with the cards. Get ready to make your tarot work for you!

# Taking Your Cards to Work

**O**kay, we have some interpretations. The next question: how the heck do you work with these cards? Deep breaths, pardner—I've got you! In this chapter we'll delve into two very important practices that are crucial to putting tarot to work for success in life and in business: Ask the Right Questions. Be Sensitive to Timing. In other words, let's jump into using **tarot spreads** to get answers, and let's see how working with your **yearly cards** can impact your timing and decision-making.

## HUH? (QUESTIONS, DUH)

Tarot cards are actually quite simple to grasp. The key is regular practice. If you work with them every day, sooner or later, it sinks in. Think about the first time you got behind the wheel of an automobile. If you were like me, you might have been scared or unsure of what to do. It's probably safe to say you weren't driving like an expert the first time. Most likely, it took a while before you knew what to do and felt confident. Any learned skill is the same—including tarot reading (or astrology).

Tarot is a practical tool for decision-making, creativity, and introspection. It can help to weigh pros and cons, explore possible outcomes, and create strategies. Tarot helps to access your own inner wisdom.

The magic isn't in the cards—it's in you.

How does Tarot work?

Here's how I explain it:

**1** First, you need a question. Once you have a question, take a minute to sit with it.

**2** Shuffle the cards while meditating on your question. When you feel ready, stop shuffling, put the deck facedown, cut them into three piles, and put them back together.

**3** You can fan them out and choose a card or series of cards, or you can take the cards from the top of the deck.

**4** Next, you'll turn them over and gaze at the images. What are the pictures saying to you? How do the cards go together or not? Are the figures interacting? What is your gut telling you? Start there and see what meanings come to the surface. If you feel stuck, grab the little white book that came with your deck—or thumb through this book for interpretations.

That's it.

You're probably thinking I'm being somewhat simplistic, but tarot doesn't need to be complicated. Frankly, when you add too many "rules," it becomes rigid. I've found that the tarot doesn't like that. It needs room to "breathe" and for the story to unfold. Keep your practice uncomplicated, and you'll get clear, helpful readings.

## Common Sixth Sense

I recommend writing down all of your readings, especially when you're a tarot newbie. You can refer back to your entries and see how things have worked out . . . or not. This will also allow you to uncover new meanings or interpretations. It's interesting when I reflect on my own tarot journals. Sometimes I see things in a whole new light!

## Asking the Right Questions

Your reading is only ever as good as your question. I'm serious about that. One of the things I've learned over the years is how to ask Tarot a question that gives a helpful answer.

For example: "will I" is not a great way to frame your question. It implies that the future is somehow out of your hands—which is a disempowering perspective. I'm also not a fan of "should I" because it puts the decision-making in someone else's hands. Taking personal responsibility for your life is essential. You don't want to become dependent on the Tarot for what you "should" do. Only you get to decide that.

That being said, Tarot can help compare options and examine possible outcomes, which puts you in the driver's seat. When you know what your situation is all about and where you're headed, you can make brave, excellent choices. This is conscious living.

What about yes/no questions? They can be helpful up to a point. Here's why: it suggests there's only one way. In some cases, that may be true. But in many others, there are shades of gray. Some "no's" can be negotiated, while some yeses may not be in your best interest. So yes/no might need a "maybe" disclaimer!

**Here are some better ways to frame your questions:**

What do I need to know about _____?

How can I _____?

What's the best way to reach my goal of _____?

What am I not seeing about this situation?

What can I expect if I do _____?

What's the hidden opportunity with _____?

What is the hidden lesson with _____?

How can I make the most out of _____?

What do I need to know about (this course of action) versus (another course
   of action)?

These guidelines can help you form excellent questions, which leads to valuable answers.

## Common Sixth Sense:

When seeking the services of a pro, it's also best to be upfront about why you're getting a reading. If you're coming in with an attitude of "I'm not telling you anything because you better wow me by reading my mind," it's not only disrespectful to the reader, but it also often leads to an unhelpful reading. For example, when I see a professional, I always let them know what I want to focus on: work and money. If I don't, I often end up getting a reading about my love life, an area I never worry about! (Some of these readers sure seem to think I've got an intriguing romantic future!)

# TAROT SPREADS

Now that you've got your question, it's time to pick a spread. What's that? When tarot readers refer to spreads, they are talking about a selection of cards laid out in a particular way. A tarot spread can be as simple as one card or a complex layout with many cards. (I've even seen a reading done with the whole deck!)

In this book, we'll cover the ones I use the most with clients (and myself) for work, vocation, and purpose. These are the go-to spreads I've been using for years—and the most reliable (psst . . . you can use them for romantic queries too if you'd like).

## One card

A one-card reading is easy and perfect for beginners. In fact, many times, all you need is one card. I'm serious! There are many symbols packed into each one—and those symbols will give you a ton of information.

How to do a one-card spread:

Get clear on your question.

Center yourself with a deep, cleansing breath.

Shuffle the cards.

When you feel ready, put the cards on the table facedown.

Cut the cards into three piles and put them back together any way you'd like.

Next, you can choose a card from the top of the deck—or you can fan them out and pull any one you'd like!

Turn the card over, gaze at the image, and take note of what pops into your mind. What does the image say to you—and how does this apply to your question?

Next, feel free to check the interpretation with the little white book that came with your deck—or this book if you're not getting a clear message.

That's it!

Here's an example. Patricia (Aquarius Sun, Taurus Moon, Cancer Rising, Aries Midheaven) is thinking of leaving her job. But she's nervous because she's been at this place for many years. Her question: "What can I expect if I decide to move on?" The card she pulled: Six of Wands. This shows an image of a victorious person on a horse. People are gathering around the figure, and the mood seems to be merry. Right away,

Patricia knows she'll be happier—and successful if she decides to leave. There will be support along the way too. Yay!

## The situation, what you need to know, advice

I created this spread many years ago and found it to be highly effective for problem-solving. This is one I use I use the most for myself and my clients.

There are three positions:

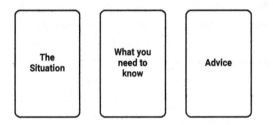

**The Situation:** this shows the energy around the question.

**What You Need to Know:** this position indicates the blind spots or things you're not seeing. If this is a positive card, it says you're in a good place, even if the situation card is challenging. If it's a tricky card, it could be a warning of possible drama you might not expect. Or maybe you do expect it, so it serves as an affirmation.

**Advice:** this card offers advice to help you make the most out of your situation, no matter what the other cards may say. This is your strategy for the best possible outcome.

The reason why I love this spread is that it puts you firmly in the driver's seat with a full view of where you're heading and a road map for any necessary detours. Let's take it for a test spin!

Wayne (Pisces Sun, Pisces Moon, Virgo Ascendant, Gemini Midheaven) is thinking of opening up a healing center. He's a Reiki Master and passionate about helping people feel better. These are the cards he drew: Three of Swords reversed, Five of Swords, Four of Cups. His question: "What do I need to know about opening up a healing center next year?"

**The Situation:** Three of Swords reversed—In my opinion, this is a great card to see for a healing center because it symbolizes relief or recovery. It says his "heart" is in the right place—and he would do a lot of good work for his community.

**What You Need to Know:** Five of Swords—This is a problematic card. It indicates dishonesty, theft, drama, and a possible backstabber. Wayne says he lives in a conservative area, and some of the people there might think this is too "woo." He worries he won't get a business license due to people's misconceptions of the work.

**Advice:** Four of Cups—I see this card two ways. One, he needs to consider his options carefully. He might need to set up a shop in a different area, for example. There may be options he hasn't yet thought of—or may not be available this year. Secondly, I see this as him having to do his part to educate people about his work. Perhaps they will open their minds if he takes an active role in reaching out to his community. Either way, this is a sign it may not happen within a year. He needs to take his time if he wants to get this setup to succeed.

## Donnaleigh's Spread

My friend Donnaleigh de la Rose created this layout, and it's one I use all the time. Like the previous spread, it gives advice but also shows a potential outcome. If you want to see where things are going and what problems you'll encounter, this is a fast way of determining what's up.

There are four positions:

**The Situation:** once again, this gives information about your question. It shows the current climate.

**The Challenge:** here are the obstacles you may encounter. If the card is positive, you're good to go. Challenging? Get ready to rumble!

**Advice:** the advice position will give you guidance on how best to navigate your situation for the most desirable outcome.

**Likely Outcome:** this is what you can expect. Remember: you can change things if you don't like that outcome card.

Here's a reading I did for myself about a year ago when I was in the middle of making a massive shift to my business. The question: what can I expect if I make this change?

**The Situation:** The Star—This hopeful card says I'll get what I want. Better yet, I may experience a healing of sorts. So interesting because I was overworked, exhausted, and feeling blue. The Star says I can replenish my well by making this decision. The figure emptying the vessels also suggests I have plenty—and it's okay to pour out what isn't needed.

**The Challenge:** Nine of Pentacles—I love this card. It's what I call the self-made person. As a challenge, it says I'm in a good position, and it's okay to make this decision. The number nine indicates completion. Coupled with the Star, I see safety, security, and abundance. Yeah!

**Advice:** Ten of Pentacles—As advice, this card says to focus on my legacy and what I want it to be. That's easy: my writing and teaching career! The Ten of Pentacles is a reminder to remain grateful and count every blessing. Being in a position where you can change is something many people do not get to experience. It's good to acknowledge how fortunate I am.

**Likely outcome:** Page of Cups—A new, happy phase is ahead. There are surprises of the delightful kind. The stage is set for a joyful new chapter—and zero regrets. If there was ever a set of cards saying, "go for it," this would be the foursome!

## Common Sixth Sense

I recommend pulling one additional "clarifier" card if the outcome sucks. A clarifier adds additional information that can help you see if there is a possibility of turning the beat around . . . or not. If the clarifier is not favorable, it affirms the negative outcome. While that stinks, it's better to know what you're getting into than remaining blissfully unaware. By the way, one clarifying card is enough.

## The Options Spread

Struggling with two (or more) decisions? This is your new go-to spread! Here's how it works:

**1** Shuffle your cards while being ultra-clear on the two options. For example, let's say you're choosing between two equally good jobs. In your mind, determine which is the first option and which is the second. As you shuffle, focus on what you need to know about each choice.

**2** Once you're ready, put the cards facedown. Cut them into three piles and put the piles back together. Take the first card off the top of the deck and turn it over. This card represents you in the situation.

**3** Now, lay out three cards for each option. There are no positions for the three cards. You simply look at how the energy is flowing to determine which may be the best.

From there, you can compare and see what stands out. If every card looks nifty, you're in the win/win position!

Kendra (Libra Sun, Capricorn Moon, Scorpio Ascendant, Leo Midheaven) is searching for a new job. She received two offers—and now she must make a decision! Here are her cards:

**The first card she pulled:** Nine of Cups. Whoa. She's in the best position possible. This is the wish card, a sign she's going to get what she wants. Yeah, baby!

**First option:** Five of Cups reversed, Seven of Pentacles, and Page of Wands. A new outlook, hard work, but lots of promise.

**Second option:** The Fool, Six of Cups, The Wheel of Fortune. A fresh start, a happy environment, and a massive opportunity. Well, duh, this is the clear winner! Two Majors trump the cards in the first spread. Go, Kendra!

# The Horseshoe Spread

I have been using this spread for almost as long as I've been reading tarot. I no longer remember where I learned it, but it's become one of my most valuable spreads. It delivers a ton of information, which makes it perfect when you need a bit more depth.

Also, this is the spread I use whenever we're talking about property, as in moving, selling, or buying real estate. The fifth card determines that. For example, you need to relocate for a job or school, it might show up here. Is it the Death card? If so, a significant change is on the way, perhaps even to a different state or country. Eight of Swords? You're stuck. Nothing is moving yet. Ace of Pentacles—a happy card to see if you're buying or selling. It's "hell yeah!" I'll also peek at the obstacle and outcome for questions like this. If they indicate conflict, it could shed light on problems that need to be overcome before the change happens.

The Horseshoe spread is comprised of seven cards laid out in a horseshoe shape. Begin laying the cards from the bottom left around to the bottom right.

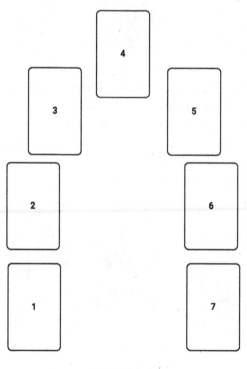

**The positions:**

    **1—The past**—allows you to see the root of the situation or where you're coming from.

    **2—The present** — this shows where you are now and how far you have to go.

    **3—The near future**—this indicates what's just over the horizon, as well as the things you need to deal with soon.

    **4—The querent**—your state of mind at the time of the reading. This is important, because if you're negatively inclined, you may have work to do around your mindset.

    **5—The environment**—the fifth card shows factors around you, including people who may be influencing the situation and the physical location. Again, if someone asks about real estate, a move, or anything like that—this is the most important position next to the outcome.

    **6—The obstacles**—if there are problems to overcome, you'll find them here. A positive card? You've got this, babe!

    **7—The likely outcome**—this is the potential future or where you're headed. Remember: you can make different decisions if you don't like the way it looks!

**How to do this spread:**

**1**   Focus on your question and shuffle the cards.

**2**   When you feel ready, put the cards face down on the table. Cut them into three piles and put them back together any way you want.

**3**   Taking the cards from the top of the deck, begin laying them out in the horseshoe position, still face down.

**4**   Turn over card number 4 first. This will show you the mindset or attitude around this question. I always begin here to see if there is resistance, fear, or any other issue that might be creating bias.

**5**   Next, turn over the cards one by one, starting from 1. I like to pause and interpret each card separately until I reach the last. Once I get there, I begin looking at the story that has unfolded—and considering the problems, possibilities, and outcome.

Mavis wants to move to a warmer climate. They've already received a green light from their employer, who has agreed to a transfer. However, their partner has been balking. They've come up with a compromise, but the negativity is still there. Here is the reading: "What can I do to make this move happen as smoothly as possible?"

**The reading:**

**The past:** The Star reversed—This card reflects Mavis's unhappiness. The current living situation makes them feel drained. Mavis said there isn't enough "green" in their environment. They are hoping to move somewhere with more nature.

**The present:** The King of Pentacles reversed—The King of Pentacles reversed might be Mavis' partner. Their biggest concern: it's going to be expensive to move, it's not practical because they have roots in the current community, etc., etc. All things Mavis affirmed.

**The near future:** Knight of Swords—A battle is ahead. They may go around and around, trying to make their points. This will be a challenge for the relationship.

**The querent:** Queen of Wands—Mavis is passionate about making this change. They see a move as an adventure and a chance to start fresh.

**The environment:** King of Cups—The ship's presence in the background says the move will happen. I think Mavis will be able to convince the partner to go along with it. Once they do, they'll probably see it's good to be in a new, spacious location.

**The obstacle:** Five of Pentacles—Again: the money! This seems to be the primary concern. But it feels more fear-based rather than reality, especially since they both have solid incomes.

**Likely outcome:** Justice—A compromise is reached, and a contract is signed. In my opinion, this will be a great change once they make the decision and go for it. (Update: they've moved and are near the ocean, which has had a great effect on the partner. Guess they have become that King of Cups!)

If someone asks about home, move, or buying real estate, the fifth card gives the clues. Is it the Death card? If so, a significant change is on the way, perhaps even to a different state or country. Eight of Swords? You're stuck. Nothing is moving yet. Ace of Pentacles—a happy card to see if you're buying or selling. It's "hell yeah!" I'll also peek at the obstacle and outcome for questions like this. If they indicate conflict, it could shed light on problems that need to be overcome before the change happens.

## The Astrological Wheel

Another spread I use for entrepreneurs is the Wheel, which is based on the houses wheel I shared on page 21. This layout will show every aspect of your business for the upcoming year. If you find astrology confusing, this tarot spin is an easier way to get helpful information.

Again, here are the positions:

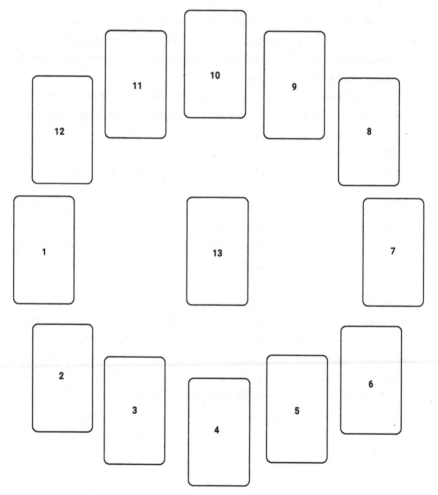

**1st**—The 1st house is your public image or brand.

**2nd**—The 2nd house is how you make money, handle it, and your business values.

**3rd**—The 3rd house is associated with writing, speaking, learning, contracts, and brand messaging.

**4th**—The 4th house is your working environment as well as your business foundation.

**5th**—The 5th is associated with creativity, speculation, monetary gain from real estate, teaching, entertainment industry, and one of the fame houses.

**6th**—The 6th house is work, routines, and health.

**7th**—The 7th house is your partnership zone. It also rules legal issues, binding agreements, joint ventures, competitors, public relations, and advertising. If you have a business enemy, observe this house.

**8th**—The 8th house is associated with business investments, taxes, joint finances, debt collection, legacy work, budgets, insurance, and loans.

**9th**—The 9th house is connected to business travel, publishers, teaching, writers, global affairs, and media.

**10th**—The 10th house is associated with reputation, fame, awards, ambition, public life, and overall career direction.

**11th**—The 11th house rules community, network, online groups, goals, associations, humanitarian work, and wishes.

**12th**—The 12th house is your self-care zone. It's associated with rest, vacations, secrets, behind-the-scenes activities, and secret enemies.


**How to do the spread:** The same routine as usual: shuffle the cards and when you feel ready, place them facedown. Cut them into three piles and put them back together any way you like. Take the cards off the top of the deck, one by one, for each position. I stop and interpret each card before I move on to the next one.

I also pull one last card for **the overall theme,** which means there are **13 cards** in all for this spread.

This example is for Clarice, who is coming off a lousy year in her business. The pandemic forced her to temporarily close the doors of her restaurant. She was able to reopen with a new takeout menu and delivery service. While her business was able to survive, she feels anxious about the following year. Here's the reading (again, the interpretations are brief to save space):

**1st**—Ten of Cups—Clarice is a beloved member of the community. Many of her customers continued to support her during the roughest times.

**2nd**—Three of Swords—This is a card of loss, which means there are still issues. While this information made her sad, I advised her to look for new ways to market—or to perhaps offer something no one else is. It's also wise to keep her expenses as low as possible until the economy improves.

**3rd**—Seven of Cups—She's got a fantastic imagination, and she's full of excellent ideas for new recipes or marketing. However, she may be uncertain which way to go. I advised her to get some mentoring to help sort out her ideas.

**4th**—Page of Pentacles—This says her business foundation is still solid. Although it may feel as if she's starting fresh, she's got great roots in the community—and a few updates to the restaurant might plant new seeds.

**5th**—Eight of Pentacles—She's working hard—and this year, she might be able to pluck many of her creative ideas and bring them down to earth. Some of her brainstorms may be profitable.

**6th**—Ten of Swords—Clarice is overworked. Right now, she may be stuck with that. However, there is a light at the end of a tunnel. It won't be like this forever. I recommended scheduling some time off wherever possible.

**7th**—The Fool—A new beginning. This might be a new partner or employee. The Fool says she'll need to be ready to take a chance in this arena.

**8th**—Three of Pentacles—The long-term financial future looks promising. Once the economy improves and she can get more help, she'll rebuild from the past year.

**9th**—Six of Cups—This can be a sweet card to see for biz travel. Maybe this year she can go home to visit the family (they live in a different country). The other way to interpret this would be doing some events in the community that could attract the media.

**10th**—The Hierophant—Clarice is a respected member of the community. People know she's a hard worker and an expert chef. No matter what has happened in the past year, her reputation remains solid (see a theme here?).

**11th**—The Devil reversed—There may be certain groups or associations which come to an end this year. Perhaps she doesn't have the time. Or there may be problems due to jealousy.

**12th**—Six of Swords—If there was ever a need for a vacation, this card illustrates that beautifully. Time away from the kitchen will do her good. It is probably not going to be easy to do that, but the Six of Swords says that she can find time to rest with the proper support.

**13th**—Two of Cups—the big takeaway: Clarice will be fine, but her business will be better once she can get more help. That help can be a partner, employees, the family, or the community.

· · · · · · · · · · · · · · · · · · · · · · · · · · · · · · · · · · · · · · · · · · · · · ·

## Tarotcise

Test drive these spreads. Which ones do you like? Is there one that speaks to you the loudest?

## THE TAROT AND ASTROLOGY MASH-UP

Remember how I said Astrology was important in the Major Arcana? Here's one of my favorite ways to play with the two: I call it the Tarot and Astrology Mash-up. This technique will help you deepen your understanding of your natal chart—and provide a visual aid.

Pull the Major Arcana out of the tarot deck, specifically the cards associated with the zodiac. That would be:

**Aries—The Emperor**

**Taurus—The Hierophant**

**Gemini—The Lovers**

**Cancer—The Chariot**

**Leo—Strength**

**Virgo—The Hermit**

**Libra—Justice**

**Scorpio—Death**

**Sagittarius—Temperance**

**Capricorn—The Devil**

**Aquarius—The Star**

**Pisces—The Moon**

Next, you'll want to match these tarot cards up with the Big Three and your Midheaven. For example, Dolly Parton is a Capricorn Sun in the 5th house, Virgo Moon in the 12th house, Virgo Ascendant, and Taurus Midheaven.

She'd pull The Devil for her Sun Sign, The Hermit for her Moon and Rising Signs, and The Hierophant for her Midheaven. So now we can use these cards as archetypes to dive deep into understanding what she's all about.

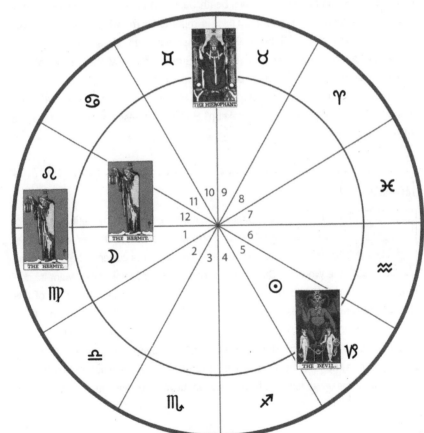

We might say she's a provocateur of sorts with the Devil as her Sun. She's here to stir up a little mischief or to explore controversial topics through her work. The double Hermit shows a need for introspection and a private life. At the same time, the Hierophant at the top of her chart indicates she's a spiritual teacher, here to share her thoughts as a way to improve the world. I find it interesting that Dolly has plenty of prim and proper Hermit and Hierophant vibes but just enough Devil to make her naughty!

One more example: I'm a Gemini Sun, Scorpio Moon, Libra Ascendant, and Leo Midheaven. This combo is The Lovers, Death, Justice, and Strength. I'm here to communicate and connect. Doing the right thing is important to me, which means my ethics lead the way in my actions. Emotionally, I'm intense, but when I surrender to that part of my nature, I can transform myself . . . or others. Strength on the Midheaven promises a spot in the sun if I'm willing to share positivity and light with the world.

**Your turn:** pull cards for your Big Three and Midheaven. What do these cards have to say about you and your cosmic makeup? How might these Major Arcana themes show up in your life?

. . . . . . . . . . . . . . . . . . . . . . . . . . . . . . . . . . . . . . . . . . . . .

# Tarotcise:

 Find out where Jupiter and Saturn are currently transiting your natal chart. Pull the Wheel of Fortune to represent Jupiter and another Major Arcana to symbolize where Jupiter is currently transiting. Use the World for Saturn and choose another Major to represent its current transit. Place these cards in your natal chart. For example, at the time of this writing, Jupiter is in Pisces in my 5th house. The Wheel and The Moon show I can expand my creativity by following my intuition. Saturn is currently in my 4th house in Aquarius, so Saturn and The Star show this is the ideal period for creating new, sound structures in my home or business. I'm in the process of renovating both! Try this out and see what these cards might have to say about your current astrological transits!

# ANNUAL CARDS

One more technique I use with my clients and myself is the Annual Cards. This is a method conceived by Angeles Arrien and Mary K Greer involving tarot and numerology and uses the Major Arcana. I highly recommend you check out Mary K Greer's book: *Archetypal Tarot* (formerly titled *Who Are You In The Tarot?*) for an in-depth exploration. This is the best book on the subject, hands down. For our purposes, we'll be concise.

The Yearly Card will give you an idea of what energies are at play for your year. When I work with entrepreneurs, I always include a Yearly Card.

It's simple addition to find out what your year might be. Here's what you do: add up your month and day of birth with the CURRENT YEAR instead of your birth year. Reduce it until you get a number from 1 to 22. If you get a number over 9, it's considered a "compound" number. You can use that interpretation or reduce it further to a single digit.

Because no one gets a zero, the Fool becomes number 22.

**Example:** Let's say you're born on May 12th, and you want to know your yearly theme for 2022.

Add up: 5 + 1 + 2 + 2 + 0 + 2 + 2 = 14.

14 is associated with Temperance. You can break it down to 5 if you like, which is associated with The Hierophant.

By the way, I have found it's best to start the year on the birthday. For example, if you are born on May 12, the yearly card kicks in on your birthday for that year.

**For interpretations, I've also included suggestions for entrepreneurs.**

**1—The Magician—☿:** This is your year to develop your talents. You might go back to school or receive on-the-job training. If you're a creative, you might be practicing more than ever. You're getting ready to up-level, and that means you cannot take your talents for granted. If you want to get the gold, you must be able to deliver the goods. The more classes you take this year, the better. Also: the Magician indicates some things may change, which will require you to be adaptable. You'll need to stand in your power at times, especially if other people doubt you. Be confident, and show 'em what you're made of. Don't be afraid to brag a bit if you can do the job better than anyone else. **For entrepreneurs,** you have great creative potential at your fingertips. You can launch new products and step up your game like never before. If you want to assume a position of power, this is the year to manifest that. You've got the skill and the will to manifest your destiny.

**2—The High Priestess—☽:** You must trust your intuition this year. Some things are developing, perhaps behind the scenes. Instead of the assertive energy of the Magician, the High Priestess is more passive. Things and people come to you—and you can offer advice, comfort, or creative ideas. Take as much time off as you can. Work in secret if you feel the need to. Learn new things but above all, learn to trust yourself. ***For entrepreneurs,*** your business instincts will be especially keen this year. At times, you may be pulling ideas out of thin air. You'll also need to know when to keep quiet. Do not reveal your plans, for others may be too happy to take them from you.

**3—The Empress—♀:** This is a prosperous, fertile, and creative year for you. You're full of ideas, and those ideas may turn out to be genius. The seeds you plant promise a big harvest. You may be unusually productive, which is fab if you're in an artistic career. Nurturing is another important aspect of the Empress. You might be taking care of others in some way. Perhaps you're raising a family, teaching, or taking care of a loved one. Give what you can, but don't forget to take care of yourself too. This card signifies abundance—you might make more money, but you may be prone to spend lavishly as well. Watch that you don't overdo the good life too much. ***For entrepreneurs,*** your muse is singing. You may create many profitable things this year. Finances improve, giving you the ability to invest back in your business.

**4—The Emperor—♈:** Get ready to work your ass off. The Emperor isn't playing around, and neither should you. Focus on the work that needs to be done, create a structure to support you, limit distractions, and get it done. You can build an empire this year if you put your mind to it. This is also your time to step into the role of authority figure. Be ready to show your expertise. Rewards come—and possibly fame. Maybe you're getting promoted or in the public eye in some way. Rules are essential in an Emperor year—you may have to follow the policies or create your own. Be ready to uphold the status quo. Life and work are often stable in an Emperor year. If you've been feeling rudderless, you can create divine order this year. ***For entrepreneurs,*** you can shine as a leader in your industry. Grab the mic where you can and share your big message. Be sure to establish good boundaries and update your policies if need be. You may receive lessons about what it means to be a good boss. Watch out for tendencies to be a control freak.

**5—The Hierophant—♉:** The Hierophant gives and receives knowledge. This year may find you back in school or sharing your wisdom with other people. Maybe both. If you're in a position to mentor others, you will find that you have plenty to share. People may also want to lay their problems at your feet. Be ready to give advice often. Like the Emperor year, rules are important in a Hierophant year, too. Conforming to fit the rules is something you'll need to do. This is not the time to upset the status quo (that's Tower year energy). Instead, you must go along with the traditions that have already been established. If you need advice, you'll have no trouble finding plenty of wise folks to guide you. **For entrepreneurs,** you'll want to step up to teach, preach, and practice out-reach. Set clear guidelines at work and uphold the rules. You may need to hire experts to help you up-level your game. Or perhaps you may join an organization for your industry. None exist? Start your own.

**6—The Lovers—♊:** While folks often associate the Lovers with romance, it isn't limited to l'amour. Although this year may be important for your romantic life, you must also look at other relationships that may benefit you. For example, you may have a kind boss who motivates you. Or perhaps you're surrounded by people who are cheering you on. Develop relationships now, and you may find they add strength and support to your life. Compromise is also a theme. You must work well with others and find ways to come together. There may be temptations around you, but don't let that distract you from your mission. A few epiphanies are possible. If your higher guides send a message, don't ignore it. This card is also associated with decisions. You may have a few meaningful choices to make this year. The selections will be impactful for your future—so choose wisely. Be careful of bad influences, which may cause you to stray from your path. **For entrepreneurs,** this card can indicate partnerships and joint ventures. By partnering up with other people, you can take your work in exciting new directions. You may also have to hire help. Strengthen relationships, take care of your people, and be sure to monitor your community to keep the troublemakers out.

**7—The Chariot—♋**: You're going far this year, kid. You've got the perfect vehicle and plenty of gas to reach your destination. The path ahead is clear for the most part. Even if you encounter an obstacle, you can swiftly discover the detours. Your will-power is unyielding. You know what you want—and you'll find a way to get it. You may experience many victories if you stay on your path and commit to your goals. Sometimes you may engage in a few battles. Are they worth it? You'll have to determine that. If someone is trying to pull you into their war, make sure it's a cause you are aligned with. You'll also need to be more aggressive at times. If you don't like asserting yourself, others will try to ride over you. Keep your boundaries high and shields up. The Chariot can also signal travel or moving on. **For entrepreneurs,** the Chariot represents a time when you need to be fierce. The competition is stiff. Blaze trails, get your work out there, and don't get distracted by others. Take the lead in your industry and leave everyone in your dust!

**8—Strength—♌**: There will be many tests coming your way this year. You will need to handle them with as much grace as possible. These tests could come in the form of exams for school—or life lessons. At times, boundaries will be part of the problem. You must assert yourself—and take command of situations as they arise. It may be hard to put your needs first, but it's too easy to become depleted if you don't. The Strength card is associated with Leo, which rules the heart. This means you'll need to check in with your feelings regularly. If something or someone no longer aligns with your heart, you may need to cut ties and move on. If you are following your passions, you will find the courage to keep going, no matter how many challenges you face. **For entrepreneurs,** this year will feel like an uphill battle. You'll need to reinforce your policies and handle situations with firmness. Question whether or not you still love what you're doing. If the answer is yes, keep at it. If not, what might make your heart happy?

**9—The Hermit—♍**: This year is best for quiet activities, time alone, and study. In some ways, you may become like a hermit, more content to be withdrawn from the world at large. This is the introvert's card and quite lovely for meditation, contemplation, and research. Some aspects of your life may be coming to a close. Use this time to tidy up and explore the new things that are piquing your interest. Take classes, work with teachers or mentors—or take on that role yourself. You may have more than one discovery this year—that could be a new path, an invention, or an entirely different perspective. Once you've found the breakthrough, be prepared to share your knowledge. Take time off from work if you can. Rest will keep you feeling replenished—and ready for next year's Wheel. **For entrepreneurs,** this is an excellent year for behind-the-scenes work, teaching, and learning new skills. You might be less visible in some ways—but that's not necessarily a bad thing. A little sabbatical from the social media world will do your soul good.

**10—The Wheel of Fortune—♃**: This is an exciting year with lots of change and opportunity. Lady Luck is on your side, bringing gifts and twists of fate. You may find yourself starting something new or finally receiving recognition for work already in motion. New directions are possible—and change feels exhilarating! You've got more choices than usual—be sure to choose wisely, for decisions made this year will be pivotal. Broaden your horizons through school, seeing the world, or engaging in new projects. The wheels are turning, momentum is gathering, and you're going far. If you feel stuck, push that wheel. Get something moving. Soon enough, you'll be on your way. **For entrepreneurs,** this year is ideal for getting your work out there in a more significant way. Up-level the marketing, publish books, broadcast your message, be SEEN. Opportunities will arrive which could prove to be fortunate. You're gaining ground—and shouldn't slow down. Raise your rates. Take bold risks.

**11—Justice—♎**: You will face significant decisions that could change the game or cement your place in the world. Which way to go? What makes sense? What do you want? What's right for you . . . and others? Consider the pros and cons, and then get ready to seize the moment! A few big things may change this year, but trust it's for the best. Karmic debts are getting paid, which means it may seem like some random events shape your world. Trust the Universe to handle things as needed. Legal issues may play a role in your year. You may be signing contracts or dealing with some other matter. If you're involved in a lawsuit, the outcome will be fair, whether you like it or not. If you've done something in error, there is no better year to course correct. Take responsibility for your goof-ups and do the right thing going forward. **For entrepreneurs,** this is your year to get your legal eagles in order. File papers, pay taxes, and update your insurance. You might sign a lot of contracts this year—be sure to have an attorney go over all the details. Partnerships must be treated with great care—if things are not on a level playing field, you may need to sever ties.

**12—The Hanged Man—♆**: This card says: let go. Trust the Universe to sort matters out. You're in suspension, and many things may be on hold. This could feel frustrating, but you must suck it up. Hang in there! You'll see things differently in a year. This is your chance to do some major decluttering in your life. What needs to go? What no longer serves a purpose? Which sacrifices do you need to make for others? Be prepared to release something. When you do, you create space for something new to arrive. In the past, the Hanged Man was associated with treason—you may experience a betrayal this year (I had a few in my last Hanged Man year). It might be shocking, but it will set you free. If someone is toxic, you can remove them from your orbit once and for all. **For entrepreneurs,** many things will be on hold. You'll be doing more waiting than usual. This is a period of incubation, going back to the womb to come up with new ideas. A rebirth is ahead next year . . . but your Hanged Man year says: chill. For some, this could indicate letting go of your business or some part of it.

**13—Death—♏**: The Death year is transformative. Significant changes will occur this year, and some things will come to an end. Do not fear those changes, even if they seem to be taking you in a whole new direction. You must let go with grace and remain open to new possibilities. Anything that goes this year is meant to go. Simplify your life and goals. Get rid of the unnecessary. Say goodbye to relationships that offer nothing. Go into therapy and clear away decades of old stories. You are being reborn, the path will change, and you will emerge cleaner and full of new life. **For entrepreneurs,** this is the year to make bold changes. You may end specific offerings, sever a few relationships, and clear your calendar for new things. If your website is outdated, tear it down and rebuild.

**14—Temperance—♐**: After last year's enormous change energy, you're finding a groove and putting everything together in a whole new way. Some aspects of the past you may keep while incorporating new things into your world. Test out the water, experiment with some things that interest you, go on a whole new path if you want to. Broaden your horizons through study and travel. See the world, explore unique philosophies, or go back to school. Above all, take it one day at a time. Reinvention doesn't happen overnight. *For entrepreneurs,* test out new products and services. Forge new partnerships, especially with business owners in different areas of the country . . . or the world. Find balance in your daily affairs and be sure to get your money in order. There is gold ahead for you—but first, you must test things out and see what makes the most sense for you and the way you want to work. If you feel unbalanced in any aspect of your work, seek support.

**15—The Devil—♑:** This card can play out a few ways. For one, it signals temptation. You may find yourself with some attractive new prospects—some of which may have a catch. You'll want to explore what you're getting into before signing on to anything. Secondly, you may be feeling materialistic. Maybe you're making more money and want to spend that cheddar. Or perhaps you feel entitled to some playtime after so much transformation. There is nothing wrong with some indulgence. Just make sure you don't go into addiction or obsession, which is the shadow side of this card. The Devil can also bring situations that feel oppressive. Other people may be throwing salt in your game. This may cause you to act out of anger, which could accelerate the problems. You'll want to make sure your anger is righteous and effective—and not just an excuse to burn it all down. Watch out for get-rich-quick schemes, dubious partnerships, and overdoing the good life. If you're making big decisions, you'll be choosing between the Devil you know and the one you don't. *For entrepreneurs,* this year could bring more money and more expenses. People may push past your boundaries—be ready to hold your ground. You might feel like doing something a little shocking. Be the Devil's advocate, poke at sacred cows, work hard, and enjoy your successes unapologetically.

**16—The Tower—♂:** In all of my years as a tarot reader, no one ever likes to see the Tower as a yearly card. It symbolizes a massive wake-up and shake-up, a time when the foundations you've depended on come crashing down. This is a revolution, liberation, and enlightenment, all wrapped up in a big storm. You will be tested, and your foundations may need to be rebuilt. Situations that are built on a faulty foundation will crash and burn—and that includes certain relationships. Many breakthroughs are possible if you lean into this vibe. You can release what's not working and start over. Better yet, once the storm clears, you'll have the clarity you always needed. *For entrepreneurs,* this is your year to shake up your industry! Stand up, take a stand, do something no one else has done before. Break free of the rigid rules and create new ones. Look under the hood of your business. Is it built on solid ground? If not, you may need to go to the root and strengthen your foundation—or start completely over from scratch.

**17—The Star—♒:** In a Star year, hope returns. You feel inspired, life seems to be getting better, and you're free to do your thing. Everything that needed to go in your Tower year is gone—and new signs of life are beginning to blossom. You're renewed, ready to plant new seeds, and more importantly, you can express yourself without fear. This is a time of great visibility, perhaps even fame. Share your unique self with the world, shine brightly, and be a source of inspiration and encouragement for others. If you're not sure of where to go, your north star will show the way. Trust your instincts, listen to your guides, and see where they take you. This is your year to think big, to focus on the collective and your role in it. As you live by your best example, the community is inspired to do the same. *For entrepreneurs,* be visible. Be unapologetically you. Share your big vision with the world. Get involved in humanitarian causes. Inspire your audience, and they will continue to reward you. Fame could happen this year—you're more than ready for that!

**18—The Moon—♓:** You might feel uncertain this year. Suddenly, nothing is clear. Whatever you worked on last year may not have panned out the way you expected . . . and now you don't know what to expect. This is a step into the unknown, a chance to explore new territory and see where the path takes you. You do not need to have every answer figured out. It's okay to get a bit lost. Confusion is part of the journey—and this year may deliver a lot of mixed messages. You might even feel let down after last year's hopeful vibe. A few situations will be revealed this year that might change your course in surprising ways. Intuition will guide you the entire time, so even if you experience a shock or two, you'll find a way to learn from it. Imagination is strong, dreams are king, and your sixth sense is operating stronger than ever. By the time the year comes to an end, you'll have clarity once again—you were never lost in the first place. *For entrepreneurs,* you'll want to try new things and remain flexible. Go with the flow and see where you need to pivot. A rebrand might be required. If something isn't working, do not fear moving on. Test out new social media platforms and learn new tech.

**19—The Sun—☉**: The Sun year is one of joy, abundance, and expansion. Everything comes together at last—and success is yours for the taking. It's also possible you are free to follow your bliss. If you're moving on, you'll be doing so joyfully. You can see the light—and step into the spotlight at the same time. Recognition is yours—and you should make sure that you make time to celebrate every win. Take time off for vacations, do things that make you happy, and bask in your success. Finances are on the upswing, which means your income might rise. Creativity is on fire—you can make all sorts of beautiful things. *For entrepreneurs,* claim your spot on the main stage. Extensive PR campaigns, media blitzes, and being "seen" as much as possible will raise your visibility to star levels. People love to be around you now—and your audience is bound to grow. Lucky breaks will come—be ready to say yes!

**20—Judgement—♇**: Something is changing. Maybe it's you. This is the wake-up call, the cosmic nudge to something greater, the message from the Universe. You must be ready to accept the call, to rise up to the next level. Shed the old parts which you've outgrown. Like a phoenix, you are rising from the ashes. There may be significant endings in your life this year. They may feel scary at first, but once you accept them, you'll experience true liberation. Everything in your world is ready to shift. Let go of the old and let the real you shine forth. This is transformation time—or awakening. Watch out for getting judge-y with others. Even though you're on a mission or upgrade, not everyone else is there yet. *For entrepreneurs,* you must market your work widely. PR needs to be your top priority. Toot your horn, spread your message, amplify your outreach efforts. Do not be shy! If something in your business comes to an end, let it. This would be an excellent year for a rebrand.

**21—The World—♄**: This year brings something to a successful close. Perhaps you're graduating or completing some other milestone. Big projects are finished, a chapter ends, and you're ready to start something new soon. You can rise up to a new level—and find worldly success. Stand out, be proud of what you've accomplished, and ready to make your mark on the world! If you're thinking of traveling or studying abroad, go for it! Be global in your approach to life. Do not think small—think big. The accolades and opportunities that come your way are richly deserved. *For entrepreneurs,* you need to finish up big projects. Be global with your brand. Clear space for a new beginning and fine-tune your bigger vision. Much success can be yours this year. Travel for work, connect with people at a distance, and take your place on the world's stage. Seek fame—but fame may also be seeking you.

**22—The Fool—♓**: The Fool year promises to be full of adventure. Everything is new, your baggage is light, and you can start off on any path you desire. If you want to leave the past in the past, you can. Nothing will hold you back except you. Don't be afraid to look foolish. Some people may assume you're being too carefree. They may expect you to knuckle down and toe the line. But you're not ready to be tied down just yet. Inspiration is around every corner; there is much to discover and plenty of sacred cows to be poked. Have fun, see where life takes you, and feel free to thumb your nose at other people's expectations. *For entrepreneurs,* this year is perfect for doing something radical. Start a new podcast, rebrand your entire business, create a new line, or take your industry into bold new directions. Walk all the paths that no one else dared to do—blaze all the trails.

. . . . . . . . . . . . . . . . . . . . . . . . . . . . . . . . . . . . . . . . . . . . . .

# Tarotcise

Alrighty—add up your year and find out what's up. Look back at past years and see how the cards applied!

**And for extra credit:**

Each of the Major Arcana cards has been listed with its astrological correspondence. Look at your Yearly Card for this year—let's say it's 16, The Tower. The Tower corrresponds to Mars. Where is Mars transiting in your chart? Reduce your year card to 7, The Chariot, corresponding to Cancer. Do you have any planets in Cancer? What house does Cancer occupy in your chart?

Go back through the astrological section of this book and puzzle through all the different ways your Yearly Card impacts who you are, who you are right now, and how that might impact the decisions you make for who you want to be.

# PART THREE

# Make
# Intuition
# Do Its Job

# Listen to Your Gut

n my introduction to this book, I told you I would give you techniques to navigate the hard stuff and carve out a destiny you love. By this point, you've learned how powerfully intertwined astrology and Tarot can be. I have always said that **astrology creates the map; Tarot shows you the detours**. But there is one more crucial element— your intuition. Your intuition deepens your ability to read the map. Your intuition drives the decision-making necessary to recognize and take the detours. I would be remiss if I didn't speak a bit about the role intuition plays in decision-making. While tarot and astrology have been trusted tools on my own journey, my instincts have trumped every-thing every time.

Whenever I got a "feeling" about a situation or person, I didn't ignore it. I paid atten-tion, even if I didn't have the facts to back it up. Every time I went with my gut, those decisions became pivotal—and some of the best choices I ever made.

For example, starting my own business happened on a "whim." There were no plans, no MBA, no capital to support me . . . nothing. In fact, I was pretty lost at that time in my life. I was drifting along, trying to figure out what I should be doing with my life . . . and how to make a living. I began bartending, because the hours were decent and the potential to make tips meant cash in my pocket every day.

I was placed on a dead shift, probably because my drink-making skills were pretty bad. Bored, I brought my tarot deck to work, and it wasn't long before I had a packed house every shift. My tip jar was full every night.

Between slinging drinks and cards, customers asked if they could get a private reading outside the bar—and they offered to pay me. One day, I mused to my boss about starting a tarot business. He went behind my back and told a few folks I would fail and that "nobody would pay for such a thing."

When this information was relayed back to me, I felt an intense sensation in my body—and I got mad. I have a red-hot Scorpion Moon temper—and when I get angry, watch out! A bridge is about to get torched! Something switched on inside of me. I quit my job immediately and began reading tarot full time. I never looked back. (Fun fact: his business closed two years later, which I knew it would, because he didn't know how to run a bar.)

Any wise business advisor would have probably told me to wait, take some business courses, and put some money aside before making such a bold move. While that would have been a prudent path, I knew it was now or never. My gut said "go," and that was the only advisor I needed.

Over the years, my sixth sense has only gotten sharper. Every time I went against my inner guidance, I quickly learned not to do that again. Remember, every brainstorm didn't come to life, and not every red flag was urgent. With time and practice, I've become better at discerning which situations require immediate attention and which don't require a response.

In this section, I'll share a few ideas that might help you get intuition confident. Because when you develop your instincts, they become the secret sauce to your success. Let's go!

## WHAT IS INTUITION ANYWAY?

You might be wondering that question yourself. Perhaps you assume it's only for the gifted (wrong). Or maybe you think it's some sort of carnival trick (nope). Hear this: intuition is a practical tool that everyone possesses. Some of us tune in and follow it, while some choose to ignore it. Still, others pooh-pooh the whole idea. (Psst . . . your GPS is always on.)

Intuition is the ability to know something without any logical reasoning. It's that moment where you get a "feeling," but don't have the facts . . . yet on some level, you know what's up.

Sometimes intuition is based on previous life experiences. This creates a certain familiar feeling when you're in a similar situation. For example, let's say you had to work with a jealous coworker who continuously sabotaged you. You moved on to a new job and found yourself working with a person, who outwardly seems friendly, but you feel anxious around them. There is something about them that reminds you of your past coworker. Later on, this person turns out to be a backstabber. The instinct you felt was because you've been in that situation before. You know those red flags all too well.

Other times, intuition doesn't seem to have any rhyme or reason. You've never been in that situation, you have no lived experience, but you know there is something there to explore . . . or avoid. When you follow that, you might stay out of trouble or, if you're getting a green light, might land the most fantastic opportunity.

I'll never forget the time a publisher started hinting around about working with me. This seemed to be a respected publishing house, but something didn't sit right with me. I politely declined. A few years later, I was approached by a different acquisition editor, and I immediately had a great vibe. This was an instant yes—and I got my first book deal shortly afterward. The book was a success, and more opportunities flowed my way. Later on, I learned the first offer was from a "vanity publisher," which offered zero royalties and produced formulaic books, something that wouldn't work with my independent spirit.

## INTUITION BASICS

Intuition is different for everyone. You may experience it like I do—or have your own unique way of interpreting your intuitive impressions. Don't expect yours to be like anyone else's.

Some people will sense something strongly, while others might experience intuition as a "gentle knowing." It's all good and all individual.

While there are many ways to experience intuition, the three "clairs" are the most common:

1. **Clairvoyance**—the ability to "see" information. This could come in the form of images in your mind or lucid dreams that hold clues. Think of it as a little movie or snapshot in your mind.

2. **Clairaudience**—the ability to "hear" information. If you get a random word in your mind or hear a voice, that's clairaudience. Just to be clear, this is not the same as "hearing voices" ala Son of Sam. For example, sometimes, I will be doing a tarot reading, and a song will pop into my mind. There is no radio on, I haven't thought

about the song in eons, and it doesn't seem to have anything to do with the cards in front of me. I mention it to the client, and later on, they tell me how that one statement turned out to be especially relevant.

**3** **Clairsentience**—the ability to "feel" information. Ever meet someone, and the hair rises up on the back of your neck? That's what I'm talking about! Clairsentience can be like a funny feeling in your stomach, your skin crawling, a warm fuzzy vibe—those feelings give clues to whether a situation is right for you . . . or not.

Although I work with all three clairs, the last one is my most developed. I feel things in my body all the time. When I say "I have a good feeling about something" or a "bad" one, this is what I'm talking about—and it usually turns out to be accurate.

## HOW TO DEVELOP YOUR INTUITION

Simple. Keep track of every "download" you receive. If you get a feeling about any situation, write it down. You can keep notes in your tarot and astrology journal—or have a special book solely for your intuitive hits. Up to you. I prefer to keep separate journals because I like seeing how these different modes work on their own. (I have a dream journal as well, which I use to write down any visits I get from loved ones on the other side.

The reason why it's crucial to track your hunches is twofold. For one, you will discover exactly which of the clairs is more robust for you. Second, you can get an idea of your accuracy. In the beginning, you might not feel confident, but after some time, you will see your abilities getting stronger. You'll also start to learn which personal signs and omens are relevant for you.

For example, I'm often amused at how many times I write down random song lyrics—and later on, I can see exactly what they were trying to tell me. Other times, I'll page through my dream journal and feel amazed by the messages my departed loved ones shared with me.

If you keep track, you'll have a record that will help you to understand your instincts and make better intuitive decisions going forward. Also, the more you pay attention, the faster and more accurate your insights will be. Why? It's because your sixth sense likes it when you pay attention to it.

## INTUITIVE DECISION MAKING

I have something to confess: I'm a horribly indecisive person. Sit next to me in a restaurant, and you'll see what I mean. Suddenly, I am overwhelmed and not sure what to order. If the menu is too extensive, I'm stressed and worried I'll make the wrong choice. A small menu isn't any better, because suddenly, I'm anxious there aren't enough choices.

I'll ask everyone else what they're ordering or appeal to my husband to make a decision for me. Then I end up getting the opposite of what he suggested. I'm eyeing everyone else's plates during the whole meal and secretly wondering if he was right.

Yeah, dining out is my idea of decision-making hell!

One thing I've learned to do to lessen the stress: research the restaurant well before my night out. I'll study the menu and give myself time to ponder the options and what I want to try. When I sit at my table, I have it narrowed down. I ask the waiter to give me a few minutes, and then I take a moment to quietly consider how each dish might taste or make me feel. I give my body and emotions enough time to feel a certain way—then I choose.

Good, intuitive decision-making comes down to the right mindset (and sometimes a little market research!).

If you want to develop your intuition, you need to start with the most important thing (next to your journal): a calm mind. Here's why:

When your mind is frazzled, you're more likely to make emotionally fueled, impulsive decisions. Making a choice under duress, especially when it comes to your career or purpose, rarely leads to a good one. Even if things pan out, you'll always wonder: did I do the right thing? Pressure creates a feeling of urgency, which activates the primal mind.

Think of it this way: we're hardwired to run from danger. Our ancestors knew a charging lion meant they might get killed. On a cellular level, we can still feel that surge of adrenaline when a threat approaches. But we also live in a different world with different stressors. In fact, many of us are constantly on edge, which puts us in that fight or flight mindset all the time. When the pressure mounts, we want to get out of the line of fire as quickly as possible. So once again, we're running. Except now we're running all the time—and there's no lion behind us.

After a while, the intuition gets overridden by the fear factor. Don't get me wrong: sometimes fear is real and valuable—even in work situations. But constantly operating from that mindset will get in the way of your practical intuition.

Quieting your mind can be as simple as sitting alone for a few minutes, taking a couple of deep breaths, or going outside for a walk. My husband finds his intuition sharper in the bathtub. I know many people who get those 'aha' moments in the shower. Something about soaking in water seems to clear energy, unclog the intuitive faculties, and get the imagination flowing.

Whatever works for you, get your mind calm first.

Now, let's say you are choosing between two jobs and you're not sure which one is best. They both have pros and cons, which makes it hard to determine what choice to make.

Begin by quieting your mind. Sit in a peaceful place—or lie down—and take a few slow, deep breaths. Then, visualize one of the options. Notice how your body feels. Do you feel warm or cold? Do you feel a charge running through your body—or nothing at all? Can you picture yourself enjoying the work? Write down whatever comes to mind without stopping to edit yourself. Let the words flow from your heart.

Next, do the same thing with your other option.

Once you've completed this, look over your notes. Read them out loud. As you do that, once again, pay attention to how you feel. If you're getting a strong feeling about one versus the other, that's your decision. (Fun twist: pull a card for each option for additional guidance!)

If you don't get any feelings at all, leave it alone and come back to your notes a day or so later. Sometimes sitting on the information will give you more insights.

In fact, this is a similar technique I often recommend with tarot: write down your reading, leave it alone a day or two, then revisit it. It's one of the best ways to make tough choices.

# QUESTIONS INSPIRE ANSWERS

I've always been an inquisitive sort of person. "Why" was my favorite word (my poor parents!). I needed to know why things were the way they were—or what people's motives might be. I was the annoying kid who would probe, poke, and research.

Here's the thing: if you don't ask questions, you never get answers. Your sixth sense is very much like that. It wants to find solutions for you.

One of the techniques I use is so simple: I ask the Universe a question. Once I put it out there, the Universe starts looking for the answers.

What's important is how I phrase the question:

**Here's my format:**

How did I _____?

Ex: *How did I get such a fantastic book deal?*

**or**

Why did I _____?

Ex: *Why did I finish writing my book in record time?*

I say the statement out loud and then wait. The answer will often come within days or weeks. What I mean by that is that I'm shown the way to make something happen. This is different than affirmations, which states I already have what I want. Instead, I'm formulating my question as if I already have what I want or have reached my goal—but I'm asking how or why everything happened. I want to see the best path for making my goals a reality.

This may seem counterintuitive, but it works.

For example, many years ago, my father needed to sell his house. It was a tiny home with plenty of problems, and the market crashed as soon as he put it up for sale. This home sat for an entire year. We had Feng Shui experts look at the house, did staging, and even lowered the price. Not one nibble.

Finally, I decided to plant St. Joseph in the ground (this is a Catholic superstition) and walked through the house, asking aloud, "How did this house sell so quickly and happily?"

Two weeks later, we had a bid from an older couple who happened to drive by randomly on the way to visit their daughter who lived nearby. They were looking for a home closer to her because they lived almost three hours away. We jumped on that offer and signed the papers a few weeks later. They were happy, Dad was relieved, and I was secretly thanking the Universe for showing the way.

## RECOGNIZE WHAT OTHERS NEED

So many times, I hear entrepreneurs complain that they can't figure out what their clients want. This same dilemma faces people in many work situations—they're at odds with a coworker, employee, or boss—and they don't know why. This can lead to a lot of stress or pain.

For example, if you don't know what your clients want or need, your business may not succeed. Not being able to figure out your boss/employee/coworker's agenda can create a toxic environment.

Here's something that every intuitive person does well: we listen.

We listen to the signs from the Universe, our bodies, and emotions—and other people.

When I work with a client, I usually have a notepad nearby. I cannot see them since I don't work in person. Instead, I listen carefully, not just to what they are saying but how they deliver their story. I'm not thinking about my response, nor am I staring at my cell phone (all distractions are shut down).

Sometimes I'll repeat things back for clarification. If something seems "off" or catches my attention, I'll write it down. This note is for me only—it may lead to another question, or it may be the information I need to know to help my client.

When you are working with people, the greatest gift you can give them is your undivided attention. That will also turn out to be a gift for you. Listening allows for gathering information, which helps you give people what they need the most, which isn't always what they want.

That's the thing when you're working with people: so often, we're in our own little zone, and we're not paying attention to what people want or need. The more attentive we are, the better we can be as entrepreneurs, coworkers, partners, and humans.

# WHEN YOUR INTUITION IS DEAD WRONG

Ever take a wrong turn and end up on the other side of town? Or how about your GPS gets goofed up, and suddenly, you are going in circles and don't know how to get off? Sometimes intuition is like that: you get a feeling but misinterpret the signs—and what you thought was a sure thing turns out to be a disaster.

Sometimes decisions "seem" good at the time, and maybe they are . . . but things change. Or perhaps you get a great job, and it all starts off fine—but then a new boss comes into the picture and turns out to be the boss from hell.

Things can change, you can make mistakes, and sometimes you realize you want something different.

When you've experienced a dead-end or decide to pivot, you'll want to do an inventory of what happened. I usually find that when I do this, I'll look back and find instances where I missed something. There were early warning signs, and I didn't follow them. I take stock of the issue and learn from it.

# STICKY SITUATIONS

Sometimes you may get into a situation that turns out to be a nightmare. The creepy coworker, the inappropriate client, the sudden lay-off—bad things can happen to good people. There is no way to "put love and light around it."

It's frustrating when that happens. You might kick yourself for "not seeing it," but here's the thing: you won't anticipate every problem, no matter how psychic you are. People can be unpredictable, and no one can "see it all."

Sometimes, tarot and astrology are NOT the answer either. There are times when you need to bail, report the issue to a higher authority, or ask for help. If you are in a situation where you are being harmed or oppressed, please look for the proper support. Seek the professionals and take good care of yourself.

# SPEAKING OF PROFESSIONALS . . .

My goal in this book is to provide you with a whole bunch of practical, mystical tools so you can find a meaningful path or vocation—and navigate problems as swiftly as possible. But there are times when you might be better served by working with a professional tarot reader, astrologer, or sacred artist.

For example, if you cannot be objective. Or if you're overthinking it to the point where you feel paralyzed and unable to make a decision. If you find yourself in those headspaces, a talented reader will be able to help you cut through the fog and find the nuggets of wisdom so you can get on your right path in a happy, healthy way.

Tarot and astrology are more popular than ever, so it's easy to find a pro these days. A click of the mouse or a referral from a friend could point you in the right direction. But if you're not sure, here are a few tips on what to look for.

Take your time getting to know the person before you hire them. Most professionals have a website and a solid social media presence. Spend some time in their orbit and see if you like their personality.

Also, be clear on what you are looking for. For example, if you want a business astrology reading, do your due diligence to find someone who offers that service. Not every reader reads for every topic, and you cannot assume every tarot reader understands astrology and vice versa.

Don't hesitate to reach out and ask questions about their services. Most professionals will have a FAQ page—but they'll also be more than happy to sort things out for you.

Get a few referrals or check out their testimonial page. Find out what it's like to work with them. Sometimes hearing someone else's experience can help you make a great decision.

When you choose your reader, don't forget to be respectful. Let them know what you want to work on. Don't come in with a closed mind or a "guess my problem" attitude. That never leads to a helpful reading. The more upfront you are, the more likely you'll walk away with a good experience and great information.

PART FOUR

# Twist Your Fate

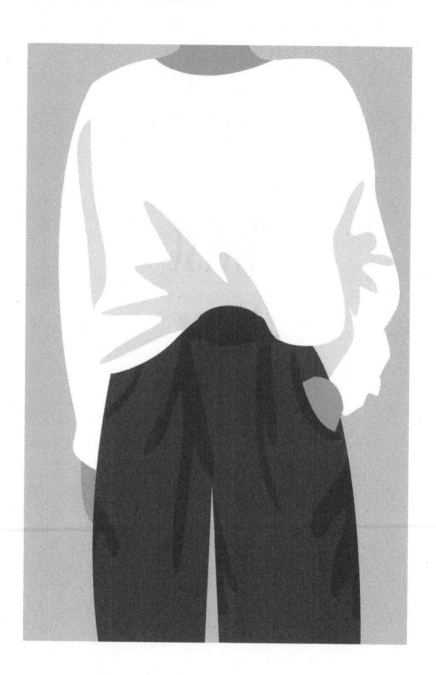

# The More You Know . . .

hope this book provides you with a wealth of helpful tools and food for thought. This is by no means an exhaustive exploration of tarot or astrology for vocation, life paths, or business. While I've provided you with the basics, it's only the tip of a gigantic iceberg.

Keep in mind, the information I'm sharing is what has worked for me and my clients. There is so much more to learn and many other concepts and theories, and so on. Other astrologers and tarot readers may have different opinions or may place emphasis on other points. You might, too, after further studies. (Psst . . . be sure to check out all the books I've listed for you. There are so many amazingly talented and wise people whose work I deeply respect.)

The more you know, the further you'll want to go.

Let's end with one last exercise to bring it all together.

To your successful and happy life,

—Theresa

. . . . . . . . . . . . . . . . . . . . . . . . . . . . . . . . . . . . . . . . . . . . . . . . .

## Astro-Tarot-Intui-cise!

One last masterclass exercise for you! This is a three-parter. Come back to it again and again to hone the skills you've learned in this book. In order for you to follow along with how to do this exercise, I'm going to use a sample chart calculated for December 5, 1992, 2:45 am EST. This is how one individual, using this book, completed this exercise. The notes are from the querent, Gabby.

# Step one: Pull out your natal chart.

If you have your chart calculated online, filling in some of this info will be easier, since it will be listed in a table to the left of the chart. This one was calculated by *astro.com*.

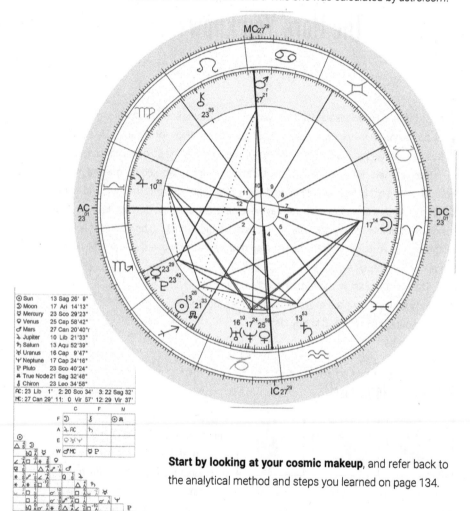

| ⊙ Sun | 13 Sag 26' 9" |
| ☽ Moon | 17 Ari 14'13" |
| ☿ Mercury | 23 Sco 29'23" |
| ♀ Venus | 25 Cap 58'42" |
| ♂ Mars | 27 Can 20'40"ℝ |
| ♃ Jupiter | 10 Lib 21'33" |
| ♄ Saturn | 13 Aqu 52'39" |
| ♅ Uranus | 16 Cap 9'47" |
| ♆ Neptune | 17 Cap 24'16" |
| ♇ Pluto | 23 Sco 40'24" |
| ☊ True Node | 21 Sag 32'48" |
| ⚷ Chiron | 23 Leo 34'58" |

AC: 23 Lib 1' 2: 20 Sco 34' 3: 22 Sag 32'
MC: 27 Can 29' 11: 0 Vir 57' 12: 29 Vir 37'

**Start by looking at your cosmic makeup**, and refer back to the analytical method and steps you learned on page 134.

1. Look at the Big Three. This will give you an idea of what you need to be fulfilled. The Sun is what you're here to do, the Ascendant shows the best way to do the work of your Sun Sign, and the Moon represents what your soul needs.

2. Find the Midheaven. This is your potential. The Midheaven indicates how you need to share yourself and your gifts with the world.

3. Elemental Makeup. The Elements shows the "weather patterns" in your chart.

4. Check to see if there are planets in your 10th house. If there are, they could impact how the world sees you and indicate possible career options . . . or problems.

5. Lastly, check the Nodes for karmic lessons and patterns.

**Next fill in the blanks. For this natal chart, Gabby filled in the information as follows:**

1. The Big Three:

   My Sun is in sign *Sagittarius*. It is in the *2nd* house.

   My Moon is in sign *Aries*. It is in the *6th* house.

   My Ascendant is in sign *Libra*.

2. Find the Midheaven: My Midheaven is in sign *Cancer*.

3. My elemental makeup:

   **Elements:**

   For the Big Three - Fire: *2* Air: *1* Earth: *0* Water: *1*

   For all the planets: Fire: *2* Air: *2* Earth: *3* Water: *3*

   **Qualities:**
   For the Big Three - Cardinal: *3* Fixed: *0* Mutable: *1*

For all the planets: Cardinal: **6** Fixed: **3** Mutable: **1**
(North Node: Mutable, Ascendant: Cardinal, Midheaven: Cardinal)

**4** The tenth house: *Chiron*. [Also: Mars is conjunct the Midheaven].

**5** My north node is in *Sagittarius*. My south node is in *Gemini*.

**Note any extra info that jumps out at you.** Gabby noted:*

*My Ruling Planet* is Venus—it's in the 3rd house. Both my Ascendant and Venus are in Cardinal signs.

*Transits:* I ran a chart for my transits and noticed I'm smack-dab in the middle of my Saturn return! This means I'm setting the foundation for my future—and I need to get serious! I noticed it's in my 4th house, which is associated with home and family. I'm going to be making a decision about a big move soon, so this makes a lot of sense. I'll consider all options carefully because this may impact a lot of things in my life.

*Solar Return:* I decided to look at my Solar Return to see what themes are operating. The Sun is in my 3rd house, which means I'm expressing myself powerfully this year. It's conjunct Mercury, a combo that bodes well for short trips. The Moon is in Sagittarius and also situated in my 3rd house. This feels like a quest for truth or knowledge! My Ascendant remains in Libra, so no changes there. Jupiter and Saturn are both in my 5th house, which is pretty good for performing artists. I'm an actor and this shows opportunity and discipline. All in all, this feels like a strong year—and I didn't have to travel anywhere to get what I wanted!

---

* For this final "astro-tarot-intui-cise" sample, Gabby went the extra mile. She could have stopped with the Big Three and the elements, but she dug down a little deeper and decided to research the extras: transits, ruling planet, and solar return. Because this exercise is meant to be done multiple times, you might want to start with the basics, and as you continue to go back through this book (as well as the other resources I've provided!), you'll learn more and can add more to your analysis.

## Step two: Pull out your favorite Tarot deck.

We'll practice using Donneleigh's spread for advice and outcomes. We've had Gabby write down a question; right now she's in the middle of a job change, possibly going up to a managerial role. This is new to her.

*What can I expect if I accept the job I'm applying for?*

| The Situation | The Challenge | Advice | Likely Outcome |

Now go to the card descriptions starting on page 147 and copy down the salient keywords.

**The Situation: The Moon.** The Moon is a tricky card. It shows a path, but that path is shrouded in darkness. Nothing is straightforward or easy. While there are options and the right track, it's hard to see which way to go. You'll need to trust your instincts. **Pisces**.

**The Challenge: Five of Wands.** The Five of Wands signals a competition is ON. You may be in the running with other qualified candidates for a position. Throw your hat in the ring and bring your A-game. Do not play shy—show what sets you apart from the rest. **Fire element.**

**Advice: Justice.** You may have to make some sort of choice—and there may be significant consequences. You'll want to gather all the facts and look at every side of the coin before making your move. **Libra**.

**Likely Outcome: Nine of Pentacles.** Living large! The self-made success story. You've created incredible abundance. Goals have been reached. Financial success is yours. **Earth element.**

# Step three: Let your intuition guide you.

**1** **Start by figuring out your annual card** to give everything context.

*What's my annual card for this reading?*

Dec 5, 2022 = 1 + 2 + 5 + 2 + 0 + 2 + 2 = 14 Temperance. **Or** 5: The Hierophant.

**Temperance**: *For entrepreneurs.* Forge new partnerships, especially with business owners. Find balance in your daily affairs and be sure to get your money in order. There is gold ahead for you—but first, you must test things out and see what makes the most sense for you and the way you want to work.

**The Hierophant**: *For entrepreneurs.* You'll want to step up to teach, preach, and practice outreach. Set clear guidelines at work and uphold the rules. You may need to hire experts to help you up-level your game. Or perhaps you may join an organization for your industry. None exist? Start your own.

**2** **Now consider who you are:** Again, this is Gabby's intuition filling in the blanks here.

*What I know about myself:*

- Libra Ascendant: people see me as fair and balanced. I'm diplomatic and a great team player. I know how to work well with others. They may also view me as decisive, although I sometimes sit on the fence far more than I'd like to admit. I present a polished, harmonious front to the world.

- Sun in Sagittarius: I'm totally incapable of lying. I believe in justice and my moral standards are high—am I stubborn? Do I sometimes seem self-righteous? Maybe. But I'm excited to see what the future holds and ready to go forth to blaze all the trails!

- Moon in Aries: Ok, I can be emotionally intense. Aries is passionate, intense, fiery, and proactive. I do love to take the initiative and would love a position of leadership. I will have to check my impulsiveness.

- Cancer on Midheaven: Careers for me indicate I like taking care of others—social work, caregiving. Does this job fill that need? I'll need to inquire further.

- Elementally I'm pretty balanced, but my Sun and Moon are both fire. My Ascendant is air and my Midheaven, water—perhaps these will tamp down my fiery nature!

- Sun in the 2nd house aligns with my Sagittarian sense of values and my desire to make money. Also, I need to have some freedom at my job if I want to be happy. Too many routines and I'll climb the walls!

- Moon in 6th: I'll be pretty intense at pursuing work, but I have to remember to put my health first. It's too easy for me to overwork, which leads to burnout.

- My Ruling planet is Venus and it's in the 3rd house—this is associated with learning, communication, and brand messaging. I love to learn and I do have a way with words. I can deliver my message with creative flair!

## What kind of weaknesses are in my chart?

- That Sun/Moon thing: I *am* impulsive. I'm usually in perpetual motion—I have a need to be the best and to outshine others. Perhaps I'm not super at being a team player after all?

- Libra Ascendant: I think I have a tendency to be too accommodating to the wishes of others, and I neglect to put myself first. And I think this is made worse by my Ascendant opposing my Moon—I need to be needed. Yet I also need to be first! Guess that Libra balance thing is going to be something to work on.

- Sun in the 2nd house: I need to be careful about taking any old job just for the sake of the money. I must remember my values and need for freedom.

- Saturn in the 4th house: I definitely have some childhood baggage there—feeling like I never stacked up to expectations. The perennial parental question: "What are you going to fall back on when acting fails?" Perhaps Chiron in the 10th is telling me to look at this a bit more? And that pursuing this job now is establishing my financial safety net while I pursue my creative goals.

- Mars in Cancer: This ties into my Ascendant/Moon opposition, plus it sits directly on my Midheaven. I also see it opposes my natal Venus! I need to be aware that my emotions can get in the way, and in business, I may be a people-pleaser who gets taken advantage of. In business, I can turn this around and make it a positive on the sales floor by recognizing what people want and focusing on making that sale. Meanwhile, I need to be mindful to not get sucked into coworkers' emotional drama.

## So . . . what about those cards?

Based on everything Gabby knows at this point, this is what she feels her intuition is telling her and how she interprets the card spread.

**The Situation:** The Moon card is the unknown and is also connected to Pisces. I have nothing in Pisces, no aspects there. But Pisces is in my 5th house of creativity and fame. Perhaps I should go into this job interview without preconceived notions, keep my ears open and trust my instincts. Right now the Sun and Jupiter are transiting my 5th house—a fantastic time for business or professional development . . . and for anything related to the entertainment industry. But also in terms of my situation: I'm pursuing an acting career—what if part of the unknown means landing a role? Easy—I can always take this job now and give it up if I strike it big.

**The Challenge:** Five of Wands: Competition! It looks like there may be a lot of promising candidates for this job. But I'm an out-front Sag, and fire is my element! My challenge is to bring my A-game. I got this.

**Advice:** Justice (associated with Libra): What if I get this job offer? Libra is my Ascendant, so perhaps I'll be a good face for this company. But is this job going to be fulfilling? Will I get sucked into a situation where I have no control? I think I need to research this company and make sure it's a good fit.

**Likely Outcome:** Nine of Pentacles: My gut says, take the job! Pentacles are earth element, and my Venus (relationships) and Uranus (shake-it-up) are in earth and also in the 3rd house—communication and brand messaging. I've got mean skills there! Plus Nine of Pentacles is pointing toward abundance. I'm going to give this a go—and I think both the company and I will be happy.

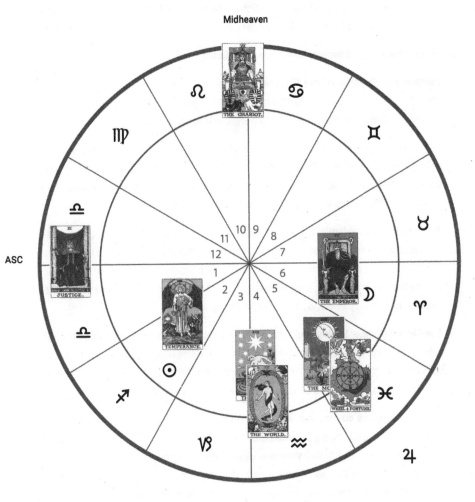

Refer back to the discussion of this exercise on page 208. This exercise provides you with a visual aid to keep on hand, kind of like an astro-tarot mandala. This mandala highlights your Big Three and your Midheaven, and we're also adding current transits for Jupiter (talents, luck) and Saturn (limitations). The more you learn, the more you will add to your mandala, and the more you will deepen your understanding of your natal chart.

**This is how I would interpret this mashup for Gabby:**

**Temperance (Sagittarius Sun):** She's here to heal, inspire, and innovate. Bit by bit, she'll find perfect harmony. She should experiment with new things, test the waters, learn new skills—try it all out. The more she learns, the more she can teach others.

**The Emperor (Aries Moon):** Gabby's emotional foundation is sound, her leadership is strong, and she's confident. Others look up to her—and she has the power to achieve every one of her ambitious goals. She's an authority—or ready to be soon enough. This is her time to stand out. She feels good when she's independent and in control.

**Justice (Libra Ascendant):** People see Gabby as decisive and fair. She loves to gather all the facts and look at every side of the coin before making a move, so that fits. She has big decisions ahead, and, no doubt, there may be significant consequences. However, she's ready to carve out her own destiny. She'll put things on hold if she needs to and forge ahead when she sees opportunity. She should take nothing for granted.

**The Chariot (Cancer Midheaven):** This confirms Gabby's role as a leader. She's on the right path. She's found the perfect vehicle to realize her goals. She needs to look ahead, take command, and keep going. Eyes on the prize. It won't be long before she scores an important victory. Progress is assured, and success is hers for the taking. The key is to remain disciplined.

**Finally, look at the current transits.** Find where Jupiter and Saturn are currently moving through your chart. Why are we looking at these particular transits? Transits of Jupiter show where you can expand. Wherever Jupiter moves through, it can bring good fortune. Transits of Saturn show where you need limitations, boundaries, or where you can experience growth if you are disciplined. Now, take the cards that symbolize the signs associated with the current Jupiter and Saturn transits (Wheel of Fortune—Jupiter, and The World—Saturn) and place them on your natal chart.

At the time that Gabby is preparing this astro-mandala, these are the transits:

**Jupiter** is in Pisces in Gabby's 5th house, so I'm combining the Wheel of Fortune with the Moon (Pisces). This means changes are happening in Gabby's creative life that could be fortunate and surprising. She may be going into uncharted artistic territory. A role may come up that changes the game for her.

**Saturn** is currently in Aquarius in her 4th house. The cards are The World and The Star (Aquarius). There may be a significant move ahead and one that makes her happy. The Star seems to imply Gabby will be bicoastal.

# Recommended Reading

*Predictive Astrology: The Eagle and the Lark* by Bernadette Brady

*The Ultimate Guide to Tarot* by Liz Dean

*Choice Centered Astrology: The Basics* by Gail Fairfield and Donna Cunningham

*Every Day Tarot: A Choice Centered Book* by Gail Fairfield

*Mindful Astrology* by Monte Farber and Amy Zerner

*Archetypal Tarot* by Mary K Greer

*Planets in Transit* by Robert Hand

*Vocational Astrology* by Judith Hill

*78 Degrees of Wisdom* by Rachel Pollack

*Astrology for Real Life—A No B.S. Guide for the AstroCurious* by Theresa Reed

*Tarot: No Questions Asked—Mastering the Art of Intuitive Reading* by Theresa Reed

*Pathworking the Tarot* by Leeza Robertson

*The Astrologer's Handbook* by Francis Sakoian and Louis S. Acker

*Tarot for One* by Courtney Weber

*Holistic Tarot* by Benebell Wen

*Astrology for Happiness and Success: From Aries to Pisces, Create the Life You Want—Based on Your Astrological Sign!* by Mecca Woods

# For Focused Study

### The Big Three
*Mindful Astrology* by Monte Farber and Amy Zerner

### The Houses
*The Twelve Houses* by Howard Sasportas

*The House Your Stars Built* by Rachel Stuart-Haas

### The Nodes
*Astrology for the Soul* by Jan Spiller—this is the best book on the Nodes, hands down.

### Retrograde Planets
*The Mercury Retrograde Book: Turn Chaos into Creativity to Repair, Renew and Revamp Your Life* by Yasmin Boland and Kim Farnell

### Planetary Returns
*How to Get More Love, Money, and Success by Traveling on Your Birthday* by Bob Marks

*Planets in Solar Returns: Yearly Cycles of Transformation and Growth* by Mary Fortier Shea

*Saturn Return Survival Guide: Navigating this cosmic rite of passage* by Lisa Stardust and Emmy Lupin

### The Moon
*The Moon in Your Life: Being a Lunar Type in a Solar World* by Donna Cunningham

*The Moon Book* by Sarah Faith Gottessdeiner

*Lunar Abundance* by Ezzie Spencer

*New Moon Astrology* by Jan Spiller

### Annual Cards

*Archetypal Tarot: What Your Birth Card Reveals About Your Personality, Your Path, and Your Potential* by Mary K Greer

## Software for Astrology:

Solar Fire for PCs

Time Passages for Mac

## Websites for Astrology Charts:

AstroDienst: *www.astro.com/horoscope*

AstroLabe: *alabe.com*

# Acknowledgments

**O**f course, my deepest gratitude to Weiser Books for bringing this book to life. I'm especially grateful to Kathryn Sky-Peck for always believing in me.

Super thankful to Megan Kenney for your sharp eyes and Easter Eggs.

Also a few tips of the hat to some of my biggest supporters while I cranked out another book (and had zero time for fun): Megan and Brandon, Nicholas Lang, Jessica Schumacher, Shaheen Miro, Briana Saussy, Chris Zydel, Tanya Geisler, Alexandra Franzen, Alexis Fischer, Tonya Huskey, Monte Farber, Amy Zerner, and Simone Salmon. Deep bows to Damien Echols and Lorri Davis for always reminding me of what true grace looks like. Much gratitude to my Patreon crew and yoga students. So much love for my teachers and mentors: Rachel Pollack, Mary K Greer, Rebecca Gordon, Ruth Ann and Wald Amberstone. There are many more folks I'd love to thank but there is not enough space for every single one—but you know who you are.

The biggest applause for my ever-patient Virgo husband, Terry, who made sure the house didn't fall completely apart while I worked twelve-hour days again (I promise not to do this ever again).

And lastly, thank you to Dad (another Virgo!). I remember you working three jobs one time just to make ends meet. You never complained about that and always had a candy bar in your pocket on Fridays. You passed on your impeccable work ethic and generosity to me and my siblings. I'm forever your daughter.

# About the Author

Theresa Reed (aka "The Tarot Lady") worked as a full-time tarot card reader for thirty years. She is the author of *Tarot: No Questions Asked—Mastering the Art of Intuitive Reading, Tarot for Kids,* and *The Tarot Coloring Book,* an illustrated tour through the world of Tarot with coloring sheets for every card in the deck. Theresa is also the author of *Astrology For Real Life (A No B.S. Guide for the Astro-Curious),* and the coauthor of *Tarot for Troubled Times* with Shaheen Miro.

In addition to writing, teaching, and speaking at tarot conferences, Theresa also runs a popular website—*TheTarotLady.com*—where she dishes out advice, inspiration, and tips for tarot lovers of all experience levels.

# To Our Readers

Weiser Books, an imprint of Red Wheel/Weiser, publishes books across the entire spectrum of occult, esoteric, speculative, and New Age subjects. Our mission is to publish quality books that will make a difference in people's lives without advocating any one particular path or field of study. We value the integrity, originality, and depth of knowledge of our authors.

Our readers are our most important resource, and we appreciate your input, suggestions, and ideas about what you would like to see published.

Visit our website at *www.redwheelweiser.com* to learn about our upcoming books and free downloads, and be sure to sign up for our newsletter and exclusive offers.

You can also contact us at *info@rwwbooks.com* or at

Red Wheel/Weiser, LLC
65 Parker Street, Suite 7
Newburyport, MA 01950